AA

CW00375712

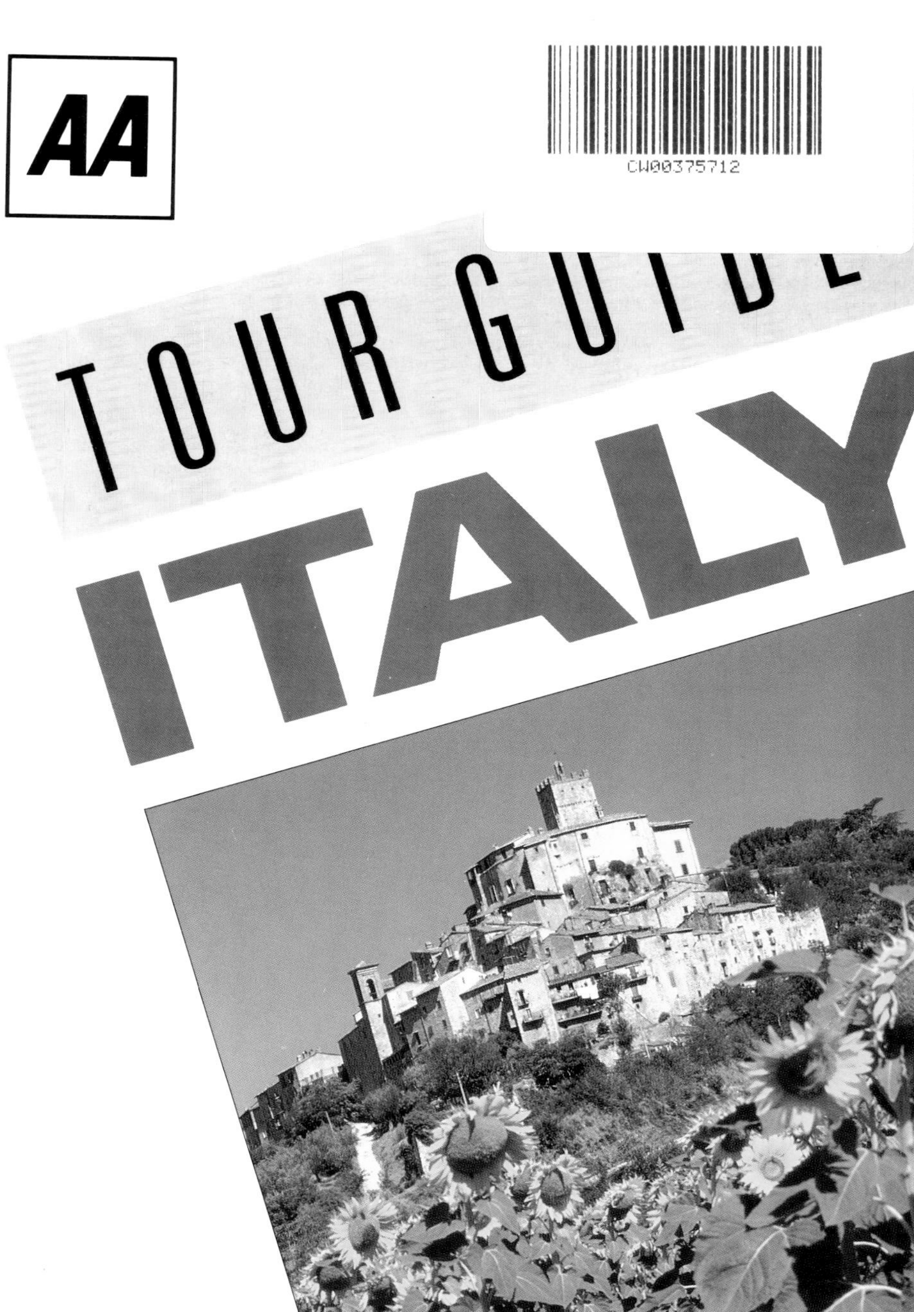

Produced by AA Publishing

Written by Paul Duncan
Original photography by
Anthony Souter

Revised second edition 1995

First published January 1991

Edited, designed and produced by AA Publishing.

Distributed in the United Kingdom by AA Publishing, Norfolk House, Priestley Road, Basingstoke, Hampshire, RG24 9NY.

A CIP catalogue record for this book is available from the British Library.

ISBN 0 74951041 2

The contents of this publication are believed correct at the time of printing. Nevertheless, the publishers cannot accept responsibility for errors or omissions, or for changes in details given in this guide or for the consequences of any reliance on the information provided by the same. Assessments of attractions and so forth are based upon the author's own experience and, therefore, descriptions given in this guide necessarily contain an element of subjective opinion which may not reflect the publishers' opinion or dictate a reader's own experiences on another occasion. **We have tried to ensure accuracy in this guide, but things do change and we would be grateful if readers would advise us of any inaccuracies they may encounter.**

Published by AA Publishing (a trading name of Automobile Association Developments Limited, whose registered office is Norfolk House, Priestley Road, Basingstoke, Hampshire RG24 9NY. Registered number 1878835).

Colour separation: Scantrans Pte Ltd, Singapore

Printed and bound in Italy by Printers SRL

Front cover: *Firenze, morning view*
Title page: *Narni in Umbria*
Opposite: *Napoli: Galleria del Umberto I*

CONTENTS

INTRODUCTION

This book is not only a practical touring guide for the independent traveller, but is also invaluable for those who would like to know more about the country.

It is divided into 5 regions, each containing between 3 and 6 tours. The tours start and finish in the major towns and cities which we consider to be the best centres for exploration. Each tour has details of the most interesting places to visit en route. Side panels cater for special interests and requirements and cover a range of categories – for those whose interest is in history, wildlife or walking, and those who have children. There are also panels which highlight scenic stretches of road along the route and which give details of special events, gastronomic specialities, crafts and customs. The numbers link them to the appropriate main text.

The simple route directions are accompanied by an easy-to-use map of the tour and there are addresses of local tourist information centres in some of the towns en route as well as in the start town.

Simple charts show how far it is from one town to the next in kilometres and (miles). These can help you to decide where to take a break and stop overnight, for example. (All distances quoted are approximate.)

Before setting off it is advisable to check with the information centre at the start of the tour for recommendations on where to break your journey and for additional information on what to see and do, and when best to visit.

PUBLIC HOLIDAYS

1 January – New Year's Day
6 January – Epiphany
Easter Monday
25 April – Liberation Day (1945)
1 May – Labour Day
2 June – Proclamation of Republic (celebrated on following Saturday)
15 August – Ferragosto (Assumption)
1 November – All Saints
8 December – Immaculate Conception
25–26 December – Christmas

MOTORING

Documents

Tourists taking their own (therefore foreign-registered) car to Italy must be at least 18 years of age, and in possession of the vehicle's registration document, an international green card or other insurance, and a valid, full driving licence. A green UK or red Republic of Ireland licence is acceptable in Italy provided it is accompanied by an official Italian translation, available free from ACI affiliated motoring clubs or from agents of the Italian State Tourist Office. The translation is not required for holders of the pink EU-type UK or Republic of Ireland licence.

Route directions

Throughout the book the following abbreviations are used for Italian roads:

A – Autostrada (motorway)
SS – Strada Statale (state road)
dir, ter, bis, q, qu – suffixes to state roads (SS) relating to links and extensions of major roads
minor roads – unnumbered roads.

Breakdowns

In case of breakdown dial 116 at the nearest telephone box. Tell the operator where you are, the registration number and type of car; the nearest ACI office will be informed for immediate assistance. The use of a warning triangle is compulsory in the event of an accident or breakdown. It must be placed on the road not less than 50m (55 yards) behind the vehicle. Motorists who fail to do this are liable to an administrative fine.

Accidents

In the event of an accident, a report must be made to the insurance company. If the accident involves personal injury, medical assistance must be sought for the injured party, and the incident reported to the police. On some *autostrada* there are emergency telephones as well as emergency push-button call boxes.

Speed limits

In built-up areas 50kph (31mph); outside built-up areas 90kph (56mph); on motorways 130kph (81mph). For cars towing a caravan or trailer the speed limits are 50kph (31mph), 80kph (49mph) and 100kph (62mph) respectively.

Driving conditions

Vehicles must keep to the right-hand side of the road or street and close to the nearside kerb, even when the road is clear. Side mirrors are compulsory on the left-hand side of the car, also for right-hand drive vehicles. The wearing of seat belts is compulsory.

Visitors who take their car to Italy are entitled to reductions on the normal price of petrol (supergrade only) and on motorway tolls. This concession applies to all cars and

Centre of the Roman Catholic world: Piazza San Pietro, Rome

motorcycles with a foreign registration number, but it excludes commercial vehicles and hired ones. Visitors interested in this concession can buy the petrol coupons and obtain at the same time the motorway vouchers towards payment of tolls. The concession is available in the UK to GB-registered vehicles only.

Car hire and fly/drive

Car hire is available in most cities and resorts. Many international firms operate this service. Rates generally include breakdown service, maintenance and oil, but not petrol. Basic insurance is also included but additional cover is available at fixed rates. Most firms require a deposit equal to the estimated cost of hire. Some firms restrict hire to drivers over 21 years of age. Generally you must have had a valid driving licence for at least one year before applying for car hire. People travelling by air or rail can take advantage of special inclusive arrangements.

HEALTH

Health insurance is recommended, but visitors from other EU countries have the right to claim health services available to Italians. For British travellers this means obtaining, prior to departure, Form E111 from the post office.

To find a doctor or dentist, consult the Yellow Pages or your hotel. The high cost of treatment makes insurance essential if you are a non-EU citizen. For medical treatment and medicines, keep all bills and claim the money back later.

Vaccinations are unnecessary unless you are travelling from a known infected area. However, it is advisable to drink bottled water and to wash all fruit and vegetables.

If your ailment is a minor one, chemists (*farmacia*) can give advice and dispense prescriptions.

TIME

Local standard time is one hour ahead of Greenwich Mean Time (GMT). Italian Summer Time (when clocks go forward an hour) is in operation from the last weekend of March to the last weekend of September. The time is one hour ahead of Britain except for a few weeks from late September to late October when the time is the same. Local time is also six hours ahead of New York time, nine hours behind Sydney and 11 hours behind New Zealand for most of the year.

CURRENCY

The unit of currency is the *lira* (plural *lire*). Notes are issued in denominations of 1,000, 2,000, 5,000, 10,000, 20,000, 50,000 and 100,000 lire. Coins are issued in denominations of 5, 10, 20, 50, 100, 200 and 500 lire. You will find lire is abbreviated to 'L' in shops.

Bernini's ornate canopy in St Peter's in Rome

CREDIT CARDS

All principal credit cards (eg American Express, Diners Card, Access, Visa) are accepted by most establishments, but not petrol stations.

BANKS

Usual banking hours are from 8.30am to 1.30pm and 3pm (or 3.30pm) to 4pm (or 4.30pm) Monday to Friday. Check locally as times vary in the afternoon from bank to bank. All banks are closed at weekends and on national holidays. On weekdays, evenings and holidays money can be changed at main railway stations and airports.

ELECTRICITY

The current is 220 volts AC, 50 cycles, with plugs of the two 'round' pin type. British, Australian or New Zealand appliances normally requiring a slightly higher voltage will work. For visitors from the US and Canada with appliances requiring 100/120 volts, and not fitted for dual voltage, a voltage transformer is required.

The Fontana del Nettuno, one of three fountains in Rome's popular Piazza Navona

POST OFFICES

Post offices are open from 8.15am to 12.30pm Monday to Friday and 8.15am to noon on Saturday. On the last day of the month offices close at noon. Times do vary, however, from place to place.

TELEPHONES

Some phones still take tokens called *gettone* which cost 200 *lire* each and can be purchased at post offices, tobacconists, some bars or slot machines. However, it is much easier to use a *carta telefonica* (a pre-paid telephone card) which you buy at the same outlets. They have a value of either 5,000 or 10,000 *lire* and can be used for international calls. Call boxes also take 200 and 500 *lire* coins which you insert before lifting the receiver. The dialling tone is short and long tones. To call abroad, first dial 00, then the country code, followed by the city code and the number itself. The prefix for the UK is 0044; for Eire 00353; for the US and Canada 001; and for Australia 00 61. If you wish to make a reverse charge or person-to-person call you will need to go through the operator – dial 15 for European countries or 170 for elsewhere.

TOURIST OFFICES

The Italian State Tourist Office (ENIT) is represented in many countries abroad including the following:
Australia and New Zealand – c/o Alitalia, AGC House, 124 Phillip Street, Sydney, New South Wales (tel: 02 221 3620)
Canada – 1 Place Ville Marie, Suite 2414, Montreal 113, Quebec H3B 3M9 (tel: 514 866 7667)
UK – 1 Princes Street, London W1R 8AY (tel: 0171 408 1254)
US – 630 Fifth Avenue, Suite 1565, New York 10111 (tel: 212–397 5294).

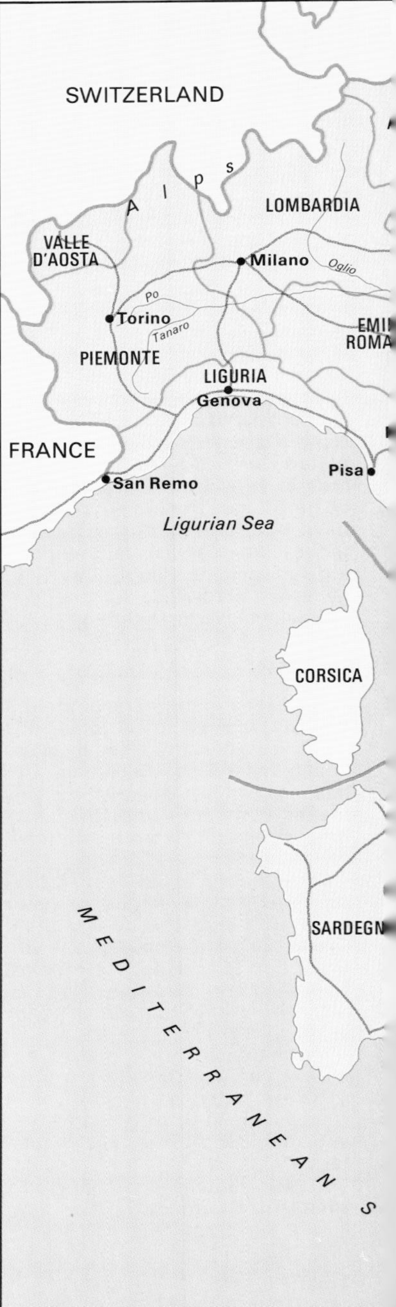

ENTRY REGULATIONS

The only document necessary for UK, Irish, Commonwealth and US citizens is a valid passport for any stay that does not exceed three months. For visitors from EU countries, a visitor's card is sufficient.

CUSTOMS

Items for personal or professional use may be brought into Italy free of charge. Duty free allowances for UK residents going to or returning from Italy are: 200 cigarettes or 100 cigarillos or 50 cigars or 250g of tobacco; alcoholic drinks over 22 per cent volume, 1 litre, or not over 22 per cent volume, 2 litres of fortified or sparkling wine plus still table wine, 2 litres; perfume, 50g, and toilet water, 250cc; plus other duty free goods to the value of £32 or the equivalent in other currencies. Travellers under 17

USEFUL WORDS

English Italian
yes si
no no
please per favore
thank you grazie
good morning buon giorno
good afternoon or evening buona sera
small piccolo
quickly presto
cold freddo
good buono
do you speak English? parla Inglese?
open aperto
closed chiuso
near vicino
far lontano
on the left a sinistra
on the right a destra
straight ahead diritto
how much? quanto?
expensive caro

Detail from the façade of the magnificent Duomo in Firenze

are not entitled to liquor and tobacco allowances. Allowances for duty- and tax-paid goods obtained in EU countries are slightly greater. For non-Europeans all tobacco product amounts shown above are doubled. Visitors may import an unlimited amount of Italian and foreign currency and export up to 1,000,000 *lire* and up to 5,000,000 *lire* in foreign currency. If you wish to export amounts in excess of the above you must declare the amount on entry using form V2 obtainable at frontier customs posts. You must then show the form to customs when leaving the country.

EMERGENCY TELEPHONE NUMBERS

Fire, police and ambulance tel: 113.

PIEDMONT, LOMBARDY, EMILIA-ROMAGNA, VENETO

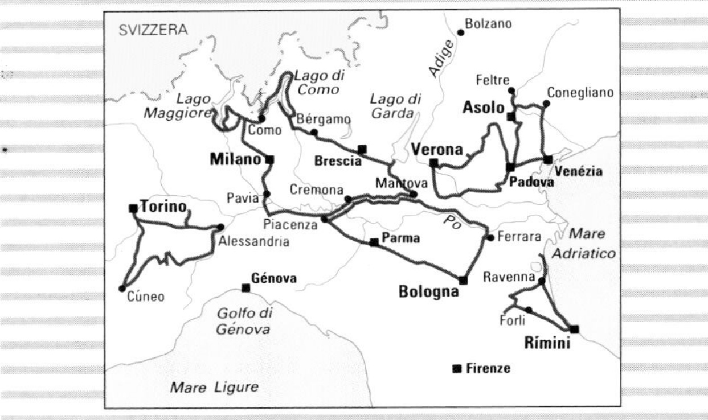

Italy is separated from the rest of the continent by the massive bulk of the Alps. The great range's southernmost peaks and valleys encroach upon Piedmont and Lombardy and on a clear day, from Torino (Turin), Piedmont's capital, and the centre of an arena of mountains, it is possible to look back to Mont Blanc and admire its magnificent snow-capped peak.

From Torino to Milano (Milan) there is a gradual flattening of the landscape as it descends gently towards the Po, the river that divides Piedmont practically in half. It continues into Lombardy which, with its five magnificent lakes, its rivers and its canals, is endlessly watery and enviably fertile. The Po forms the region's southern border with Emilia-Romagna before it flows out to the Adriatic at the bottom of the Veneto.

Piedmont and Lombardy combined are the cradle of Italy's industry and the source of much of its wealth. Its inhabitants are the industrious descendants of invaders from northern Europe. It is not by accident that here are the huge Fiat works (Piedmont), some of Europe's best design studios and manufacturers (in Lombardy, especially Milano), the vineyards that produce some of Italy's most excellent wine (eg Barolo from Piedmont) and the vermouth industry (Torino).

The great plain of the River Po, which continues southwards into Emilia-Romagna, was once northern Italy's greatest attraction. Hordes of invaders since time immemorial managed to work their way across the dangerous Alpine routes simply because the riches at the other end were immeasurable. Every inch of the plain of Emilia-Romagna right up to the Apennines in the south is still under cultivation. So prolific is the area's produce, so big the vegetables and succulent the meat and poultry, that Bologna, Emilia-Romagna's capital, is known as 'La Grassa', 'The Fat'.

The Veneto is as lush as any of the other regions mentioned. From the flat plain of the Po to the Dolomites of the eastern Alps and the marshy lagoons around Venice, the Veneto is also just as varied. But its reputation has more to do with art and architecture, particularly of the Renaissance, than culinary activities and geography. Its hills and southern plain are filled with towns and villages whose past affinities with Venice are acknowledged usually by an ancient stone-carved lion of St Mark – the Venetian symbol – placed conspicuously in the centre of the town. Even the cultural activities of this great northern city spread to the remotest corners of the Veneto. You will still find its country churches and museums filled with masterpieces of Venetian art.

Torino

Torino is one of the most intellectually active cities in Italy. This, mixed with a dose of Piedmontese sobriety, has provided Italy with marvellous museums, libraries, theatres, exhibitions and a university. Torino's Egyptian Museum is the second most important in the world (after Cairo's), while its Armería Real (Royal Armoury), the Museo dell'Automobile (Motor Museum) and Museo del Cinema are stacked with varied treasures. A baroque-style centre contributes to an almost courtly atmosphere in this elegant and dignified city.

Milano

Milano, capital of Lombardy, is also the economic capital of Italy, and is unquestionably northwest Italy's major art centre. In the Castello Sforzesco (Sforza Castle), the Pinacoteca di Brera (Brera Gallery), Museo Poldi-Pezzoli and the Pinacoteca Ambrosiana (Ambrosia Gallery), you will find endless works by the 'greats' of the history of Renaissance painting. The Duomo

Statues atop the pinnacles of the cathedral gaze over Milano

Verona, setting for Shakespeare's tragic tale of Romeo and Juliet

(cathedral) of Milano is the most striking example of northern Italian Gothic architecture that you will see anywhere.

Bologna

Bologna has a well-deserved reputation as Italy's culinary capital: if you like dishes with cream, butter and cheese, or succulent red meat, this is where you will find them at their best. There is a feast of architecture too, as Bologna's medieval and Renaissance centre is still intact. Its old streets are lined with arcades which come into their own when it rains. Museums, galleries, an ancient university, nightclubs and shops are Bologna's other attractions.

Rimini

Rimini has one really important monument, the 15th-century Tempio Malatestiano (Malatesta Temple), with a famous Renaissance façade designed by Leon Battista Alberti for Sigismundo Malatesta. Otherwise, Rimini is famous for its entertainments of the not so intellectual sort. Sunbathing, nightclubbing and lazy days contribute to Rimini's reputation as one of the Adriatic's most seductive resorts.

Asolo

Not only does the small hilltown of Asolo preserve the memory of famous inhabitants such as Robert Browning and Eleanora Duse, but its ancient centre is full of well maintained medieval and Renaissance buildings and villas. It has a good monthly antiques market.

Verona

Verona's many treasures include the 14th-century tombs of the Scaligeri, noble medieval palaces, Roman ruins such as the famous Arena (the best preserved amphitheatre in Italy after the Colosseum) and a clutch of medieval and Renaissance churches.

Duke Emanuele Filiberto of Savoy in Piazza San Carlo, Torino

3 days – 411km (255 miles)

THE FOOT OF THE MOUNTAINS

Wild mushrooms, one of Piedmont's many gastronomic delights

Torino • Moncalvo • Asti • Alessandria Acqui Terme • Alba • Serralunga d'Alba • Barolo La Morra • Cherasco • Cuneo • Torino

Piedmont is the most western region of Italy and is enclosed on three sides by mountainous Alpine countryside. Here you will find some of the best known ski resorts in Italy. To the east is the great plain of the Po river beyond which are the hilly and fertile Langhe and Monferrato districts, memorable for their picturesque hilltowns and their wine. More or less in the middle is Torino (Turin), the region's capital, with its baroque architecture, a well preserved city centre, Roman remains and an active street life.

ⓘ Via Roma 222, Torino

*From Torino, take the **A21** towards Asti, about 60km (37 miles). Leave the autostrada at the Asti Est exit taking the **SS10** towards Asti, then the **SS457** going north to Moncalvo, about 22km (14 miles).*

Moncalvo, Piedmont

1 Moncalvo is where you will get a real taste of the Piedmontese countryside. Terraced vineyards and tidy, ordered rows of poplar trees climb the slopes on the edge of town. Situated in the middle of the immensely fertile **Monferrato** district, it is a gastronome's delight – a good place to try the local truffle crop at the annual auction. Moncalvo itself has the pretty Gothic Church of **San Francesco**, which, along with the remains of an old moated **castle**, towers over the surrounding countryside. The old centre of town has some 14th-century houses.

From Moncalvo, retrace the route to Asti.

Asti, Piedmont

2 Asti is full of places to see and awash with festivals. Once the city rivalled Milan, and it is well worth spending some time in its old centre. The Gothic **Duomo** (cathedral) contains fonts made from Romanesque capitals supported on inverted Roman capitals and 18th-century inlaid choir stalls. Other churches include **San Pietro in Consavia** with its 10th-century circular baptistery and little adjacent **archaeological museum** housed in the cloisters. In Piazza San Secondo is the large Gothic Church of **San Secondo** in which you can see an altarpiece by Ferrari who was much influenced by Leonardo. The **Torre San Secondo**, a Romanesque tower on a Roman base, is the belltower for the Church of **San Caterina**. In

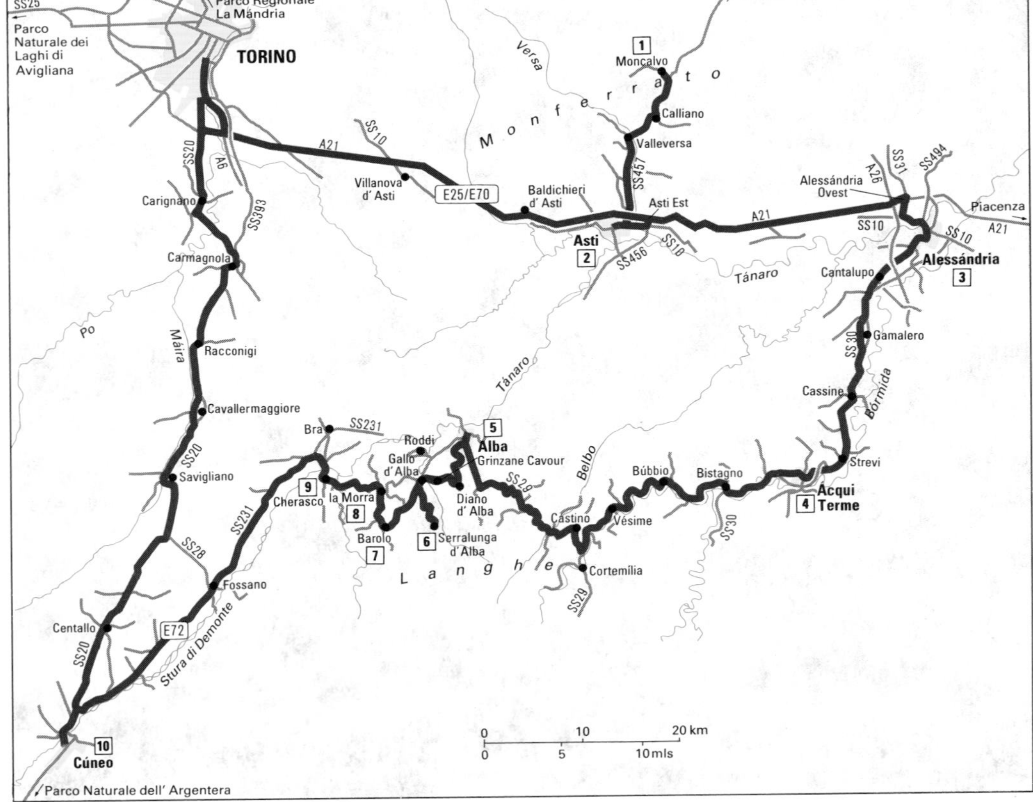

fact there are quite a few towers scattered around Asti – the medieval **Torre Troiana**, and the octagonal **Torre dei De Regibus** are just two. The town is the scene of a great wine fair at the end of September.

[i] Piazza Alfieri 34

From Asti, return to and take the ***A21*** *going east to Alessandria, about 36km (22 miles).*

Alessandria, Piedmont

3 Alessandria is the centre for the manufacture of the *borsalino*, the ubiquitous felt hat – in fact the city has the world's best hat museum, **Museo del Capello Borsalino**. Not much of old Alessandria has survived except in the 18th-century **Duomo** (cathedral) and the older Church of **Santa Maria di Castello**. Among the city's palaces is the **Palazzo della Prefettura**, designed by Benedetto Alfieri. The 18th-century Cittadella (citadel) is particularly well preserved. The countryside all around Alessandria is as fertile as anywhere in Piedmont, supporting rice fields, wheat, fruit and acres of poplar woods which are used in the making of furniture.

The bold red wine Barolo takes its name from this hilltop town

[i] Via Savona 26

From Alessandria, take the ***SS30*** *for about 34km (21 miles) to Acqui Terme.*

Acqui Terme, Piedmont

4 Acqui Terme is noted for its **hot sulphuric springs**, in particular one which bubbles up out of the ground in a fountain at the centre of town. The hottest spring, **La Bollente**, is housed in a special pavilion, the Nuove Terme. The Romans were aware of its properties but all that remains from their time here are four arches of an **aqueduct**. The Romanesque **Duomo** (cathedral) has a very fine 17th-century loggia (gallery), and a good entrance portal. Next to the cathedral are the remains of the **Castello dei Paleologi** (Castle of the Paleologi) in which there is now an **Archaeological Museum** containing the finds from the old baths of Acqui – including mosaics.

From Acqui Terme, go via Bistagno, Bubbio and Castino (west) across country to Alba, about 60km (37 miles).

Alba, Piedmont

5 Alba is the capital of the Langhe district, an area famous for its vineyards and its white truffles (*tartufi bianchi*). Set beside the Tanaro river, Alba has buildings of terracotta-coloured brick. The **Duomo (cathedral) of San Lorenzo** was rebuilt by Bishop Novelli in 1486 and inside is Barnardino Fossati's chancel with its 35 carved and inlaid wooden stalls. Other churches include **Santa Maria Maddalena** and the baroque Church of **San Giovanni**. Inside the latter you can see the *Madonna delle Grazie* by Barnarba da Modena, 1377. The Council Chamber of the Town Hall, the **Palazzo Comunale**, houses the *Virgin Crowned* by Alba's greatest painter, Macrino (dated 1501). Much of Alba is still medieval – there are narrow arcaded streets and old doorways. In the old centre is a Saturday market which has been held on the same spot since 1171.

From Alba, follow the signs pointing to Diano d'Alba, about 8km (5 miles). From there proceed via Gallo d'Alba to Serralunga d'Alba, about 12km (7 miles).

Serralunga d'Alba

6 This picturesque place is dominated by a stately **castle** built between 1340 and 1357 to support the castle at nearby Barolo (see over). These two buildings, as well as other local castles built for the same family, were aligned so as to allow a system of communication using torchlight at night and coloured drapes during the day. The entire town retains its medieval character. Little houses cluster in circles around the castle and nearly every one has an amazing view of the surrounding countryside. **San Sebastiano**, the parish church,

SPECIAL TO . . .

2 In Asti, the **Palio** is held in the Campo del Palio on 18 September. This event dates back to the Middle Ages and consists of a colourful horse race, ridden bareback. The 'offering of the Palio' takes place in May. The events include flag-tossing and participants wear medieval costume.

5 Alba has another **Palio**, this time a donkey race. Held in October, it is supposed to parody the Asti Palio, and to keep alive the memory of a horse race staged by the soldiers of Asti around the walls of Alba in 1275, when they were laying siege to the town.

9 Cherasco holds the National Gathering of Snail Breeders on the second weekend in June with associated gastronomic events.

SCENIC ROUTES

The most scenic parts of this tour are the views from La Morra, which is known as the 'Belvedere of the Langhe' – you can see for miles from the highest point in town, the edge of the open-ended main square in the centre; on a good day you can even see the snow-capped Alps in the distance. The countryside all around Barolo, and especially the approach to the town from Alba, is scenic. Take a picnic. The roads are small and under-used and there are clumps of woodlands and views to distant hilltowns.

RECOMMENDED WALKS

There are special walks from La Morra following designated **wine routes** which take you through vineyards to winetasting points. Each path is identified by a different colour according to its destination. The routes also go past inns and local wine cellars where you can sluice your parched throat with the local brew.

BACK TO NATURE

10 Cuneo is practically on the edge of the **Parco Naturale dell'Argentera** (Argentera Natural Park), a protected mountainous area which is home to various wild alpine animals and birds. Ibex and chamois are among the rare species sometimes seen. Alpine marmots are widespread in the alpine meadows and birdlife includes citril finches, Alpine accentors, griffon vultures and ptarmigan.

FOR CHILDREN

Just to the north of Turin is **Parco Regionale La Mandria** (La Mandria Regional Park). Part of it is a sanctuary for animals – deer in particular, but there are horses and unusual cattle as well. Also near Turin, just to the west, children might enjoy a visit to the **Parco Naturale dei Laghi di Avigliana** (Avigliana Lakes Nature Park). Here the specialities are ducks, moorhens, kingfishers and other waterfowl.

FOR HISTORY BUFFS

5 The Langhe countryside around Alba is dotted with little towns, each one dominated by a castle. They do not necessarily have any particular sites of interest, but the towns themselves are picturesque and worth visiting if you have time. Among the best with interesting and dramatic-looking castles are Grinzane Cavour, whose castle was lived in by the Marquise of Cavour – the family of the prominent 19th-century statesman Camillo Cavour – about 6km (4 miles) from Alba on the way to Barolo and Roddi. Roddi's castle passed through a variety of noble ownerships, ending in 1836 with King Carlo Alberto. Today the property of the Catholic Church, it is about 6km (4 miles) from Alba.

was reconstructed in about 1630, but is far older and still preserves its 14th-century belltower.

From Serralunga d'Alba, return in the direction of Gallo d'Alba, turning left before the village to Barolo about 6km (4 miles) further on.

Barolo, Piedmont

7 Tiny Barolo is perched on a hill overlooking countryside filled with vineyards. Dominated by a vast castle, the **Castello Faletti**, it gives its name to one of the most renowned Italian red wines. The castle itself is no longer a private home, but the centre of the Barolo wine production and housed in it is a **museum**, a **vintage cellar** and an ***enoteca***, a place for tasting the local wine. The castle is open to the public and has interesting furnished rooms with perhaps the best views in Barolo. The town is a picturesque place, predominantly terracotta-coloured. You could walk around it in about half an hour. The local **parish church** is Romanesque and was most probably once the castle chapel – it is filled with the memorials to the Faletti family who once owned the castle.

Cherasco, Piedmont

9 Cherasco is famous as the centre of the National Association of Snail Breeders. Not that you will meet any snails within the precincts but the town is the centre of gastronomic events relating to edible snails. The **Torre Civico**, a 36m (118-foot) high tower, is the most important monument here. It sports a rare clock (1552) showing the phases of the moon. Among Cherasco's churches, **Sant'Agostino**, with its baroque altar, and **San Pietro**, the oldest church in the town, are the most interesting. In the **Palazzo Fracassi** you can see treasures dating from when the Holy Shroud was housed in the town in the early 18th century. In fact, in 1706, the Shroud itself was kept in the **Palazzo Salmatoris**. The 14th-century **Castello** (Castle of the Visconti) still survives in excellent condition

It is a short distance to the SS231 which leads directly to Cuneo, about 48km (30 miles).

Cuneo, Piedmont

10 Cuneo is an important market town. The huge **market**, which swamps the town's centre every Tuesday, filling every corner of the

Picturesque La Morra is a popular stop-off for wine-lovers

From Barolo, travel north to La Morra, about 6km (4 miles).

La Morra, Piedmont

8 La Morra has two churches, the bigger one dedicated to **San Martino**, the town's patron saint, and the smaller to **San Rocco**. However, the principal reason for coming to La Morra is not to look at old monuments, but to indulge in winetasting. There are plenty of places in which to do this. Apart from the **Enoteca Civica** with its exhibition and sales of *Barolo* wine produced by local vineyards, there are smaller, private cellars all over this small hilltown. Even the most obscure wines can be found here and the range of prices is huge. Near by is the **Museo Ratti** (Ratti Wine Museum), housed in the former Abbey of the Annunciation.

From La Morra, cross the River Tanaro, to Cherasco, about 6km (4 miles) away.

porticoed Piazza Galimberti, is best known for its chestnuts and raw silk. There are porticoed streets all over town, Via Mondovi being the most characteristic. In the centre, too, is the 13th-century Church of **San Francesco**, which also houses the local **museum**. Many of the Piedmontese towns have festivals, relating to the consumption of food and drink and Cuneo is no exception. At the **Piedmontese Cheese Exposition** held here in November you can taste locally produced cheeses – some of which you will never find anywhere else in Italy.

i Corso Nizza 17

From Cuneo, take the SS20 back to Torino, about 85km (53 miles).

Torino – Moncalvo 82 (51)
Moncalvo – Asti 22 (14)
Asti – Alessandria 36 (22)
Alessandria – Acqui Terme 34 (21)
Acqui Terme – Alba 60 (37)
Alba – Serralunga d'Alba 20 (12)
Serralunga d'Alba – Barolo 12 (7)
Barolo – La Morra 6 (4)
La Morra – Cherasco 6 (4)
Cherasco – Cuneo 48 (30)
Cuneo – Torino 85 (53)

4 days – 728km (452 miles)

OF ALPS, LAKES & PLAIN

Lago Maggiore, with its 'Beautiful Isle', Isola Bella

Milano • Sacro Monte Varese • Lago Maggiore Como • Lago di Como • Lecco • Bellágio • Bergamo Lago di Garda • Mantova • Cremona • Pavia • Milano

Lombardy is crossed by the huge River Po and studded with great lakes – Maggiore, Garda, Como, Iseo and Lugano. Since the Middle Ages it has been a prosperous commercial region – reflected in the quality of its surviving period architecture. Milano (Milan) nowadays is the thriving economic capital of Italy but the traces of its cultural past are everywhere: the art in the Castello Sforzesco (Sforza Castle), Leonardo's *Last Supper* in Santa Maria delle Grazie, the Pinoteca di Brera (Brera Gallery) and Teatro La Scala, the world-famous opera house. The other historic towns in the region have much to offer. This tour highlights the best and provides an opportunity to view the lush Lombardy countryside.

[i] Via Marconi 1, Milano

*From Milano, take the **A8** going north (via Legnano and Gallarate) – the latter about 38km (24 miles) – to Varese, about another 17km (10 miles). About 10km (6 miles) north of Varese lies Sacro Monte Varese.*

Sacro Monte Varese, Lombardia

1 The 'Sacred Mountain of Varese', with its narrow passages and ancient covered alleys, is only the backdrop for a **pilgrimage route** more famous nowadays for its art than for its saintly connections. It is supposed to have been founded by St Ambrose in thanks for Lombardy's deliverance from the Arian heresy (the doctrine put forward by the 4th-century theologian Arius, that Christ is not one body with God). From the bottom of the Sacro Monte to the top, about 800m (2,625 feet), is a cobbled route with 14 **chapels** at intervals along the **Sacred Way**, each one dedicated to the Mystery of the Rosary. The shrines are the work of Bernascone and each is filled with lifesize terracotta figures, by Bussola, acting out some religious episode. At the top is the lavishly decorated Church of **Santa Maria del Monte**. The views from the Sacro Monte are wonderful and, to restore you after the climb, you will find cafés and restaurants in the town.

*From Sacro Monte Varese, go back to Varese, then continue on the **SS394** to Lago Maggiore, about 22km (14 miles).*

Lago Maggiore, Lombardia

2 Only the eastern shore of Lago Maggiore (Lake Maggiore) is in Lombardia. Its western shore is in

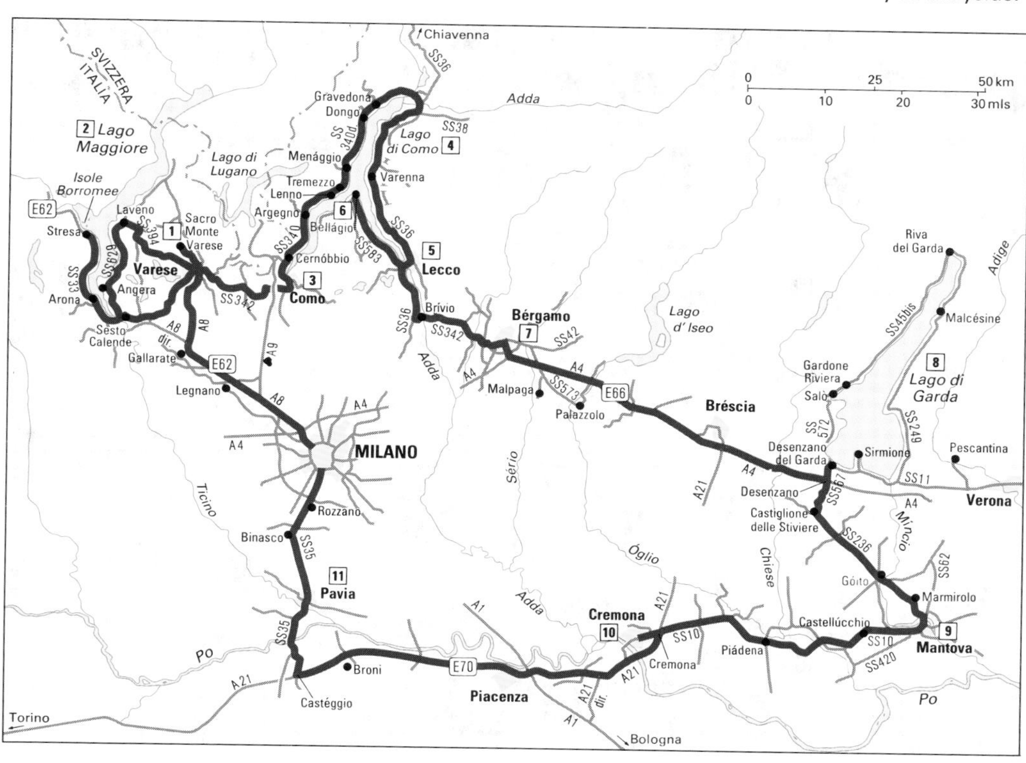

Fine olive oil and wine on sale in the lake resort of Stresa

Piedmont and its northern part in Switzerland. It would take days to drive around the lake seeing all that there is to look at. The highlights are the towns of Angera, Arona, Stresa and Isole Borromee (the Borromean islands) in the middle of the lake opposite Stresa. At Angera is the Visconti **castle** (open to the public), which contains well-preserved 14th- and 15th-century frescos. At Arona is another **castle**, this time ruined. Visit the Church of **Santa Maria** with, in the Borromeo Chapel, an altarpiece of 1511 by Ferrari. Stresa is the largest resort on the lake. Full of Victorian-style hotels, it is also dotted with old-fashioned villas and luxurious gardens running down to the water's edge. Some gardens are open, including the **Villa Pallavicino**. But the real gem of Maggiore is the Borromean islands. Isola Bella, perhaps the best known, is a huge private garden surrounding a palace (**Palazzo Borromeo**) – both open to the public. The gardens were laid out for Count Carlo III Borromeo in the 17th century by Angelo Crivelli. The elaborate complex includes white peacocks, grottoes, fountains and statuary. Isola Madre is another of the islands, famous for its large botanical garden which, with its palace, is well worth a visit. Boats to these islands leave from Stresa.

*Make for Varese from Stresa, take the **SS33** to Sesto Calende at the very foot of the lake, about 25km (16 miles) then follow the signs to Varese, about 23km (14 miles)]. From Varese, take the **SS342** to Como, about 28km (17 miles).*

Como, Lombardia

3 Como was the birthplace of the Roman writer Pliny the Elder. In fact you will see signs dotted around Lago di Como (Lake Como) pointing to the sites of the various villas the Pliny family owned here. One of the most elegant towns on the lake, Como has, facing the water, a huge **Promenade** which fills with people at dusk. There are busy cafés, palm trees and parks. The **Duomo** (cathedral) dates mainly from the 14th century. The rose window on the façade is Gothic in style and there is excellent carving by the Rodari brothers of Maroggia, about 1500. Other relics of old Como include the churches of **Sant'Abbondio**, and **San Fedele**, which was once the cathedral, and the **Porta Vittoria**, the late 12th-century city gate. In the **Museo Civico** (Civic Museum) you will see objects dating from the neolithic period to World War II. See also the Museo Alessandro Volta which houses equipment used by the man who gave his name to the electric volt.

[i] Piazza Cavour 17

*From Como, drive around the lake, starting on the **SS340** up its left-hand side.*

Lago di Como, Lombardia

4 All around the lake you will see vast villas and castles overlooking the water. Cernóbbio is a pretty town about 7km (4½ miles) from Como. Here is the grand **Hotel Villa D'Este**, once the home of the English Queen Caroline. At Tremezzo is the **Villa Carlotta**, once lived in by Princess Carlotta of Prussia, who laid out its gardens in the 1850s. You can visit this as well as the **Villa Arconati**, just a few kilometres outside Tremezzo, at Lenno. The parish Church of Lenno has an ancient **crypt** that is well worth a visit. Further on around the lake are Menaggio and Gravedona. The latter has the interesting Church of **Santa Maria del Tiglio** which contains early frescos of St John the Baptist. At nearby Dongo, Mussolini was captured by the partisans in 1945. On the other side of the lake, at Varenna, visit the **Villa Monastero** with its formal gardens and the Romanesque Church of **San Giorgio**. One really good way to see the lake – and admire the towns from a distance – is to take a boat trip

SCENIC ROUTES

The most scenic parts of this tour are the following:

– From Sacro Monte Varese, drive to Monte delle Tre Croci (the Mount of the Three Crosses) where you will have wonderful views of the surrounding countryside. Another 200m (220 yards) further up, at **Campo dei Fiori** – a long ridge – an even wider panorama can be enjoyed.

– From Stresa on Lago Maggiore, take a cablecar to **Mount Mottarone** and see the views to the Alps and to Lake Garda.

– On the west shore of Lago di Como, at Argegno, there are views to the northern snowy mountains.

– The **SS45bis** for the last 11km (7 miles) before you reach Riva del Garda on Lago di Garda, is one of the most spectacular stretches of road on the lake, should you elect to drive rather than take the steamer.

around it. It is possible to take one that stops at a number of places, using it like a bus. Begin at Como.

Lecco lies at the foot of the eastern arm of Lake Como, from Como itself, a direct distance of 29km (18 miles).

Lecco, Lombardia

5 Lecco is in direct contrast to its illustrious neighbour Como. More industrial than prettier Como, Lecco's claim to fame is that it was the birthplace of Alessandro Manzoni, the great 19th-century Italian novelist. The **Villa Manzoni**, his former home, is now a museum – you will find it in **Via Promessi Sposi**, named after the writer's most famous novel which, translated, means 'The Betrothed' (the street is also known as Via Amendola). While you are in town, visit the **Duomo** (cathedral), with its 14th-century frescos in the style of Giotto, and the **Ponte Azzone Visconti**, a medieval bridge over the Adda river. Although much altered (it no longer has any towers) and enlarged, it still has much of its early character.

*From Lecco, take the **SS583** up the western edge of Lecco's portion of Lake Como, called the Lake of Lecco, to Bellágio.*

Bellágio, Lombardia

6 Bellágio is one of the most beautiful points on Lake Como. Not only is it an interesting old town, but it is splendidly sited on a promontory overlooking the three arms of the lake. There is plenty to do here apart from just sitting in the sun enjoying the view. The 12th-century Church of **San Giacomo** has good carving in the apse and on its capitals. There is the **Villa Serbelloni**, with good gardens which can be visited, and the **Villa Melzi d'Eril**, which is open to the public and contains a collection of sculpture from Egypt. If time is short, the Villa Sebelloni gardens, supposed to stand on the site of the younger Pliny's villa 'Tragedia', are the more interesting.

*Return to Lecco, then take the **SS36** going south for about 15km*

BACK TO NATURE

There is plenty of birdlife to observe on and near Lakes Maggiore and Como. Black kites scavenge along the shoreline and herons and egrets are found in undisturbed spots. Ducks and grebes can be seen on the open water and swallows and alpine swifts hawk for insects over the water's surface.

Bergamo's splendid Piazza Vecchia is the town's historic centre

FOR CHILDREN

8 At **Pescantina**, about 12km (7 miles) from Lazise on the bottom eastern edge of Lago Garda, is a zoo and reptilarium, and a dinosaur park – although the dinosaurs are the concrete kind.

SPECIAL TO . . .

9 In Mantova is the **Good Friday Procession** on 1 April. Sacred vases which, according to tradition, contain earth soaked with the blood of Christ, are carried in a procession around the town.

RECOMMENDED TRIPS

Walking is not the best way to explore this area – take a boat trip instead. That way you will get a much better feel of what the lakes on this tour are about. Steamers run to all corners of Lago Maggiore and Como – there are well organised schedules run much like a bus service. Take a short trip to a destination down either lake, have lunch, then return in the afternoon.

(9 miles) until it cuts the SS342. Take the latter to Bergamo, about 24km (15 miles).

Bergamo, Lombardia

7 Bergamo is divided into the **Città Alta** and the **Città Bassa**, the Upper City and the Lower City. The former is the more interesting, as well as being the older. Its best monuments are in the **Piazza Vecchia**. In it is the **Biblioteca Civica** (Civic Library), a late 16th-century building modelled on Venice's great library building, designed by Sansovino. Across the square, past **Contarini's fountain** surrounded by stone lions, is the 12th-century **Torre Civica** with its 15th-century clock that still tolls the curfew hour (10pm). Behind the 12th-century **Palazzo della Ragione** are the **Duomo** and the ornate **Colleoni Chapel**. You can just see the base of the latter through the pointed arched loggia beneath the Palazzo della Ragione. Built in 1476, the façade of the Colleoni Chapel is a mass of sculptured decoration and coloured marble. Inside is the tomb and a statue of Bartolomeo Colleoni, who controlled Venice's armed forces in the 15th century. The ceiling fresco is by Tiepolo. The Church of **Santa Maria Maggiore**, in Piazza Duomo, is a fine Romanesque building. Also in the Upper City is the **Cittadella** (citadel), which contains the **Natural History Museum**, and the **Museo Donizetti** – this great composer was born in Bergamo, and you can visit the **Teatro Donizetti** in the Lower City. Between the Upper and Lower Cities is the **Galleria dell'Accademia Carrara**, a first-class collection of art, well worth taking in.

[i] Via Paleocapa 2

*From Bergamo, take the **A4** via Brescia to Lago di Garda, about 78km (48 miles) – at Desenzano del Garda at the foot of the lake.*

Lago di Garda, Lombardia

8 The most interesting ports of call around Lago (Lake) di Garda are Salò, Gardone Riviera, Riva del Garda, Malcesine and Sirmione. All are accessible by the steamer, and rather than drive around the lake, you could leave the car at Desenzano del Garda and go by boat. Salò has a fine Gothic **Duomo** (cathedral) with a noteworthy Renaissance portal. At Gardone Riviera, most things to visit have something to do with Gabriele d'Annunzio (1863–1938), one of the greatest writers and poets of his generation. His villa, **Vittoriale degli Italiani** was specially built for him and can be visited. The villa and grounds are filled with an extraordinary array of bits and pieces, like the great ornate organs in the music room, among which the writer chose to live. There is also a **museum** and a **mausoleum** in the villa's grounds. At Riva del Garda, right at the northern tip of the lake, about 95 breathtaking kilometres (60 miles) away from Desenzano del Garda up the western edge of the lake, and actually in the Trentino region, is a 13th-century tower, the **Torre Apponale** and a clutter of other ancient edifices of which the **Palazzo Pretorio** and the 12th-century **Rocca** (fortress) are the most interesting. The town's **Museo Civico** (Civic Museum) contains an interesting collection of armour and archaeological finds from the area, housed in the Rocca. Malcesine, halfway down the eastern edge of the lake, is the proud possessor of the magnificent **Castello Scaligero** (Scaliger Castle) dramatically situated at the water's edge. But the **castle** at Sirmione is more remarkable. Also from the 13th century and one of the Scaligeri castles, its battlements and its dramatic situation half in the water

The shores of Lake Garda are dotted with pleasant resorts

makes it possibly the most memorable sight on the Lago di Garda.

*From Desenzano del Garda, take the **SS567** for 11km (7 miles) to Castiglione delle Stiviere, at which branch on to the **SS236** and continue on to Mantova, about 37km (23 miles).*

Mantova, Lombardia

9 Mantova (Mantua) sits on a swampy, marshy bend in the Mincio river. Its claim to fame is that it was the seat of one of the most intellectually active and refined courts of the Italian Renaissance. The Gonzaga family were the rulers and they embellished the town with a remarkable **Palazzo Ducale** (Ducal Palace) that still contains some of their art collection. The neo-classical rooms have a set of early 16th-century Flemish tapestries and the duke's apartments have a fine collection of classical statuary. Here you will see Rubens' vast portrait of the Gonzaga family. The **Camera degli Sposi** in the **Castel di San Giorgio** is world famous for its brilliant frescos by Mantegna, finished in 1472. Apart from a series of portraits of the family, there are others of their favourite dwarfs. In the **Casetta dei Nani**, the House of the Dwarfs, you can see the miniature rooms where the latter were once thought to have lived. The **Palazzo del Tè** is another Gonzaga palace built by Giulio Romano in 1527 for Federico II Gonzaga's mistress. The **Sala dei Giganti**, the Room of the Giants, is its masterpiece: huge frescoed fighting giants seem to bring down the ceiling. The Basilica of **Sant'Andrea**, designed by Leon Battista (1472), houses a chalice of Christ's blood, a relic once much venerated by the Gonzaga.

[i] Piazza Mantegna 6

*Take the **SS10** for about 66km (41 miles) to Cremona.*

Cremona, Lombardia

10 You cannot come to Cremona and not visit the **Museo Stradivariano** (Stradivarian Museum). For the modern violin was developed in this city in 1566, and one of the great masters of violin-making here – though much later – was Antonio Stradivarius. There is also the **Museo Civico** (Civic Museum) in which much space is devoted to Roman Cremona. Here, too, are works of art from defunct local churches. The **Duomo** (cathedral) has five wonderful 17th-century Brussels tapestries as well as a series of frescos by local artists. Among the town's most interesting churches is **Sant'Agostino** with, in the fifth chapel on the south, a *Madonna and Saints* by Perugino, who was once Raphael's teacher.

[i] Piazza del Commune 5

*From Cremona, take the **A21** via Piacenza 33km (20 miles) as far as the Casteggio turning, 82km (51 miles), for the **SS35** to Pavia, a further 21km (13 miles).*

Pavia, Lombardia

11 Pavia was at one time an important Roman city (*Ticinum*). Not a lot remains from this period, though the **Museo Civico** (Civic Museum) does contain finds from Roman times and earlier Pavia. On an upper floor you will find the **picture gallery** with works by, among others, Bellini and Van der Goes, the latter one of the most important of the Netherlandish Renaissance painters. But in Pavia, the most noteworthy monument to visit is the **Certosa di Pavia**, a remarkable and highly decorative Renaissance monastery complex, situated just on the outskirts of town. A tour will take in the vestibule, the Little Cloister, the Great Cloister and the church with Gothic, Renaissance and baroque decoration. Back in the town once again, Leonardo was partially responsible for the design of the **Duomo** (cathedral), begun in 1488, and in addition to the cathedral, there are about six other churches worth seeing in the city.

The Palazzo del Comune in Cremona, home of fine violins

[i] Via Fabio Filzi 2

*Take the **SS35** back to Milano, about 35km (22 miles).*

Milano – Sacro Monte Varese 65 (40)
Sacro Monte Varese – Lago Maggiore 32 (20)
Lago Maggiore – Como 76 (47)
Como – Lecco (around Lake Como) 109 (68)
Lecco – Bellágio 22 (14)
Bellágio – Bergamo 61 (38)
Bergamo – Lago di Garda 78 (48)
Lago di Garda – Mantova 48 (30)
Mantova – Cremona 66 (41)
Cremona – Pavia 136 (84)
Pavia – Milano 35 (22)

FOR HISTORY BUFFS

7 Near Bergamo, just off the SS573 south of the city, is **Malpaga**, in whose castle you can see frescos of Bartolomeo Colleoni hosting a banquet in honour of a visit by the King of Denmark in 1474. This is fascinating if you have already seen Colleoni's grandiose tomb in Bergamo.

3 days – 378km (234 miles)

LA GRASSA – THE 'FAT' COUNTRY

Frescos from the baptistery in Parma – a glimpse of medieval Italy

Bologna • Ferrara • Piacenza • Parma Reggio nell'Emilia • Modena • Bologna

This tour reveals two of the finest Romanesque churches in Italy, well preserved fortified cities – one with a moated castle – great Renaissance painting and sculpture, grand opera, thermal spas for therapeutic or self-indulgent breaks, Parma ham and a sparkling local wine – Lambrusco – which is never at its best outside the region. Bologna is the most cosmopolitan city on the tour. It has a huge, ancient university, its shops mirror those of Milan and it has a wide range of excellent restaurants giving it its nickname 'La Grassa' – 'Bologna the Fat'. From Bologna, the route passes through the vast flat plain which makes up the region, wedged in between the Apennines in the south and the borders of Lombardy and the Veneto in the north.

FOR HISTORY BUFFS

3 In the province of Parma are two interesting castles that would make a detour from Parma more than rewarding. Northwest of the city, at Fontanellato (take the A1 westwards for 20km/12 miles, as far as the Fidenza-Salsomaggiore Terme exit), is the moated **Castello di Sanvitale**. It has good frescos by Parmigianino, and is open to the public. Just to the north of this, at Soragna (only 8km/5 miles), is the furnished and frescoed **Palazzo di Soragna**. The castle, begun in the 8th century and converted into a palace in the 19th century, contains fine period furniture and art. This is also open to the public.

[i] Via Marconi 45, Bologna

*The autostrada **A13** goes north from Bologna for about 42km (26 miles) until the Ferrara Nord exit.*

Ferrara, Emilia-Romagna

1 The centre of Ferrara is dominated by a vast castle, the **Castello Estense**. Begun in 1385, it was the backdrop to the splendid court of the Este family, the rulers of Ferrara. It was designed to ward off any potential threat to this little city state, and its moat, drawbridge and military bulwarks are still formidable and do nothing to relieve its prisonlike appearance. A tour round the castle includes the dungeons in which Nicolò III d'Este imprisoned his lovely young wife Parisina Malatesta and her lover before they were beheaded. After these, the various decorated chambers of the castle are a welcome relief. Nicolò III's son Ercole I (1471–1505) was responsible for an addition to the medieval town known as the '**Herculean Addition**', making Ferrara the first 'modern' town in Europe. At the heart of the Herculean Addition is the extraordinary **Palazzo dei Diamanti** whose façade is studded with 12,600 stone 'diamonds', the Este badge. On the other side of the castle is the **Duomo** (cathedral). Begun in 1135, it has a lovely sculpted portico, with scenes from the Last Judgement. Inside, look for the painted *Martyrdom of St Lawrence* by Guercino in the south transept. But it is the **cathedral museum treasury** that contains splendid works, including a marble *Madonna of the Pomegranates* (1408) by Jacopo della Quercia, the greatest Sienese sculptor of the early Renaissance. Back outside in the Piazza Trento e Trieste which abuts the long flank of the cathedral, you come down to earth at the colourful market. There is also the **Museo Archeologico** (Archaeological Museum), housed in the Palazzo di Ludovico il Moro, with its collection of vases from the Greek and Etruscan necropolis of nearby Spina. See also the Palazzo Schifanoia with its lovely Renaissance frescos by Cosimo Tura.

[i] Piazzetta Municipale

*Leave Ferrara on the **SS16** going north. After crossing the Po, turn left towards the **A13**. Cross the motorway and continue west to Ostiglia, 56km (34½ miles). The **SS482** continues to Mantova, a further 33km (20 miles). From Mantova, the **SS10** continues west for 62km (39 miles) to Cremona immediately before which the autostrada **A21** branches southwest for 30km (19 miles) towards Piacenza. Leave the autostrada at the Piacenza Est exit and follow the signs into the city.*

Piacenza, Emilia-Romagna

2 This is a town that visitors to Emilia-Romagna tend to ignore unwittingly: its treasures and attractions are less obvious and less well known than those of other places. It has an interesting old centre filled with churches including a 12th-century Romanesque **Duomo** (cathedral) with a belltower topped by a gilded angel and interior frescos by Guercino, a notable baroque illusionist painter of the 17th century. The cathedral stands at the top of the Via XX Settembre looking down to the Piazza Cavalli, named after its equestrian statues of Alessandro Farnese and his brother Ranuccio. These early 17th-century statues by Francesco Mocchi, a pupil of Giambologna, who was the most famous sculptor in Florence after the death of Michelangelo, are the pride of Piacenza. The 16th-century **Palazzo Farnese** is a huge unfinished palace of the Farnese family which houses the **Museo Civico** (Civic Museum) containing works by Botticelli and the school of Botticelli. It also has another very peculiar relic known as *Il Fegato di Piacenza*, 'Piacenza's Liver', an Etruscan bronze sheep's liver marked with the names of local deities. To the south of the Piazza Cavalli, in a warren of little streets near the cathedral, is an early 19th-century **theatre**, an elegant neo-classical building still used during the various seasons of cham-

The fertile land of Emilia-Romagna, source of the region's prosperity

ber and orchestral music and ballet. It has an eccentric little museum attached to it containing relics from the theatre's past. Near by, the **Galleria d'Arte Moderna Ricci Oddi** (Ricci Oddi Gallery) contains a collection of modern art, including work by Boldini (1845–1931), a fashionable portrait painter who was the Italian equivalent of Sargent.

ⓘ Via San Siro 17

Leave Piacenza by the ***SS9*** *which runs directly to Parma 49km (30 miles).*

Parma, Emilia-Romagna

3 Parma is built on the flat so visiting its monuments is not such a strain on the calf muscles. Bigger than either Piacenza or Ferrara it has much more to see. If you start in the heart of the city, in the Piazza del Duomo, you will see the two buildings for which Parma is best known – the 11th-century **Duomo** (cathedral) and the 12th-century **baptistery** alongside it. The exterior of the cathedral is richly patterned, and the interior contains work of the painter Correggio who was influenced by Michelangelo. In the cathedral his *Assumption* (1526–30) can be seen in the vault of the dome: notice how the painted

SPECIAL TO . . .

5 Modena has an important **Antiques Fair** on the fourth Saturday and Sunday of every month, held in the Piazza Grande. It is best to go early in the morning, firstly to spot the hidden treasures before anyone else does and secondly to avoid the crowds who come in from all over the countryside to stroll among the stands.

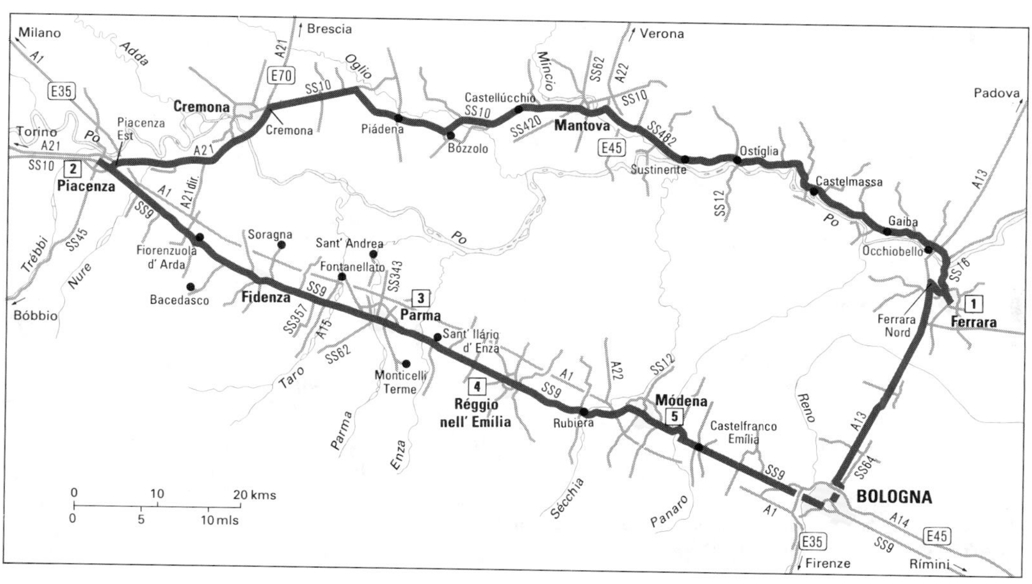

Although not Italy's most spectacular region scenically, Emilia-Romagna is rich in history

'architecture' and the apparently three-dimensional clouds and angels almost seem a part of the real world. In the **Church of San Giovanni Evangelista** just behind the cathedral, you can see Correggio's *Vision of St John* (1520), also in the dome. While you are here, take a look at the work of Parmigianino, a pupil of Correggio, to be seen in the first two chapels on the northern side of the interior. In the **Camera di San Paolo** you can see Correggio's very earliest documented works, painted in about 1518 for the abbess of the now defunct convent of San Paolo. The little Church of **SS Placid e Flavia** is one other place to see his work and so is the **Pinacoteca** (National Gallery), housed in Palazzo della Pilotta. Back in the Piazza del Duomo, the **baptistery** is well worth a visit. Most of the sculpture, both inside and out, is by Antelami (12th-century) and there are interesting frescos in the vault. For a complete change of scenery, visit the **Teatro Regio**, one of Italy's great theatres. The great conductor, Toscanini, who was born in Parma, played in the orchestra here. There is another theatre in Parma, called the **Teatro Farnese**. Built entirely of wood by Aleotti (a pupil of Palladio) in 1618, it is part of the Palazzo della Pilotta along with the **Museo Archeologico Nazionale** (National Museum of Antiquities). In its majestic interior performances took place in honour of the ruling family of Parma – the Farnese. Have prosciutto di Parma (Parma ham) as an antipasto for lunch and sprinkle Parmigiano (Parmesan) cheese on your pasta. Both are local favourites.

[i] Piazza Duomo 5

*The **SS9** leaves Parma going southeast to Reggio nell'Emilia 28km (17 miles).*

Reggio nell'Emilia, Emilia-Romagna

4 This town, almost halfway between Parma and Modena, is another centre of Parmigiano cheese manufacture. Here, so good is the cheese, and so well does it mature, that it goes up in value. People buy huge

RECOMMENDED WALKS

5 If you want some of the best walks in Emilia-Romagna (60 per cent of which is flat and rather uninteresting to look at), drive from Modena to **Sestola**, just off the **SS12** about 50km (30 miles) to the south. Here, at the base of Mount Cimone, the tallest peak in the Northern Apennines, there are lovely walks in mountain scenery. You could even stay at Sestola – it has a reputation as a good mountain resort.

BACK TO NATURE

The floodplain of the River Po is an area of rivers, wetlands and cultivated rice fields. The latter are especially rewarding for the birdwatcher: look for little egrets, grey herons, purple herons and squacco herons. Harvested fields attract ducks and wading birds, including lapwings, snipe, ruff and spotted redshanks.

cakes of it as an investment. Reggio nell'Emilia, sometimes known as Parmigiano-Reggiano, is a thriving bustling little capital. You would not really need to spend more than a morning here. Like the rest of this part of the region, it is completely flat. Also, like the other towns, it is built of characteristic small red bricks. Perhaps the most interesting – and the oldest – historic relic to be seen here is the mysterious '**Venus of Chiozza**', reputedly 12,000 years old. You can see it in the **Museo Civico** (Civic Museum) along with a great many other ancient pieces. Reggio was once an important Roman city, *Regium Lepida*, which was cut in two by the great ancient Via Emilia, also built by the Romans. In the public gardens behind the theatre is a Roman family tomb (**Monument of the Concordii**), dating from AD50. In the **Museo Numismatico** (Coin Museum) are the finds from a 5th-century treasure dug up in the locality of the city in the 1950s. Reggio nell'Emilia's **Duomo** (cathedral), while as old as any others on the tour, has fewer artistic treasures. However, the Church of the **Madonna della Ghiara** is full of the work of the Emilian painters, particularly those of the 17th century. All over town are unexpected architectural treasures, such as the courtyard of the baroque **Palazzo Sormani-Moretti**. Another baroque building is the **Palazzo Spalletti-Trivelli**. There are also a great many lovely neo-classical buildings from the 19th century, including the **Palazzo Corbelli** and the **municipal theatre** whose season of opera, concerts and plays runs from December to March.

[i] Via Guido da Castello 7

*From Reggio nell'Emilia, the **SS9** runs straight to Modena.*

Modena, Emilia-Romagna

5 Modena vies with Parma for status as the most prosperous city in the region, though Modena has a head start over Parma due to the existence of the Maserati and Ferrari car works on its territory. Modena was once an Etruscan colony then a Roman city, but the earliest apogee of its power was under the 11th-century Canossa Countess Matilda, a powerful ally of the Pope. Until the middle of the 19th century, the Este family, through a variety of judicious marriages, were its rulers. The **Duomo**, dedicated to **San Geminiano**, built between 1000 and 1200, was constructed largely from material taken from the old Roman city. The external sculptures are worth examining in some detail, particularly those on the west portal and on the apse. The tomb of the patron saint of the city, San Geminiano, is in the crypt, and a wooden statue of the saint lurks in the shadows of the north aisle. Just beside the cathedral is the **Museo Lapidario del Duomo** (Lapidario Museum) which contains finds from the necropolis of the old Roman city. Also close to the cathedral is the medieval **Ghirlandina Tower**, which contains an eccentric relic in the form of an old wooden bucket which, as an act of rivalry, was stolen by the people of Modena during a 14th-century raid on Bologna. If you want to see it, you may have to ask for the key to the tower at the Comune. Most interesting is the town's **Palazzo dei Musei**. This contains the **Biblioteca Estense** which has a famous collection of illuminated manuscripts including the Bible of Borso d'Este. In the same building is the **Galleria Estense**, with a fine collection of paintings including works by El Greco Correggio, Velázquez and Tintoretto, as well as a bust of Francesco I d'Este by Bernini. Here, too, is the Museo d'Arte Medievale e Moderne e Etnologia.

[i] Corso Canalgrande 3

*From Modena, return to Bologna on the **SS9** – 39km (24 miles).*

Bologna – Ferrara 53 (33)
Ferrara – Piacenza 185 (115)
Piacenza – Parma 49 (30)
Parma – Reggio nell'Emilia 28 (17)
Reggio nell'Emilia – Modena 24 (15)
Modena – Bologna 39 (24)

SCENIC ROUTES

For the most scenic drives between towns on this tour, you must really veer off the given route and take to the mountains immediately to the south. Among the mass of the Apennines, which follow the route from Piacenza to Bologna, you are never very far from deep wooded valleys and views to the snow-covered highest peaks of these.

FOR CHILDREN

1 There are few activities specifically designed for children in this part of Emilia-Romagna; your best bet is to take them to see the displays of puppets and dolls for sale in Ferrara, in the Circus Atelier in Via Mazzini.

Piazza Garibaldi, Parma, a popular spot for meeting friends

2/3 days – 258km (160 miles)

OF MOSAICS, SUN & SEA

Rimini • Cesenático • Ravenna • Comácchio Faenza • Brisighella • Forli • Rimini

With one or two exceptions, the towns on this tour are the antidote that every trip needs to a surfeit of culture. Whereas the interior of Emilia-Romagna contains the cultural capitals, the coast has all the playgrounds. Miles of sandy coastline usually mean miles of burning oiled bodies, but there are also places where you can escape the masses to burn in solitude. Restaurants, nightclubs, hotels – all these are in good supply, and there is an overabundance of them at Rimini in particular. And if you have had a surfeit of lazy days, there is still plenty of sightseeing to do.

FOR HISTORY BUFFS

2 The Church of **Sant'Apollinare in Classe** is worth the short detour from Ravenna, and completes the tour of Ravenna mosaics. In particular it has a wonderful apse with a depiction of the Transfiguration of Christ attended by Sant'Apollinare.

ℹ Piazza C Battista 1, Rimini

From Rimini, the coast road, the ***SS16****, leads north to Cesenático.*

Cesenático, Emilia-Romagna

1 Just a short way from Rimini on the Adriatic coast, Cesenático was built in 1302 as the harbour of Cesena, a town about 14km (9 miles) inland. It seems to have spent its days being destroyed by the enemy, each time being faithfully rebuilt. Césare Borgia did much to prevent the sea knocking down the fortifications. These were built to the plans of Leonardo da Vinci, the originals of which are kept in the National Library in Paris. Cesenático nowadays is a seaside resort often crowded in the summer by people attracted by the fact that the beach gently slopes into the water and there is good swimming. There are in fact about 6.5km (4 miles) of sandy beach sometimes 200m (656 feet) in width, so there is room for everybody. While this stretch of beach has the usual array of tall new hotels, there are also little shaded streets in the old town where there is a lively and colourful market. The town was once a canal port and here you can still see the yellow and brown sails of the *bragozzi*, flat-bottomed boats with colourful designs painted on them. Brightly painted fishermen's houses with canvas canopies leaning out over the pavement line the waterfront. Hidden among these are the **Antiquarium**, the **Seamanship Museum** and a large variety of typical restaurants selling unpretentious local food.

The Arch of Augustus in Rimini, where ghosts of the past rub shoulders with sun-seekers

ℹ Viale Roma 112

From Cesenático, the ***SS16*** *goes straight towards Ravenna – about 30km (19 miles).*

Ravenna, Emilia-Romagna

2 This is the most important place in Italy for mosaics of the Byzantine era (5th and 6th centuries). They adorn the interiors of the octagonal **Church of San Vitale**, the **Mausoleo (mausoleum) di Galla Placidia**, and the **Church of Sant'Apollinare Nuovo**, built by Theodoric. There are more in the **Battistero degli Ortodossi** or Neonian Baptistery (named after Bishop Neon who commissioned the mosaics) and the **Oratorio di Sant'Andrea**. Even if you see nothing else of the town of Ravenna but the mosaics, you will not go away disappointed. Those of San Vitale are the best and they include the portraits of Emperor Justinian and his wife Theodora, located in the apse. Justinian offers a gift to the new church; his wife is covered in extravagant jewellery and both are surrounded by retinues of servants. The Mausoleum of Galla Placidia is a jewel-like little building. Inside is on one of the most beautiful mosaics in the world. The interior is entirely taken up by this sumptuous mosaic – geometric patterns and flowers, as well as animals and religious imagery. There are also three hefty tombs, one of which contains the remains of Galla Placidia's second husband Constantius III. Galla Placidia was one of the patronesses of early Ravenna though she was in fact buried in Rome.

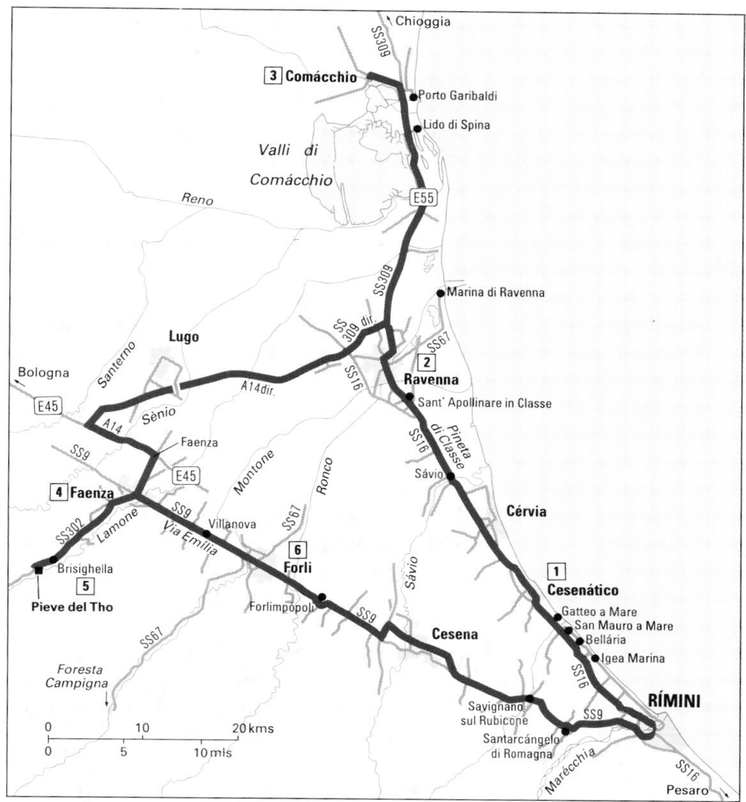

Sant'Apollinare Nuovo has two long mosaic processions running the length of its nave – male and female martyrs. Other sights include, not far from the central Piazza del Popolo, **Il Sepolcro di Dante** (the tomb of Dante), housed in a little neo-classical mausoleum. Italy's greatest poet Dante died here in exile in 1321. There is also a variety of little museums, including the **Museo dell'Arcivescovado** which contains the exquisite 6th-century ivory throne of Maximian and the silver cross of Sant'Agnello. The **Museo Dante** tends to close rather erratically and you might not get in. The **Accademia delle Belle Arti** (Fine Arts Academy)

Mosaic splendour fills the Mausoleum of Galla Placidia, in Ravenna, with gleaming colour

SPECIAL TO . . .

The Adriatic coast has a huge number of very popular beaches. The best among these are the **Marina di Ravenna** with its backdrop of pine woods and **Cervia**, with possibilities for windsurfing, sailing and other summer sports.

2 At Ravenna is a **summer school of mosaics**. Here you learn the art and technique of mosaic on a 15-day course. Enquire for details at the local tourist office. And there is the **market** on the third weekend of every month – an antiques fair which sells a huge variety of things from carved wooden angels to gilded clocks to wooden breadboards from the 19th century.

FOR CHILDREN

1 There are plenty of very safe beaches on this tour, where the water is shallow for a good stretch from the shoreline. In particular, **San Mauro a Mare**, about 4km (2½ miles) south of Cesenático, and **Bellaria-Igea Marina** (just further on) are ones to aim for. **Gatteo a Mare**, just south of Cesenático, has a special games park for children.

has good Venetian paintings including works by Vivarini and Bellini.

ⓘ Via San Vitale 2

*From Ravenna, the **SS309** goes north for about 32km (20 miles) to the turning for Comácchio, a further 5km (3 miles).*

Comácchio, Emilia-Romagna

3 Comácchio is situated a few miles from the coast, just north of Ravenna. It is a kind of little Venice with the town sitting among a series of canals. Even its bridges, of which the most famous is the Trepponti which spans three of the waterways, have a Venetian look about them. But the resemblance stops here. Comácchio is a rural place, home to fishermen who sail down the canals, past the lagoon to the sea at Porto Garibaldi. It is famous for its eels: they are farmed in the nearby Valli di Comácchio and you can have them cooked with tomatoes or grilled and washed down with a Trebbiano wine called Vino di Bosco. You can watch the fishermen catch the eels in huge square nets suspended in the water. The season for eels is October to December. Grey mullet and bass, produce of the lagoons and canals of the area, are also often found on the menu at Comácchio, and you can visit the **Peschiera** (fish market), housed in a restored 17th-century building. Until the beginning of the 16th century the town was a flourishing place with a healthy commercial life. Fearing competition, the Venetians destroyed it and it was later rebuilt. Thus the look of the town today is fairly uniform because many of the buildings were constructed more or less at the same time. Find time to visit the churches of the **Carmine** and **Del Rosario** and the restored Cathedral of **San Cassiano**.

*The quickest way to Faenza is to go back towards Ravenna on the **SS309** and to continue on to the **SS309dir**, which quickly becomes the **A14dir**. Turn left on to the **A14** and exit at the Faenza turnoff. Follow the signs to Faenza.*

Faenza, Emilia-Romagna

4 Faenza has been one of the most important centres of the ceramic industry in Italy for about 1,000 years and gave its name to the type of glazed pottery called faïence. Early faïence ware is much sought after and nowadays is the kind of thing found gracing the cabinets of international museums, not least of which is the **Museo Internazionale delle Ceramiche** (International Museum of Ceramics) in Faenza itself. Here there are examples with designs by Picasso, Chagall and Matisse. Faïence ware is a majolica with characteristic yellow and blue patterns. There are traditional versions of it, modernist reinterpretations of it and you can eat off it, drink out of it or simply put it on a shelf and admire its colour and texture. You can even decorate your house with it as did the

RECOMMENDED WALKS

6 South of Forli, in the Emilian Apennines, there is the famous Campigna forest, a vast parkland of beech, maple, fir, hornbeam and chestnut. This is an idyllic place to walk. Take the **SS67** going south from Forli. At Rocca San Casciano (about 28km/17 miles), follow the signs to Santa Sofia, about 16km (10 miles). From there take the **SS310** to Campigna (about 14km/8½ miles).

Pieve del Thò, an ancient Romanesque church, stands on the edge of the town at Brisighella

Shops selling colourful enamel-glazed pottery abound in Faenza, the home of faïence

owners of the Art Nouveau **Palazzo Matteucci**, using ceramic tiles of decorative patternwork including flowers and plants. There are shops selling it all over town, and the workshops are interesting to visit. There is even an Institute of Ceramics where works have been documented and technology tries to discover new and exciting ways of manipulating the raw material. If you can tear yourself away, visit the **cathedral**, which contains some good Renaissance sculpture, and the **Palazzo Milzetti** with its 18th-century Pompeian-style ceiling decorations by Felice Gianni.

Close to Faenza is Brisighella, 13km (8 miles) to the southwest on the SS302.

Brisighella, Emilia-Romagna

5 In the last century, the discovery of the therapeutic efficacy of the waters in the nearby Lamone Valley put Brisighella back on the map. It is a pretty little town, dwarfed by the great quarries that produced the clay for the Faenza workshops. It never grew much in size but it is the proud possessor of one or two interesting and unusual monuments. Perhaps the most noteworthy is the strange little Romanesque **Pievo del Thò**, a church which incorporates Roman fragments. Above the town is the 12th-century castle, the **Rocca**, which was built to guard the Lamone Valley. It was radically modified by the Venetians, who added cylindrical towers. Nowadays it contains the **Museo del Lavoro Contadino** (Museum of Country Life), covering the Lamone, the Senio and Marzeno river valleys.

Return to Faenza, then follow the SS9 for about 15km (9 miles) as far as Forli.

Forli, Emilia-Romagna

6 Forli is another old brick town with an ancient Roman heritage. Once known as the *Forum Livii*, it was an important post on the old *Via Emilia* which still bisects the town. A large part of Forli still retains something of its old character, but much of it suffered under Mussolini. Still, you can ignore the surroundings and visit the interiors of the Romanesque Basilica of **San Mercuriale**, the **cathedral** and the Church of **Santa Maria dei Servi**. The first of these three churches has a lovely red brick interior. If you can get into the crypt, look out for the remains of the 11th-century church. The Cathedral of **Santa Croce** has been much rebuilt and most of what you see now dates from the middle of the 19th century. A piece of the old fabric of the church survives in the apse and is adorned with a huge tempera painting of the *Assumption* by Cignani. In the **Pinacoteca Saffi** (Picture Gallery), apart from the work of local artist Marco Palmezzano, there are paintings by Lorenzo di Credi and Fra Angelico. The **Museo Archeologico** (Archaeological Museum) contains the finds from a variety of prehistoric and Roman sites in and around Forli.

[i] Corso della Repubblica 23

From Forli, take the SS9 back to Rimini, bypassing Cesena, a distance of about 47km (29 miles).

Rimini – Cesenático 22 (14)
Cesenático – Ravenna 30 (19)
Ravenna – Comácchio 37 (23)
Comácchio – Faenza 81 (50)
Faenza – Brisighella 13 (8)
Brisighella – Forli 28 (17)
Forli – Rimini 47 (29)

BACK TO NATURE

3 The **Valli di Comácchio**, a vast wetland area, is the haunt of breeding terns, gulls and waders. Coots and great crested grebes commonly nest among the waterside vegetation and small flocks of penduline tits can be found in reedbeds. View this area from any accessible part of its perimeter.

SCENIC ROUTES

The road from Ravenna to Classe and to Cervia has a remote eerie flatness which is very typical of this stretch of the coast. Here there are pine groves. On the road from Brisighella to Faenza, the countryside is dramatically different around each of these towns; the former is deep in the Apennines, the latter on the plain. The road weaves through the Lamone Valley's pretty mountain scenery, keeping to the River Lamone.

3 days – 274km (170 miles)

THE GENTLE VENETO

A visit to Venice can quite easily go to your head

Asolo • Possagno • Feltre • Conegliano Treviso • Venezia • Murano • Burano • Torcello Castelfranco Veneto • Asolo

This tour takes you through one of the most popular parts of the Italian peninsula. If travellers are not chasing the memory of a famous writer or painter linked to a particular town in the flat cypress-strewn countryside, they are in search of the sublime beauty of the watery landscape of Venice and its islands. Asolo, where the tour begins, claims Robert Browning as her most famous inhabitant and there are references to him all over the town – his writing instruments are in the museum and there are streets named after him. From Asolo you can visit the Renaissance villas among the vineyards that produce some of Italy's most characteristic white wines.

From Asolo going north, follow the signs to Possagno.

Possagno, Veneto

1 The first thing you will notice about Possagno is the huge mausoleum, the **Tempio**, of the sculptor Canova, who died here in 1822. You can see this building for miles around. It sits on a hill overlooking the town with the snow-covered heights of Mount Grappa looming behind it. Designed by Canova himself, the Tempio is based on the Pantheon in Rome. Canova's house is not far away, at the bottom of a wide straight road leading down from the Tempio. His rooms are preserved in the pretty courtyard house, now partly an art gallery, and there is a **Gipsoteca** (gallery of casts) where examples of his work, as well as full-scale plaster models for pieces now in museums or abroad, can be seen, including the *Three Graces.*

From Possagno, follow the signs for about 9km (6 miles) to the SS348, then branch north on this, along the River Piave, to Feltre, about 22km (13 miles).

Feltre, Veneto

2 You enter old Feltre, squatting on a low incline, through the Imperial Gate. From here, a road rises gradually to the Piazza Maggiore, passing on

Venice: gondolas at rest, San Giorgio Maggiore in the background

the way a series of palaces some of which, like the **Casa Franceschini**, have frescos by Morto da Feltre painted on their external façades. The **Piazza Maggiore** itself is full of old buildings, mainly from the 16th century. Apart from the Church of **San Rocco** and a lovely central fountain by Tullo Lombardo there are the remains of the town's old **castle** with its clock-tower. Surveying the entire scene is an enormous column on top of which stands the Lion of St Mark, the symbol of Venice. A large ornate palace to one side is the **Palazzo Municipale**, which has a striking Palladian portico of a type fairly common in this part of Italy. Beyond the piazza is the **Palazzo Villabuono** in which is the **Museo Civico** (Civic Museum). Here you will see paintings representative of the region's famous art history, in particular works by Gentile Bellini and Cima da Conegliano. The **Museo Rizzarda** contains a collection of wrought-iron work, much of it locally made by Carlo Rizzarda. Just below the spur on which Feltre is situated, and close to the site of the weekly market, is the **Duomo** (cathedral) with a 15th-century façade. Make a point of seeing the **Byzantine cross** of AD524 housed here. It is carved with 52 scenes from the New Testament.

ℹ Largo Castaldi 7

*Go back to the **SS348** and follow it south to Funer, at which turn left on to the Strada del Vino Bianco to Conegliano, a total of 56km (35 miles).*

Conegliano, Veneto

3 Conegliano is the centre for a wine-producing region. It was also the birthplace of the painter Cima da Conegliano, the great rival of Bellini. Preserved here is Cima's home, restored and filled with copies of his greatest work. In the Gothic **Duomo** (cathedral) is one of Cima's greatest works – an altarpiece dated 1493. Near by is the important **Sala dei Battuti**, a guildhall whose walls are covered in 16th-century frescos by, among others, Francesco da Milano. The details are extraordinary and the countryside scenery recognisably Venetian. Above the town, standing on a cypress-covered hillock, is the **castle**, which has been turned into an art gallery. This is full of interesting works of art, including paintings by Palma il Giovane, a late 16th-century painter who once worked in Titian's studio, and sculptures by the Florentine sculptor Giambologna.

*From Conegliano, the **SS13** goes straight down to Treviso, about 28km (17 miles).*

Treviso, Veneto

4 Treviso is a bright, busy provincial capital, crossed by rapidly flowing canals that once fed the moat beneath the town's walls. There is plenty to see, although the town suffered much damage during World War II. In the **Duomo di San Pietro** (St Peter's Cathedral), which has seven domes, is an *Annunciation* by the greatest Venetian painter, Titian, who died in 1576 at the age of 99. The 12th-century crypt is also interesting for its sea of ancient columns and its fragmentary mosaics. In the Museo Civico (Civic Museum) is the town's art gallery with works by Venetian artists such as Bellini, Guardi and Tiepolo. Of Treviso's churches, perhaps the large Dominican Church of San Nicolò, with its fine apse, and decorated columns, is the most interesting. In the restored 13th-century Church of San Francesco you will see the tomb (1384) of Francesca, daughter of the poet Plutarch. Out in the

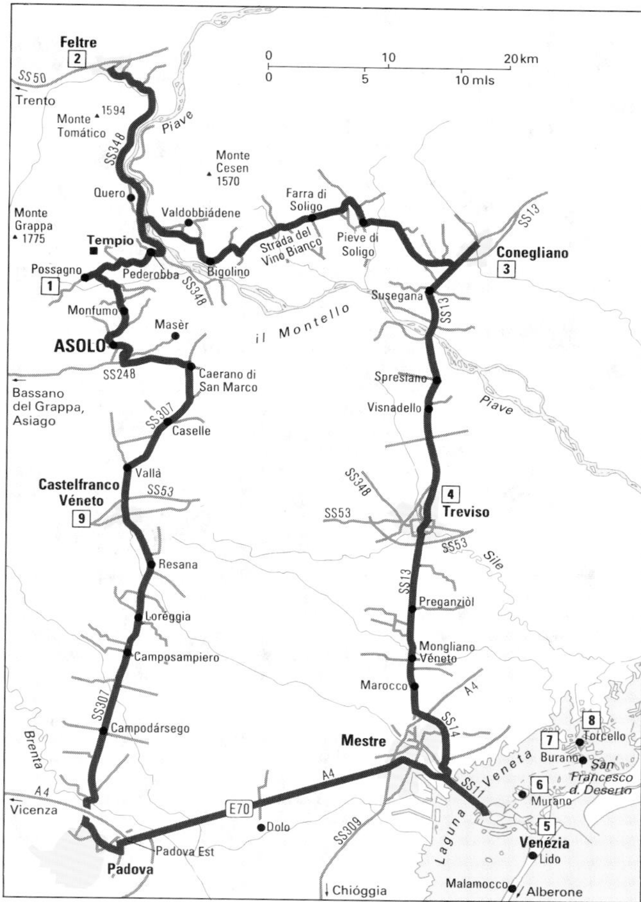

streets of Treviso the arcades are full of cafés, and here and there you will see frescos painted on the walls of the older houses.

ℹ Via Toniolo 41

*From Treviso, take the **SS13** towards Mestre, about 18km (11 miles), then via the **SS14** and the **SS11** to Venezia. At Venezia you must leave your car in a specially provided garage.*

Venezia, Veneto

5 Venezia (Venice) is one of the great 'art cities' of Italy, and its churches and galleries are still crammed with magnificent paintings. To see the city's many treasures, you must take to the water – the *vaporetto* (water bus) is the main means of transport through the canal system and the lagoon. In Piazza San Marco (St Mark's Square) is the **Basilica di San Marco**, the chief glory of Venice, which was built after the original burned down in 976. Mosaics, coloured marbles, ancient columns and the famed bronze horses of St Mark are its chief attraction. The lat-

SPECIAL TO ...

3 In Conegliano is the **Strada del Vino Bianco** (the Road of White Wine), a 42km (26-mile) wine route that encompasses some of the main vineyards between Conegliano and Valdobbiadene. You can taste such wines as the *Prosecco di Treviso* and *Prosecco di Conegliano*, two delicious sparkling wines, at various stops along the way. There is also a **Strada del Vino Rosso** which starts at Conegliano.

5 In Venice the great **Carnevale** festival is held annually in the days preceding Lent, when the streets are thronged with people dressed in wild, extravagant costumes and masks. In the streets there are concerts and dancing and there are more formal concerts in the Teatro La Fenice (Fenice Theatre). The carnival food speciality is apple fritters.

FOR HISTORY BUFFS

You cannot go on this tour and not visit at least one villa designed by the great architect Andrea Palladio. His designs, based on the architectural principles of the ancient world, were immensely influential throughout Europe and in the United States. Indeed, this influence is apparent in neo-classical buildings built even in the present century. The **Villa Barbaro** at Maser, about 10km (6 miles) east of Asolo, is the very best of his houses. Still a private residence, it has fabulous frescos by Veronese, as well as original furnishings and lovely gardens. There are other villas; in fact you could go on a special villa route, seeing most of them.

ter are copies of the 3rd-century BC originals, kept in the Basilica's **Museo Marciano**. Next door is the **Palazzo Ducale** (Doge's Palace) which took on its present appearance in about 1309. It has a lovely façade of lacy Gothic tracery and decorative brick-work. Look for the two reddish pillars on the front said to have acquired their colour from the tortured corpses that used to hang there. Behind the palace is the **Ponte dei Sospiri** (Bridge of Sighs) leading to the prison and just across the water of the Giudecca canal and standing on a separate little island, is the **Church of San Giorgio Maggiore** (1565), built by Palladio, one of Italy's most influential architects. Other great sights are the **Ca' d'Oro**, a former palace on the Grand Canal with a picture gallery, the **Ponte di Rialto** (Rialto Bridge) across the Grand Canal, and the **Galleria dell' Accademia**, the art gallery with some of the greatest masterpieces of Venetian art.

i San Marco Ascensione 71c

From Venezia take a vaporetto from Fondamenta Nuove to the island of Murano.

Murano, Veneto

6 Murano has been famous for its glass-blowing workshops since the early 13th century. Many palaces in Venice contain elaborate multi-coloured chandeliers from this island and nowadays you can visit the descendants of the glass-blowers in their forges and workshops. In the **Museo Vetrario** (Museum of Glass) are the best examples of the work of the Murano glass-blowers and the **Modern and Contemporary Glass Museum** contains more up-to-date pieces. There are even fine pieces from Roman times. Glass objects can be purchased here in a large variety of shops. In the **Church of Santi Maria e Donato**, built at roughly the same time as St Mark's in Venice itself, you can see fragments of Murano glass in the 12th-century mosaic floor.

Murano and Burano are connected by boat. You can do a round trip that includes both, or else you can visit either on a

None of Venice's grandeur on Burano, but plenty of colour

single trip from Venice. The distance from Murano to Burano is about 6km (4 miles).

Burano, Veneto

7 Lace-making is to Burano what glass-blowing is to Murano. All over the island you will find exquisite examples of it for sale. In the local Lacemaking School, the **Scuola dei Merletti**, you can watch women at work. This school was established late in the last century to rejuvenate the craft, which had all but died out. Burano is a very pretty island and its town, also called Burano, is like a miniature Venice. In the Church of **San Martino**, is a *Crucifixion* by Tiepolo, the last of the great Venetian painters, who died in 1770. While here, you could visit the little island of **San Francesco del Deserto**, about 20 minutes by ferry to the south of Burano. Here you can visit the little **monastery** with beautiful gardens said to have been founded by St Francis of Assisi in 1220.

From Burano, the boat goes to the island of Torcello, a few miles further north.

Torcello, Veneto

8 All that remains of this once great city, the first settlement in the lagoon in the 5th century AD, and once a serious rival to Venice itself, are two beautiful churches. One, the Byzantine-style **Duomo di Santa Maria dell'Assunta**, founded in 639 but rebuilt in about 1008, has splendid mosaics covering the floor as well as the walls. The *Last Judgement*, done by Greek artists in the 11th century, is particularly noteworthy. In the apse, the mosaic of the Madonna on a stark gold background, is one of the finest examples of Byzantine art anywhere. The other church, **Santa Fosca**, is just as ancient. In the garden outside is a stone seat known as 'Attila's chair', the exact origins of which are unknown. Near the cathedral is the **Museo dell'Estuario** which contains finds from the ruins of the old city. There is a silver altarpiece from the cathedral and some Roman remains from the ancient city of *Altinum*, which once stood near the present-day town of Mestre (seen on the way to Venice). Malaria virtually wiped out the population, bringing life in Torcello to an end.

From Torcello, return to Venice. Here take the A4 to Padua 35km (22 miles), then go north on the SS307 to Castelfranco Veneto, about 31km (19 miles).

Castelfranco Veneto, Veneto

9 This little town's claim to fame is that it was the home of Giorgione, one of the most mysterious painters of the Venetian Renaissance. Very few of his works survive (nobody knows why) and those whose authorship has been authenticated are very precious. You can see one in the town's **cathedral**. The *Madonna and Child with Saints*, dated 1504, has a typically lyrical Venetian landscape in its background. The old town of Castelfranco was once surrounded by a battlemented brick wall. One chunk of this – the **Torre Civica** – survives in the centre of town, and there is another length of moated wall to the west. Visit the **Casa del Giorgione** (Giorgione's house); also see if you can get inside the pretty 18th-century **Teatro Accademia**.

*From Castelfranco, the **SS307** leads northwards to Caerano di San Marco, about 15km (9 miles), where you turn left on the **SS248** to Asolo, a further 9km (6 miles).*

The cathedral on Torcello is noted for its Byzantine mosaics

Asolo – Possagno 12 (7)
Possagno – Feltre 31 (19)
Feltre – Conegliano 56 (35)
Conegliano – Treviso 28 (17)
Treviso – Venezia 31 (19)
Venezia – Murano 4 (2)
Murano – Burano 6 (4)
Burano – Torcello 3 (2)
Torcello – Venezia (return) 13 (8)
Venezia – Castelfranco Veneto 66 (41)
Castelfranco Veneto – Asolo 24 (15)

SCENIC ROUTES

The countryside is fairly flat on this tour. However, it has its scenic parts:
– the exit from Conegliano on the **SS13**: the profile of the town and its little mountain is idyllic;
– the scenery looking out over the Trevisian Plain from the castle at Asolo;
– the boat trip from Venice, to the islands of Murano, Burano and Torcello, with views of the lagoon and back over Venice.

FOR CHILDREN

5 This tour does not especially favour children. However, the **Lido**, just southeast of Venice, is a popular holiday resort with sandy beaches, including two public ones.

RECOMMENDED WALKS

There are some good, pretty walks in the foothills of the Dolomites around the little town of Asiago – about 32km (20 miles) from Bassano del Grappa, a town within easy reach of both Possagno and Asolo.

If you have time, spend as long as you can walking around the islands of the Venetian Lagoon – Murano, Burano, Torcello. Torcello in particular has little paths leading through the ghostly remains of what was once a large and important city.

BACK TO NATURE

The birdlife of the Venetian lagoons is a high spot on this tour. Boat tours and ferries allow an interesting range of birds to be seen in the Valli Venete. Mediterranean gulls are a conspicuous feature of the area but also look for black terns and whiskered terns and waders and herons on any exposed areas of mud.

2/3 days – 256km (158 miles)

BEYOND VENICE – INLAND VENETO

The restored Roman bridge, Ponte di Pietra, in Verona – one of ten across the River Adige

Verona • Montécchio Maggiore • Vicenza Marostica • Pádova • Arqua Petrarca Monselice • Este • Verona

Many of the towns in this part of the Veneto have at least one architectural gem worthy of attention. Most often it is a church or a palace by Andrea Palladio, the greatest Italian architect of the 16th century and one of the most influential architects of all time. The tour also highlights an interesting cluster of fortified towns with moats. There are castellated mansions and castles dotted about the fertile, green Venetian landscape neatly parcelled up into farms and vineyards. Verona, the starting point, is the biggest town on the tour. This pale pink city on the edge of the Adige river is second only to Venice in the importance of its cultural treasures. It is famed for its Roman theatre and early Renaissance buildings connected with the warring families who tried to gain control of the city over the centuries.

[i] Piazza Erbe 38, Verona

*Take the **A4** going east from Verona as far as the Montécchio Maggiore turning, about 40km (25 miles).*

Montécchio Maggiore, Veneto

1 Montécchio Maggiore was one of the strongholds of the legendary Montagues of *Romeo and Juliet* fame. Nowadays the little town is a quiet backwater. The two **castles** here, now restored, are the town's chief monuments, but just outside Montécchio is the large **Villa Cordellina-Lombardi**, built in the Palladian style in about 1730. The building is now owned by the province of Vicenza and is used for conferences, but you can visit it and see the vast frescos by Tiepolo in the central hall. About 6km (3½ miles) away is the castle of **Arzignano**, whose mighty black stone walls are still intact.

*Return to and take the **SS11** for about 12km (7 miles) to Vicenza.*

Vicenza, Veneto

2 Vicenza is known as the 'City of Palladio', due to the fact that many of its buildings were designed by the great architect, who was born here. Vicenza's Palladian works include the **Basilica**, the justice building, in the Piazza dei Signori. With classical statuary along the top and a two-tiered arcade along the front, it hides a much earlier collection of buildings. In the same square is his **Loggia del**

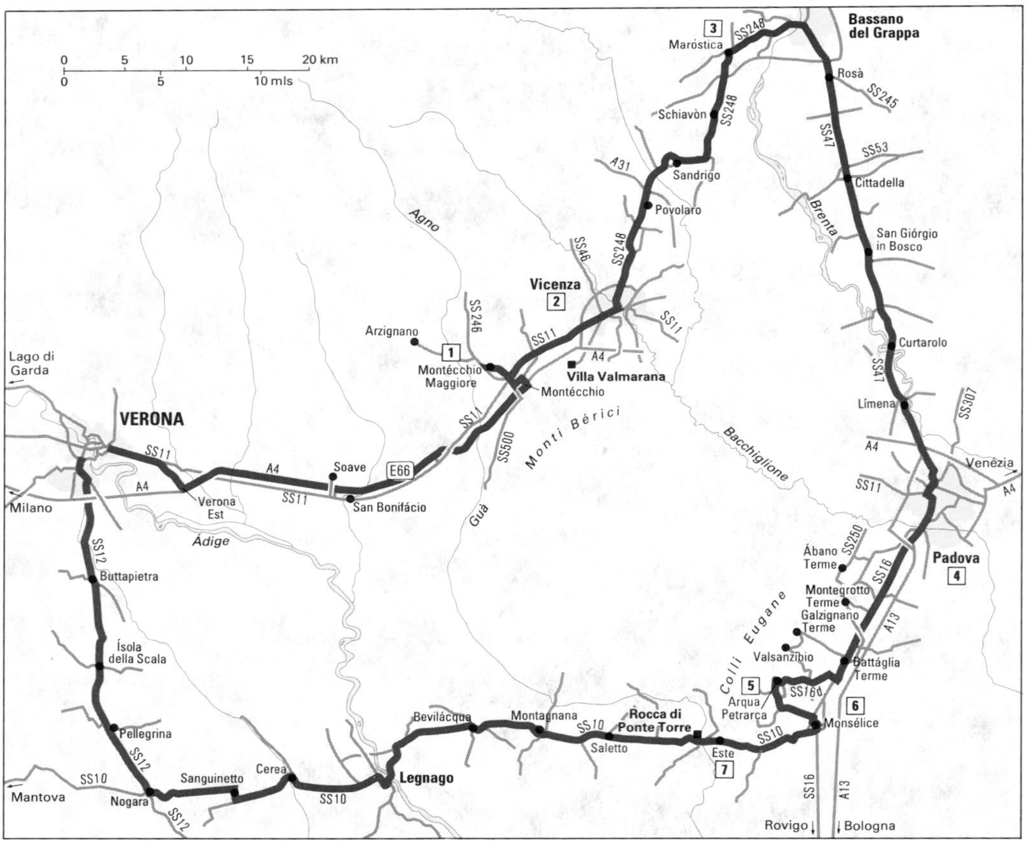

Capitano, built in 1571 to celebrate the Venetian victory at the battle of Lepanto. The Corso Palladio contains Palladio's **Palazzo Chiericati**, now the **Museo Civico** (Civic Museum) housing an art gallery in which you can see Van Dyck's *The Four Ages of Man*. But Palladio's masterpiece is the **Teatro Olimpico**, which the architect modelled on the theatres of ancient Rome. Half-moon shaped, it has a permanent wood and stucco stage set of an imaginary city in fake perspective. This is supposed to be the ideal Renaissance dream city. Don't miss it.

ⓘ Piazza Duomo 5

*From Vicenza, take the **SS248**, going northwards for about 28km (17 miles) to Marostica.*

Vicenza is a busy working city as well as an architectural gem

Marostica, Veneto

3 Marostica preserves its medieval fortifications almost intact. Not a very big town, it is centred around a large oblong square called Piazza del Castello. In the square is the battlemented **castle** building, now the town hall and all along the length of the walls are towers placed at regular intervals. The biggest, at the top of the hill up which the walls stretch, was supposed to have been the very last resort for the town's people in times of war. South of Marostica is Cittadella, another remarkable town whose walls are circular and extremely high. They are punctuated by brick towers; from one of these, the Tower of Malta, political prisoners were once flung to their deaths.

*From Marostica, continue for about 7km (4 miles) to Bassano del Grappa, then branch directly south on the **SS47** via Cittadella to Pádova, about 42km (26 miles).*

Pádova, Veneto

4 Shakespeare set *The Taming of the Shrew* in Pádova (Padua), and although the city was badly damaged during World War II, much of its southern quarters retain the kind of setting that Shakespeare might have found appropriate for his play. Arcaded streets, fountains, orange brick churches and, above all, one of the oldest and most revered universities in Italy (founded 1222), survive to be looked at and walked through. But the real treasure of this city is the **Capella degli Scrovegni**, the 14th-century chapel of the Madonna dell'Arena, which contains the most revolutionary paintings in the early history of Renaissance art. By Giotto, they are the first to tackle **problems** of three dimensional space and volume.

SPECIAL TO . . .

2 Vicenza holds the **International Palladio Study Centre** which offers summer courses in architecture. This is a very popular centre for Palladian studies and is good for a fuller understanding of the region's world-famous architecture. In the neighbourhood of Pádova are the **thermal baths** at Abano Terme, 9km (5½ miles), with 100 thermal swimming pools and a much venerated mud therapy. Others are at nearby Galzignano, Battaglia and Montegrotto.

SCENIC ROUTES

The little country roads leading through the Euganean Hills around Arqua Petrarca, Monselice and Este are laced with vineyards. Volcanic mounds, they are quite out of character with the surrounding area, which is flat.

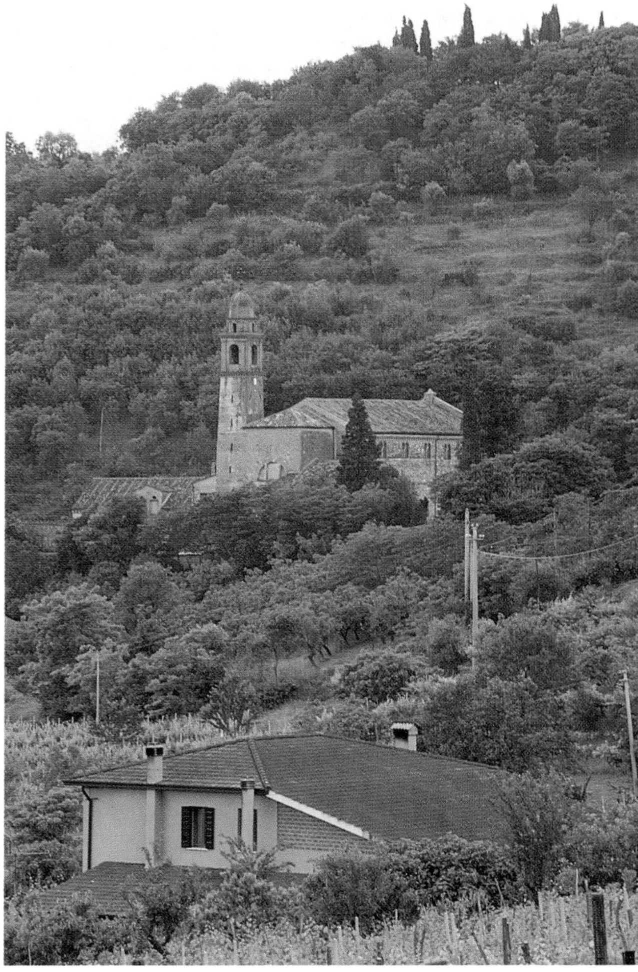

The soft landscape of Petrarch's last home, Arqua Petrarca

In particular, see the *Deposition of Christ*. Near by is the hermits' church, **Chiesa degli Eremitani**, with more early Renaissance works, this time by Mantegna. The **Museo Civico** (Civic Museum) in the old Eremitani convent of the Augustinians contains Greek and Roman finds from the area. Tours are conducted around the seat of the university, the **Palazzo del Bo'**. Here you can see the old Anatomical Theatre (1594). Other places of interest are the **Palazzo de Capitano** in the Piazza dei Signori, with Italy's oldest astronomical clock (1344), and the domed **Basilica di Sant'Antonio** in whose treasury you can see, in a precious reliquary, the tongue and larynx of Sant'Antonio of Pádova, who was canonised in 1232.

i Riviera Mugnai 8

*From Pádova, take the **SS16** south for about 18km (11 miles) until the turning on the right, the **SS16d** for Arqua Petrarca. Follow the signs for about 5km (3 miles).*

Arqua Petrarca, Veneto

5 The second part of this town's name derives from the fact that it became the home, in his last years, of Petrarch, one of the greatest early Italian writers. He died here in 1374, and apart from being able to visit his tomb in the courtyard in front of Arqua's parish church, you can visit his house, the **Casa del Petrarca**, as well. It contains furniture contemporary with his period, and it even has a stuffed cat which you will be told belonged to the great man himself. The town itself thrives on the memory of this illustrious past resident. It is pretty, well restored and has one or two chapels worth a visit.

From Arqua Petrarca, a road leads to Monselice, 7km (4 miles) to the southeast.

Monselice, Veneto

6 Monselice dominates the lovely Colli Euganei (Euganean Hills) on the edge of which it stands. Its position made it a natural fortress which was nonetheless fortified with castles and walls in the Middle Ages. Not very much of these survive because the town lost its military function in the 15th century. However, there is a lovely 16th-century fortified palace in the town, called the **Ca'Marcello**, with a magnificent collection of Renaissance arms. There is one other palace at

FOR CHILDREN

3 Try, if you are there in September, to take the children to see the open-air chess game at Marostica, called the **Partita a Scacchi**. The players, dressed in 15th-century costume, play on a 22m (72-foot) square board and the event is supposed to commemorate a contest for the hand of the daughter of the lord of Marostica. Plenty of local children are involved, dressed in Renaissance costume. As well as the chess match, there is a parade of younger people dressed as ambassadors, noblemen, bejewelled ladies, etc. This is a popular and lively spectacle.

BACK TO NATURE

To the west of Verona is Lago di Garda, a fine place to forget art and architecture for a while and do some birdwatching. Herring gulls haunt the shores of Lago di Garda in the summer and great crested grebes and ducks can be seen on the open water. Migrant waders – notably sandpipers and plovers – can be found around the margins in spring and autumn.

Monselice: **Villa Duodo**. This was designed towards the end of the 16th century by Scamozzi, the most important of Palladio's immediate followers. Only the gardens may be visited. Rising up the hill beside it is the curious **Via Sacra delle Sette Chiese** (the Sacred Way of the Seven Churches), with seven chapels spaced along it. This was also designed by Scamozzi and is linked to the town's Romanesque **Duomo** (cathedral).

*From Monselice, the **SS10** goes straight from Este, about 9km (6 miles).*

Este, Veneto

7 Este is one of the more beautiful walled towns in this part of the Veneto. Its fortifications – crenellations and towers – date from the 14th century. The walls were once over 1,000m (3,000 feet) long and there were 14 towers, of which only 12 remain. The **castle** became a pleasure palace of the Mocenigo family in the 16th century, and today its park is open to the public. Este was once protected by other out-of-town strongholds. One of these, the **Rocca di Ponte Torre**, is the most interesting. It lies just outside town on the west side. There is also the town's **Torre Civica** (Civic Tower), which was transformed from a far earlier building in 1690 into a clock tower. In the **Duomo** (cathedral) is a painting of St Tecla by Tiepolo. One of Italy's best archaeological collections is in the **Museo Nazionale Atestino** here, housed within the Palazzo Mocenigo. Note particularly the 5th- and 6th-century bronze statuettes.

*From Este, continue along the **SS10** for 53km (33 miles) until Nogara, at which branch north on the **SS12** to Verona, 31km (19 miles).*

Verona – Montécchio 43 (27)
Montécchio – Vicenza 13 (8)
Vicenza – Marostica 28 (17)
Marostica – Pádova 49 (30)
Pádova – Arqua Petrarca 23 (14)
Arqua Petrarca – Monselice 7 (4)
Monselice – Este 9 (6)
Este – Verona 84 (52)

RECOMMENDED TRIP

5 At Valsanzibio in the Euganean Hills, just a few miles north of Arqua Petrarca, is a magnificent 18-hole golf course, good for a game or a leisurely walk. Close by is the Villa Barbarigo with a lovely garden, park and labyrinth all open to the public.

FOR HISTORY BUFFS

7 If you want to see some of the best preserved medieval fortifications in Italy, then go to the little town of Montagnana, 15km (9 miles) west of Este on the **SS10**. The walls were built in the 13th century by the Paduan tyrant Ezzelino da Romano. Look out for the two wonderful original gateways into the town through the wall. Also medieval, they look like mini castles.

Verona is rich in traces of its Roman and medieval past

LIGURIA & TUSCANY

The Apennines, skirting the Gulf of Genova and the Ligurian coast, link the Maritime Alps on the Italian-French border with the mountains of Tuscany. But this, together with deep, wooded valleys and an idyllic climate, is all that Liguria and Tuscany have in common.

Liguria is better known as the Italian Riviera with, to the north of Genoa the Riviera di Ponente, famous for flowers and olives – and to the east the Riviera di Levante, with dramatic cliffs and pretty fishing villages. Justly famous, its attractions range from throbbing seaside resorts to lonely isolated coves hidden on one of the most spectacularly beautiful coastlines in Europe.

The great undiscovered secret of Liguria is, however, the hilltowns hidden among the Apennine valleys further inland. Built in inaccessible places in the Middle Ages, mostly as defence against Saracen attack from the sea, their little houses clustered together around the parish church are now mostly silent and empty. Yet, strangely, even the most under-visited of these is only, at the most, one and a half hours' drive from the coast. Mountain passes lead to them through woodland, past terraced hillsides planted with olives and vines, past banks of oleander and incredible views down through the valleys to the sea.

Parts of Tuscany enjoy the same isolation as the Ligurian hinterland. And the beauty of this region is legendary. As the Apennines sweep down towards Firenze, much of the countryside is folded into hills and valleys which hide villages and castles, known only to the few. The Mugello, in the northeast of the region, is one of these places, characterised by thick woodland. By contrast, the Chianti region, producing Italy's most famous wine, between Firenze and Siena is immensely popular and is a fixture on most travellers' itineraries. Here the lie of the land is gentler with more rounded hills covered with olive groves and vineyards. Here trails of cypresses climb hills, or run along their spines, towards ancient terracotta-coloured farmhouses and Renaissance castles.

It is difficult to appreciate that this peaceful landscape was, from the 11th to the 15th century, the backdrop to fierce wars between the independent city-states of the region before they were united as the Grand Duchy of Tuscany under the infamous Medici rulers. Remarkably, a great many towns and villages have preserved their cultural heritage intact. You can find, in remote country churches, paintings of the Madonna and saints from the very earliest days of the Renaissance, still in their original positions. Considering that so many wars, despots, invaders and calamities have each in their turn wrought havoc in this particular region, it is surprising that anything has managed to survive at all.

San Remo

There are two distinct parts to San Remo: a modern metropolis and a quaint medieval town. Vestiges of a more aristocratic period in its history survive in the grand old hotels lining the seafront, and the promenade backed by palms. But today bustling, modern San Remo, with its glossy shops, cafés and its very popular Casino, has taken over. San Remo is a fairly costly place but if you go into the old town (La Pigna) you will find less expensive restaurants. Up here the character of the old town has survived amongst the tangle of cobbled lanes and tunnel-like alleys.

Genova

Many travellers bypass Genova (Genoa), but by doing so, they miss out on not only one of the most lively cities in northern Italy but also on some unexpected monuments – especially those in the labyrinthine old quarter down by the port: in addition to the typically Genoese cathedral there are proud palaces which date from the 16th century when Genova was at the height of its power. For art lovers, the National Gallery in the Palazzo Spinolo contains some important works of art.

Pisa

Pisa contains some of the most magnificent buildings in Italy. Everyone knows about the Leaning Tower where Galileo conducted his experiments on the velocity of falling bodies, which, together with the cathedral, baptistery and the cemetery known as the Campo Santo (Holy Field) make up the Campo dei Miracoli (Field of Miracles) in the heart of Pisa. But what about the tiny Church of Santa Maria della Spina, one of the supreme examples of the Italian Gothic style? Pisa is full of surprises. In the Borgo Largo and Borgo Stretto districts there are ancient twisting alleys and an old market; here you will also find handsome squares and majestic palaces, such as the Palazzo dei Carovana and the Palazzo dell'Orologio.

In Italy's small towns, the priest is an important figure

Once a winter health resort, San Remo has changed its image

Firenze

Firenze (Florence) is Tuscany's capital and the undisputed centre of the Renaissance. In its heart, the Piazza del Duomo, is the great Duomo (cathedral), crammed with paintings, sculpture and frescos by early masters, and the Baptistery, a strange little building in green-and-white marble with its famous and much imitated 15th-century sculpted bronze doors by Ghiberti. From the art in the Galleria degli Uffizi (Uffizi Gallery) to the numerous notable churches and palaces and the antique shops, markets and restaurants, Florence's reputation rests on the fact that it can offer everything that is best about Italy.

For Florentines, the great cathedral dome is the essence of their city

2 days – 144km (90 miles)

THE LIGURIAN HILLTOWNS

The casino in San Remo, one of Italy's most elegant resorts

San Remo • Dolceacqua • Apricale • Pigna Castel Vittorio • Triora • Ceriana • Taggia • San Remo

The Ligurian interior (not that there is much of it in this narrow strip of the Italian peninsula bordering the sea) is wild and mountainous. Perched on the highest crags are remote townships, once the home of rural communities, whose subsistence existence depended on whatever the narrow man-made terraces on the side of the mountains surrounding the towns could provide. Farm animals lived in the undercrofts of the little houses to which you could – and still can in many cases – only gain access via labyrinthine vaulted passages. Many of these towns are empty now, their inhabitants having gone to earn a better living on the coast. But the windswept mountain eyries they left behind are evocative and worth visiting even if only for the magnificent views from them. By contrast, San Remo on the coast is an elegant and lively, if old-fashioned, resort full of 19th-century villas, hotels and places to swim and to eat.

[i] Largo Nuvoloni 1, San Remo

*Take the coastal **SS1** going west, from San Remo for about 12km (8 miles) to Bordighera at which follow the signs to Dolceacqua, about 10km (6 miles) via Camporosso.*

Dolceacqua, Liguria

1 This is one of the prettiest towns of the Ligurian countryside. A wide stretch of the River Nervia divides it into two parts: the higher section, dominated by the ancient **castle** of the Doria family, is the most interesting. If you happen to be in Dolceacqua in August, and are spending a few nights there, look out on the castle ramparts for the ghost of an unfortunate girl murdered by a Doria baron in the Middle Ages, when she refused him his *droit de seigneur*. The castle was partially destroyed by artillery fire in the Austrian War of Succession and is now a ruin. The Doria moved into a small palace in the main square down by the Nervia, where Napoleon visited them in 1796. Behind the palace, narrow medieval stone-paved streets, lined by tall houses straggle up to the castle gates. The atmosphere is all the more evocative for the fact that cars are not allowed into the narrow streets. A curious single-arched medieval **bridge** links the two districts of the town, the section below the castle called Borgo, the other Terra. There are interesting little churches to visit in each. But the real reason for coming to Dolceacqua is to sample the local wine called *Rossese di Dolceacqua* – a favourite of Napoleon – which can be found for sale or for tasting in any of the little shops and bars slotted into the walls of the Borgo district.

Continue along the same unnumbered country road, along the Nervia river, branching right at Isolabona, for about 6km (4 miles) to Apricale.

Apricale, Liguria

2 You can see Apricale from miles around, lodged on the top of a hill covered in olive trees, way above the upper reaches of the Nervia river. Like most of the mountain-top settlements in the region, it was built on high as defence against attack from Saracen pirate raids in the Middle Ages. These were the scourge of Ligurian life at the time; if the Saracens struck, women and children were carried off and enslaved – or worse. The ruined **castle** was another place that belonged at one time to the Doria barons. From this lair they could survey the comings and goings in the surrounding countryside. Not a great deal of it is left but its presence nonetheless gives Apricale, with its narrow dark alleys and streets, a dour air, all the more oppressive because much of the town is no longer inhabited. There is an interesting little Romanesque church dedicated to **Sant'Antonio** and there is also the Chapel of **Santa Maria Alba**.

Retrace your route to Isolabona on the Nervia river, then continue to Pigna.

Pigna, Liguria

3 Pigna's name derives from the fact that, according to the locals, it resembles a pine-cone. Pigna's reputation as a picturesque town is matched by the views from the medieval gates across the valley to the little town of Castel Vittorio. In its tightly packed centre of old stone houses are the Romanesque Church of **San Tommaso**, the parochial Church of **San Michele**, and some pretty buildings in the main square in the local vernacular style. San Tommaso is in ruins but enough architectural detail survives to be able to note that it was once an important building. San Michele is in better condition. Dating from 1450, it contains a painted wood altarpiece by Giovanni Canavesio hanging in the choir. You can see frescos, dated 1482, by the same artist, covering the walls of the Chapel of **San Bernardino** not far away. The oldest part of Pigna is also the highest. Up here is a small covered square which was used as an assembly point by the local parliament, with its old stone measures used in the sale of oil and grain.

Continue to Castel Vittorio.

Castel Vittorio, Liguria

4 In the past this hilltown had a variety of names. It was known as Castel Dho, Castel Doy and Castelfranco, only becoming Castel Vittorio in the middle of the 19th century in deference to the ruling house of Savoy, one of whose members was Vittorio Emanuele XI, King of Sardinia and later the first king of a united Italy. Today it is more a village than a town, though it is recorded as having once possessed a fortress with four towers. None of this remains, but

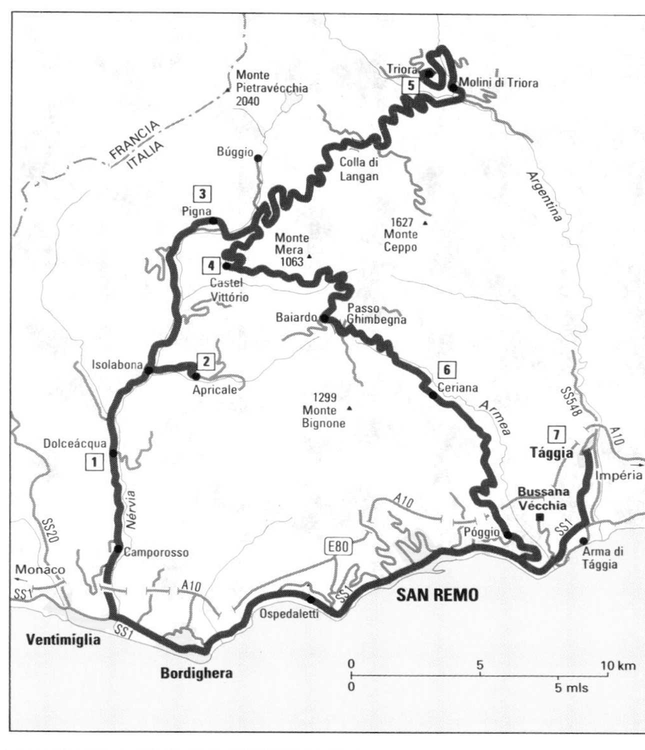

Remote Apricale is typical of Liguria's semi-deserted hilltowns

SPECIAL TO . . .

1 In Dolceacqua is another festival linked to primitive agricultural rites. On 20 January, St Sebastian's day, a man carries in procession a tree heavily laden with communion hosts of different colours. The hosts allude to Christian sacrifice but also to bread and fruits of the earth, and the man, half hidden by the tree, becomes a 'tree man', infusing the plant with his life force.

7 Taggia's mid-July festival of Saint Mary Magdalen is centred around the life-giving powers of the lavender blossom. Two men perform a Dance of Death in which the saint is 'brought back to life' by the miraculous perfume of the blossom, thus renewing the fertility of the countryside.

SCENIC ROUTES

Liguria is very mountainous and much of this tour is scenic, particularly:
– the approach to Triora on the road from Pigna; you come from the other side of the valley, above the Argentina river, level with Triora, then the road dives to the bottom of the valley only to rise gradually in a series of devious hairpin bends;
– around Apricale, where there are ever-changing distant views of other little hilltop villages and towns. Choose a particular view, park the car and sit and have a picnic among the wild flowers at the roadside.

RECOMMENDED WALKS

Make your way to the **Sanctuary of San Zane** on the summit of Mount Ceppo on the other side of the Argentina river. Park the car here where, apart from the magnificent views, there are acres of woodlands of chestnuts, beech, alder, Turkey oak and hazelnut in which to walk.

FOR CHILDREN

The beaches of San Remo are very popular, and there are also swimming pools here and at other resorts along the coastline. If you go to the part of the town, by the sea, called the Lungomare Vittorio Emanuele XI, you will find that the beach is protected by breakwaters, which means it is suitable for children. Small 'natural' sea-pools are created free from waves.

Castel Vittorio no longer has the fortress its name remembers

Castel Vittorio still merits a grinding detour in second gear to its high ramparts. Look out for the openings under the houses where the locals kept their goats and pigs. You might well see this old tradition still being carried on. If you come to Castel Vittorio early enough in the morning you will see old women in black leading their livestock down into the terraced countryside. Chickens are shooed out into the streets and there is a pungent smell of dung and hay. In the winter, logs are dragged down the covered alleys and streets and bundled into the undercrofts for use while the countryside all around is clogged with snow.

Retrace your route back towards Pigna then continue in the opposite direction for about 27km (17 miles) to Triora.

Triora, Liguria

5 Triora is one of the most fascinating towns on the tour. It is in the upper valley of the River Argentina which it overlooks from its precipitous site, 1,240m (4,070 feet) above sea-level, on the side of Monte Trono. Like so many other remote towns in Liguria, it is practically empty, many of its ancient houses locked and deserted. However, it is an interesting place to wander through. Many streets are covered over with stone vaults, the upper limits of which have been blackened by the woodsmoke of the ages. Here and there you will see carved door lintels: some are decorated with figures of saints and there are others with past owners' initials. Triora was an important walled fortress in the Middle Ages. It once had five towers but only three of these remain. In the centre of the town is a large square. It seems almost too big for a town of this size until you realise that beneath it is a vast cistern capable of holding enough water to enable the population of the town to withstand a siege of several months' duration. Also in the square are two important churches: the Church of **Our Lady** contains one of the oldest dated paintings in the district, a panel called the *Baptism of Jesus Christ*, by Taddeo di Bartolo da Siena, 1398; the Church of **San Giovanni Battista** (St John the Baptist), smaller and older, has its own curiosity, a late 17th-century statue of its dedicatee, known to the locals more colloquially as San Zane. The statue is the centrepiece of an annual procession that takes place in the town in June.

Return to Castel Vittorio, then follow the signs to Ceriana.

Ceriana, Liguria

6 Ceriana was founded in Roman times by the Celiani family. It stands on a wooded promontory covered in olive, pine and chestnut trees and is full of interesting ancient monuments. Although this spot was inhabited way before the Middle Ages, Ceriana only enters the written records in the 11th century, when it is mentioned in the history of San Remo for the courageous part its population played in the struggles against

Genova's supremacy. Of special interest are the churches of SS Pietro e Paolo and of San Salvatore, both of which lie on the outskirts of the town. **SS Pietro e Paolo**, once called Santo Spirito, is early Romanesque, and has a lovely entrance portal. Inside, the church is divided in half by a low wall running across the nave. The front part was reserved for the men, the back for the women. **San Salvatore** is an immense building with outside buttresses supporting its weight. Ceriana still preserves its labyrinthine streets and alleys – often the coolest places to be at the height of the summer. Some are lined with arcades and most are still paved with flagstones.

*The country road leads back to the coastal **SS1** (follow the signs). Follow the signs to Taggia via Arma di Taggia.*

Taggia, Liguria

7 Being very close to the coast, Taggia was forever being attacked by the Saracens. In the 16th century, their attacks were so prolific that the prior of the local Dominican convent led a team of monks and townspeople in the construction of a massive fortress near the mouth of the River Argentina. This, and the defensive walls of Taggia itself, repelled the raiders so successfully that no subsequent raids were recorded there. The castle, the walls and also the courageous prior's convent all survive. Modern Taggia is surrounded by olive groves and fields of flowers (the cultivation of which is this area's particular plus point). Right at the centre of the town are characteristic streets (some of which are arcaded), long vaulted flights of steps, little Romanesque churches, one or two tiny baroque palaces and an assortment of carved stone portals. Walk down the **Via Soleri** with its 15th- and 16th-century palaces; through the entrance portals you can glimpse ancient staircases and vaulted ceilings and most have old dappled glass in their windows. Off the Via San Dalmazzo are two very steep streets which lead up to the castle. At the top of these you can still see a huge stone, said to have been rolled down the hill to crush invaders intent on climbing to the citadel. The Convent of **San Domenico** (1490) lies just outside town. It has an interesting library and its church contains works by Giovanni Canavesio and the 15th-century Ligurian School painter Ludovico Brea, who also painted the frescos in the library of the monastery. There are also various illuminated manuscripts and *incunabula* (books printed before 1501).

[i] Via Boselli

*Return to San Remo via the town of Arma di Taggia and the coastal **SS1**.*

San Remo – Dolceacqua 22 (14)
Dolceacqua – Apricale 6 (4)
Apricale – Pigna 10 (6)
Pigna – Castel Vittoria 3 (2)
Castel Vittorio – Triora 29 (18)
Triora – Ceriana 44 (27)
Ceriana – Taggia 19 (12)
Taggia – San Remo 11 (7)

FOR HISTORY BUFFS

6 Between Ceriana and Taggia is the ruined town of **Bussano Vecchia**. This was devastated in the 19th-century earthquake which killed a large proportion of its inhabitants. Today it is officially a 'non-town' in the sense that it does not have electricity or running water provided by the local *Comune*. But you can visit it and poke about the quaint ruined streets and marvel at the fact that a colony of artists considers it safe enough to establish a community here. Look in particular at the ruins of the parish church which collapsed on that fateful Ash Wednesday in 1887. Incongruously, there is a very good restaurant here.

BACK TO NATURE

6 in the hills and valleys immediately surrounding Triora, you will find dense but beautiful forests of chestnuts, pines and firs – good places for picnics. If you are lucky, walking through this remote landscape you will see wild boar (but take care, they can be very aggressive) and birds of prey including golden eagles.

The Chapel of San Bernardino has frescos by Giovanni Canavesio

2/3 days – 267km (166 miles)

THE RIVIERA DI LEVANTE

Genova • Camogli • Portofino • Rapallo • Monterosso al Mare • Vernazza • Portovenere • Genova

The shoreline of this part of Italy is the most popular riviera on the peninsula. It is also the most beautiful. Away from the huge villas, the palaces, museums and churches, and the clamour of the bigger ports, there are hidden villages, toppling down steep cliffs almost to the sea. These are places where you could sit all day on a restaurant terrace, washing down seafood with sparkling local wine. Genova (Genoa), on the other hand, is Liguria's biggest city, though its old centre still has the flavour of a small seaport. It has big department stores as well as little traditional markets in quarters of the town where the locals all know each other.

RECOMMENDED WALKS

The most scenic part of the Ligurian coastline, on this tour, is that of the Cinque Terre. You could actually walk parts of it. From Vernazza to Corniglia, there is a good path around the cliffs. That would take about an hour and a half. From Manarola to Riomaggiore, there is another one, known as 'Lover's Way'. It, too, is a pretty walk.

ℹ Via Roma II, Genova

*Take the coastal **SS1** from Genova to Recco, branching off right on the minor road to Camogli, about 23km (14 miles).*

Camogli, Liguria

1 Camogli is one of a series of little fishing ports which dot the Ligurian coastline. Tall, brightly painted houses crowd on to the quay overlooking rows of fishing boats and small yachts. Space being at a premium along this steep crowded coastline, everything is tightly packed together. Streets are narrow and tortuous and some are really only flights of steps tunnelled beneath the buildings. The tangy smell of the sea is everywhere and so are the fishing nets, buoys, and the up-turned, brightly painted dinghies, while strollers are constantly tripping over the lines being repaired by old, bronzed seamen. Explore the town in the morning then lunch on the terrace of a restaurant, of which Camogli has many. The **Museo Archeologico** contains all the finds from old Camogli, beginning with the very earliest settlement on this seaside spot (Bronze Age). There are also a number of items taken from the water including rare Roman silver coins from about the 3rd century BC. The **Museo Marinaro** (Maritime Museum) concentrates on the maritime traditions of the town. It illustrates various aspects of Camogli's once-important fleet. There are journals, navigational equipment, maps, pictures, prints and votive offerings. There are also objects from Roman ships. A Garibaldi section is devoted to this famous national figure and his followers. Perched on a rock near the port is the 12th-century **Castello Dragono** (Dragono Castle). It once provided for the defence of the town and now it contains a seawater **aquarium** full of indigenous fish in specially recreated 'natural' habitats.

In a Cinque Terre harbour, fishing boats rest in the sun

*From Camogli, continue to rejoin the **SS1** for a short distance before branching off right to Santa Margherita Ligure about 9km (6 miles), at which turn right on to the coastal **SS227** for Portofino, about 5km (3 miles).*

Portofino, Liguria

2 Portofino is one of the tiniest ports on the coast. It is also one of Europe's costliest playgrounds. Previously a meeting place for sailors and coral fishermen, whose former homes have been transformed into sumptuous weekend retreats, Portofino is nowadays the holiday haunt of leading lights of Italian society. Prices in the local restaurants and bars, of which there are many, are, not surprisingly, extremely high. But you can always buy a cappuccino and sit for hours in the sun in the village's only square. There is no telling what celebrity might stroll by. Portofino's good fortune has always been due to its exceptional position. Even in Roman times it was an

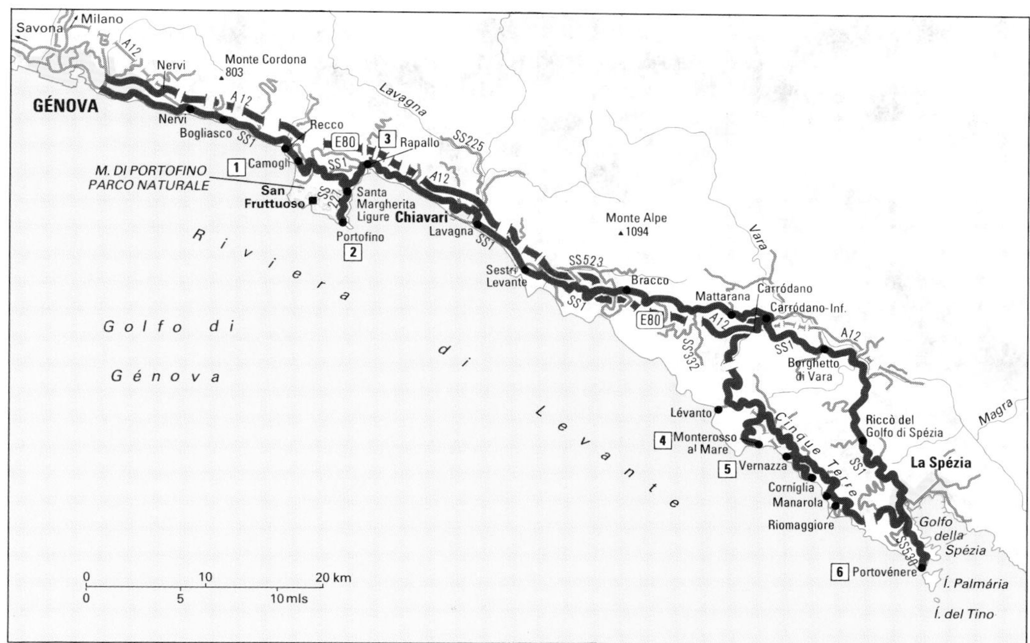

important base. Its little harbour is protected by an arm of land which stretches out, practically encircling it. At the very end of this are the remains of the 16th-century **Castello di San Giorgio**. Surrounded by gardens, the position of the old fortress is idyllic. Having been there, it is an easy walk to the Church of **San Giorgio**, which is a fairly recent rebuilding of an ancient chapel. Today its fame rests on the fact that it contains what are supposed to be the mortal remains of the patron saint of England, St George. They found their way here when returning crusaders were washed ashore with them in a storm. Needless to say bits of St George languish in other churches around Europe but this does not worry the people of Portofino who

Portofino, favourite holiday spot of the rich and famous

SPECIAL TO . . .

The **Cinque Terre** are noted for wines which are among the best you will find anywhere in Italy. Two produced here are DOC (*Denominazione d'Origine Controllata*) wines, considered to be of particular reputation and worth. The *Cinqueterre Bianco secco* is a dry white, good with seafood and liver; *Cinqueterre Sciacchetra* is rarer. It has a golden colour and varies from being sweet to almost dry. There are lots of others: look out for *Vermentino, Albarola* and *Trebbianco.*

1 Camogli holds its annual fish festival on the second Sunday in May. Here fish are cooked in the largest frying pan in the world, then freely distributed to all and sundry.

2 In Portofino are regattas and boating activities during the summer months.

BACK TO NATURE

Parco Naturale del Monte di Portofino protects one of the few remaining unspoilt coastal stretches of the Gulf of Genoa. The promontory is cloaked in *macchia* (like the French *maquis*) vegetation, comprising aleppo and maritime pines with a fragrant understorey of tree heathers, cistuses, rock-roses, junipers, strawberry trees and orchids. The birdlife includes Dartford, subalpine and Sardinian warblers.

FOR HISTORY BUFFS

The Abbey of **San Fruttuoso** can be reached on foot (a long walk from Portofino) or by boat (also from Portofino). It is a very secluded spot. The surrounding countryside and religious buildings were given to the state by the Doria family to whom they had belonged for centuries as a way of protecting them from developers. The abbey itself was founded in 711. In the 13th century the monastic complex was transformed into a secular abbey and became the traditional burial spot for members of the Doria family. There is one commoner who was allowed to be buried here – Maria Avegno, who drowned in 1855 during a noble attempt to help a shipwrecked English vessel.

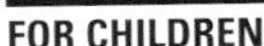

FOR CHILDREN

The little beach at **San Fruttuoso** (see **For History Buffs**) is very small and should be safe for young children to bathe from. Its scale means that toddlers cannot wander out of sight.

celebrate his feast day (23 April) with a huge bonfire in the main square. The little **Oratorio dell'Assunta** dates back to the 14th century and has Gothic and Renaissance elements. There is also the parish Church of **San Martino** to look into, an early 16th-century building that contains some interesting works of art.

i Via Roma 35

Go back to Santa Margherita Ligure and on to Rapallo.

Rapallo, Liguria

3 Rapallo is another ancient seaport once important for its local coral fishermen. Today, however, it is the major tourist and bathing resort on this stretch of the Ligurian Riviera. People favour its mild climate and its long sunny promenades overlooking the beaches. The size of the town, and its popularity, have attracted a whole range of summer cultural events. These and the town's museums are welcome relief from suntan oil and the ridiculously warm Ligurian seawater. In the **Museo Civico** (Civic Museum), you can examine collections of local pillow-lace. This art was one in which the people of Rapallo excelled. They still do, in fact, and you can see examples of it for sale in many shops in the town. The 17th-century examples are particularly important. See other specimens in the **Museo Pizzo al Tombo**, whose exhibits are more magnificent. In particular, it contains the very rare and precious liturgical works of lace belonging to Rapallo's parish churches. A school for lace-making ensures that the craft will never die in Rapallo. Despite the town's image as a modern holiday resort, it has some ancient monuments including the Church of **Santo Stefano**, a pre-1000 parish church rebuilt in the 17th century and recently restored, and the Oratory of **Santissima Trinità**. Other places of interest include the **fortress** built to deter the Barbary pirates. There is also the Church of **San Francesco**, with a lovely sculptural group by Maragliano, and the much restored 16th-century Collegiate Church of **San Gervasio e Protasio**.

i Via Diaz 9

Continue along the ***SS1*** *for about 48km (30 miles) until the village of Carrodano Inferiore, then follow the signs back down to the coast to Monterosso al Mare, about 21km (13 miles).*

It is easy to relax in Vernazza, where tourism is still a low-key affair

Monterosso al Mare, Liguria

4 Monterosso al Mare is the first town in a series with four others in what is called the **Cinque Terre** (Five Lands) region. Vernazza, Corniglia, Manarola and Riomaggiore (all within the next 15km/9 miles) are noted for their wine, their seafood catches and their wonderful secluded positions crammed to the side of precipitous hills falling dramatically down to the sea. All the towns, Monterosso included, are quite difficult to reach both by sea (in bad weather) and by land. Monterosso is perhaps the most important of the five. Its little port is usually full of brightly painted fishing boats. It has a lovely 14th-century **parish church** dedicated to St John the Baptist, two ancient oratories – **degli Neri** and **Santa Croce**, and a castle on the hill near the town, built as defence against the pirate menace.

Once a fortified settlement, Portovenere now cheerfully welcomes 'invading' visitors

Vernazza is a few kilometres further down the coast from Monterosso – use the winding cliff road.

Vernazza, Liguria

5 Vernazza is also a port – of sorts. Tiny and ancient (it was founded by the Romans), it is still used by the local fishermen. In the port is the old **fortress** whose benign existence nowadays is celebrated by the fact that it contains a restaurant. Vernazza's fine 14th-century **parish church**, with octagonal belltower, is dedicated to St Margaret of Antioch.

From Vernazza it is easy to reach Corniglia, the tiniest of the Cinque Terre, and Manarola is another fishing village with a harbour and very steep, cobbled lanes leading down to the sea. This is perhaps the most picturesque of the Cinque Terre, with its seamen mending nets, cats lying in the sun, brightly painted houses and wonderful countryside all around. You cannot take your car into the village, the streets are too narrow and too steep. So leave it in the car park specially provided for the purpose.

*Continue along the little cliff road for about 15km (9 miles) to the large industrial town of La Spezia, at which take the slightly bigger **SS530** to Portovenere, about 12km (8 miles).*

Portovenere, Liguria

6 Portovenere is a bit like Portofino though not nearly as expensive. There are one or two hotels here and a great many restaurants and bars. Another lovely Ligurian Riviera town, this one was fortified by the Genoese in the early 12th century; it has a ruined **fortress** and remote, windswept **sanctuary** to be visited. The latter is dedicated to St Peter (San Pietro), the patron saint of fishermen, and is supposed to stand on the site of an ancient temple dedicated to Venus, who may have given her name to the town itself. She, too, was the protectress of fishermen. The sanctuary is one of the most beautiful churches – more of a chapel really – along the Ligurian coastline. Built in 1277, it is constructed in black and white marble. The other coloured marble that shows through dates from a 6th-century building that once stood on the spot. From the sanctuary you can see across to the little islands of **Palmaria** and **Tino**. Just below the sanctuary very slippery steps lead down to the rocky shoreline and a cove associated with Lord Byron – it is thought to be the spot from which he swam across the sea to Lerici. Look in the Church of **San Lorenzo** and see the town's most precious relic, the **Madonna Bianca** (White Madonna), which is said to have floated into town in the 13th century, encased in a cedar log (also on view).

*Trace your route to La Spezia, then follow the **SS1** to Carrodano where you join the autostrada **A12** back to Genova.*

Genova – Camogli 23 (14)
Camogli – Portofino 14 (9)
Portofino – Rapallo 8 (5)
Rapallo – Monterosso al Mare 69 (43)
Monterosso al Mare – Vernazza 17 (11)
Vernazza – Portovenere 27 (17)
Portovenere – Genova 109 (67)

SCENIC ROUTES

On the winding road from Manarola to Portovenere (about 10km/6 miles), look out for the Sanctuary of the Madonna di Montenero on the way. There are incredible views down the steep mountainside to the sea way below.

For the same reasons, the road from Manarola to Corniglio (about 6km/4 miles) and from Monterosso al mare to Vernazza is quite stunning.

3 days – 314km (194 miles)

TREASURES OF TUSCANY

Pisa • Viareggio • Lucca • Pistoia • Prato
Poggio a Caiano • Artimino • Empoli • Certaldo
San Gimignano • Volterra • Pisa

Most of the towns on this tour made a contribution to the unique artistic achievements of Toscana (Tuscany). An incredibly rich heritage of monuments survives covering a time-span ranging from the Etruscan period to the great flowering of culture during the Renaissance. Pisa, one of the region's principal cities, competes with Florence as a showcase for the region's artistic accomplishments.

ⓘ Piazza Duomo, Pisa

*From Pisa, take the **SS1** going north for about 21km (13 miles) to Viareggio.*

Viareggio, Toscana

1 This coastal resort's scale is matched by its popularity in summer. The biggest resort on the north Tuscan coast, it has two pretty promenades beside the sea, a tremendous

How long can it stand? Pisa's Leaning Tower defies gravity

sandy beach and the kind of nightlife that people drive miles to indulge in. It has a small dockyard dominated by a 16th-century tower and in the centre of the town is a **museum** housed in the old Palazzo Comunale. **Lido di Camaiore, Marina di Pietrasanta** and **Forte dei Marmi** are other popular bathing resorts along the coast, the latter, in the shadow of an 18th-century fortress, being the most fashionable.

ⓘ Via G Carducci 10

*From Viareggio, take the **A12** about 28km (17 miles) to Lucca.*

Lucca, Toscana

2 Strangely, this is one of the more under-visited Tuscan cities, travellers preferring to stop in Pisa or Florence. Lucca is small and compact – mostly contained within massive walls – and is undoubtedly one of Italy's most beautiful cities. It has the most impressive bastions in Italy and three of its early gates are still intact. **Porta San Pietro** (St Peter's Gate), on the south side, has preserved its portcullis, **Porta San Donato** is decorated with statues of San Paolino and San Donato, while **Porta Santa Maria**, the oldest, is decorated with a 16th-century sculpture of the *Madonna and Child*. The city you walk – or cycle (as most people do) – through today has preserved its Roman street plan, betraying its origins. The outline of the now vanished amphitheatre is preserved as the **Via dell'Anfiteatro** which, lined with medieval houses, follows its original shape. The Romanesque and Gothic **Duomo di San Martino** (cathedral), is a masterpiece in the Pisan style. In it you can see a crucifix said to have been carved in New Testament times by the Jewish high priest Nicodemus and supposedly an accurate portrait of Christ. Other places to be seen are the **Pinacoteca Nazionale**, housed in the Palazzo Mansi, with paintings commissioned by the Medici family, including some by Bronzino, the **Museo Guinigi** which contains good paintings and sculpture and the new Museo della Cattedrale.

ⓘ Piazza Guidiccioni 2

*From Lucca, the **A11** runs directly to Pistoia, about 43km (27 miles).*

Pistoia, Toscana

3 Pistoia's reputation rests on its **Piazza del Duomo**, the medieval square at its ancient heart. It is overshadowed by a Romanesque cathedral, a 14th-century **baptistery** and two magnificent Gothic palaces. In the **Duomo** (cathedral) you can see a clutch of paintings and sculpture by Tuscan artists and the Dossale di San Jacopo (Altar of St James), made of solid silver. Adjacent is the Museo San Zeno with other treasures. The Gothic **Palazzo del Comune**, just beside the cathedral, has a huge collection of paintings, some of which you should go out of your way to see, for instance the *Madonna and Child* by Domenico Beccafumi. Beyond the magnificent heart of this city, famous in the past for the manufacture of weaponry, are countless churches. Among the most characteristic is **San Bartolomeo in Pantano**, where you can see a remarkable pulpit which stands on the backs of humans and lions. The pulpit in the Church of **Sant'Andrea**, by Giovanni Pisano, is one of Tuscany's finest, with scenes from the Life of Christ depicted on it.

ⓘ Via Eramsci 110

*From Pistoia, the **A11** continues to Prato, about 18km (11 miles).*

Prato, Toscana

4 Prato is a centre for textiles. As such it has been important for the last 600 years, though its stature nowadays is obscured by its more illustrious neighbour, Florence. Perhaps its principal attraction is the **Duomo** (cathedral), a great green and white striped building. The choir is decorated with frescos by Filippo Lippi, a 15th-century monk who abducted a nun by whom he had a son called Filippino, also a great painter. If you have time to wander about Prato's quiet, deserted streets, look in at the fortress built by the Emperor Frederick II, **Castello dell'Imperatore**. The **Galleria Comunale** (Communal Gallery) in the Palazzo Pretorio contains more Lippis, both father and son, while the **Museo dell'Opera del Duomo** (Cathedral Museum), in addition to yet more Lippis, contains the fine panels carved by Donatello for the pulpit which stood at the cathedral's west front. The Museo Pittura Murale contains minor artworks from churches in and around Prato.

From Prato, follow the signs going south for about 10km (6 miles) to Poggio a Caiano.

Poggio a Caiano, Toscana

5 Poggio a Caiano is a small rural town, no more distinguished than any other in Tuscany except that in its midst is a colossal late 15th-century **Medici villa** built by Guiliano da Sangallo for Lorenzo il Magnifico (the Magnificent). Its (mostly empty) rooms, open to the public, have frescoed scenes painted to the glorification of members of the Medici family by Andrea del Sarto and his assistants; incidents in Roman history are depicted as events in the lives of Cosimo il Vecchio (the Old) and Lorenzo il Magnifico. There are lovely views from a wide terrace, on a colonnade that encircles the villa – you look down into formal gardens and a park.

Follow the signs to Artimino – about 7km (4 miles) away on a ridge above Poggio.

Artimino, Toscano

6 Artimino is famous for another magnificent **Medici villa**, this one built a little later (1594) for Ferdinand I de Medici by Bernardo Buontalenti. The villa faces Artimino village, standing a little way outside of it at the end of a long tree-lined avenue. Its position is spectacular – from its front

FOR HISTORY BUFFS

1 A few kilometres to the south of Viareggio is **Torre del Lago Puccini**, on the edge of Lago (Lake) di Massaciuccoli. Here you can visit the home, now a museum, of the composer Puccini who wrote most of his operas here.

6 Rather more off the beaten track, near the village of Artimino, (or go from Empoli, whichever is more convenient) is Vinci, birthplace of Leonardo da Vinci. It has a castle and a museum dedicated to the great painter, sculptor, architect and engineer, whose birthday (15 April) is celebrated there by annual festivities.

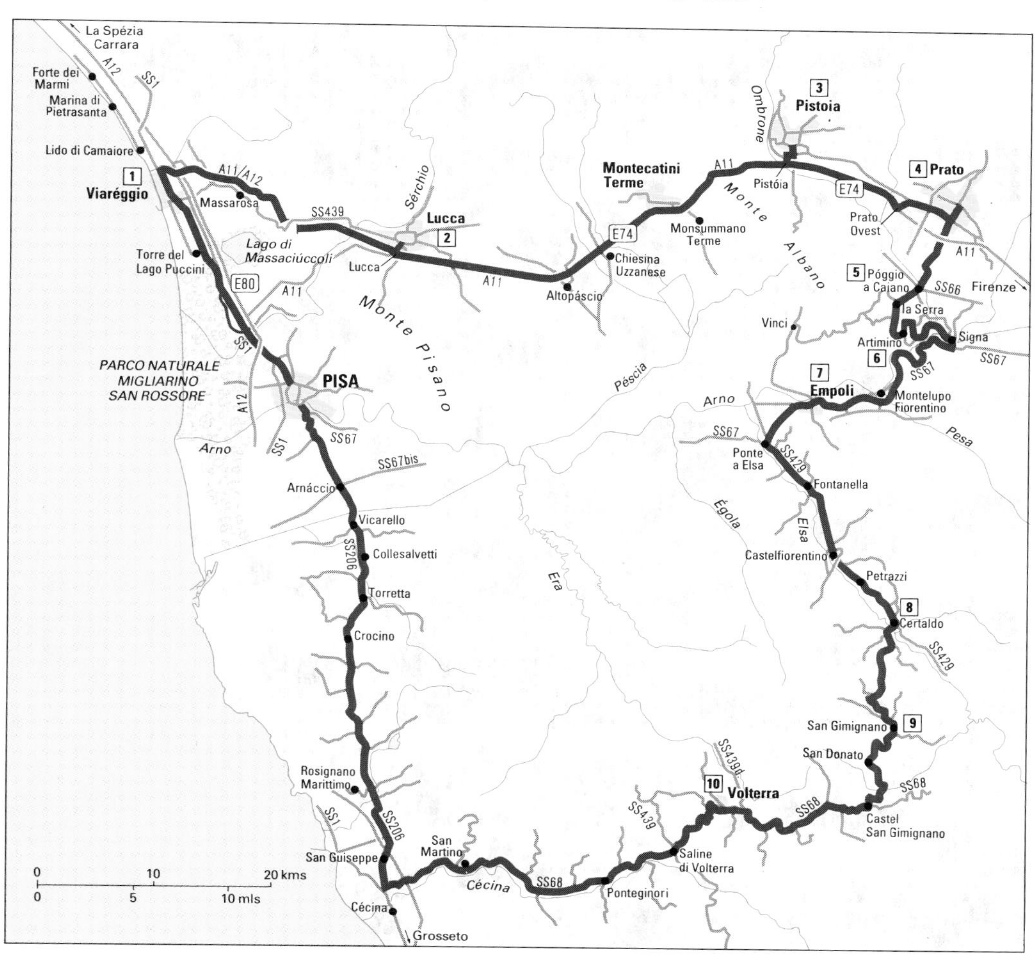

The Villa Reale, a former royal estate north of Lucca

windows you look out over the valleys and hills beyond. Artimino, more a hamlet really, is a walled enclosure in which only a handful of families now live. Its other notable monument is a Romanesque **church**, a short way out of the village, on the opposite side of the ridge from the route by which you approached Artimino. It is a pleasant, short walk to this building which seems to have been constructed from the stones of a nearby **Etruscan cemetery** (7th-century BC), discovered only in 1970.

Follow the signs to Signa then, having crossed the Arno, continue west on the ***SS67*** *to Montelupo Fiorentino. After that, it is only about 7km (4 miles) further to Empoli.*

Empoli, Toscana

7 The oldest part of Empoli dates from the Roman era though today's town centre grew up around the Church of **Sant'Andrea** (sometimes known as the Collegiata) in the 12th century. This little church has a beautiful, typically Florentine Romanesque façade – when in Florence, compare it with the church of San Miniato al Monte – in green and white marble. To the right of the church is the **Museo Collegiata** where you can see paintings by the ever prolific Filippo Lippi and other important Renaissance artists, such as Masolino and Lorenzo Monaco. While you are here you should also look at the Church of **Santo Stefano**, which was built by Augustinian monks. Most of the church's works of art have gone for safekeeping to the Collegiate Museum. Still *in situ*, however, is a *Madonna* by Masolino.

Take the cross-country road going southwest until you run into the ***SS429***. *Certaldo is 22km (14 miles) further on the latter.*

Certaldo, Toscana

8 Certaldo is one of the most dramatic hilltowns in the region. Its silhouette is the kind that immediately springs to mind when you think of a medieval Tuscan hilltown – orange-red buildings, towers and castellations crammed together on the pinnacle of a defensive outcrop. It

Treasure-cave in Certaldo – a bric-à-brac shop to tempt browsers

SPECIAL TO ...

Pisa holds its regatta on 16 and 17 June. The buildings on the banks of the Arno are lit by torches and the next day the regatta is held.

1 In Viareggio is the carnival which precedes Lent. Throughout the week there are costume balls, parties and performances, the whole spectacle topped by the parade of gigantic floats which generally present a satirical view of current politicians and events.

9 San Gimignano has scores of wine shops all over town in which you can buy the local brew – in particular the white *Vernaccia di San Gimignano*, a wine with an ancient pedigree, drunk by Dante and Boccaccio.

FOR CHILDREN

1 The beaches from Viareggio to Forte dei Marmi are popular for swimming. The beach disappears gently into the water which is shallow for some distance.

has two principal buildings: the crenellated **Palazzo Pretorio** and the Casa del Boccaccio. The Palazzo Pretorio's outside walls are covered in coats of arms, made of majolica or painted on to the wall surface, belonging to the local notables of long ago. Those on the façade above the entrance are still very brightly coloured. The **Casa del Boccaccio** was the home, until he died, of one of Italy's greatest writers, Giovanni Boccaccio (1313–75). Author of the *Decameron*, he had a profound influence on the English poet Chaucer. His home is preserved as a museum. Boccaccio was buried in the Church of **Santi Michele e Jacopo** – he himself wrote the inscription on his tomb.

Cross the Elsa river and follow the signs to San Gimignano, about 13km (8 miles).

San Gimignano, Toscana

9 San Gimignano is known as the City of Towers; though only a dozen or so remain out of an original 70 or more, it is for these that it is remembered even today. They were built for protection by the feuding families of San Gimignano. The town is easily seen at a leisurely pace in one morning. Enter at the medieval **Porta San Giovanni**, the gate which opens the way to the heart of town. Here in the Piazza del Duomo is the town's largest church, the **Collegiata**, in which are spectacular frescos by early Renaissance artists including Benozzo Gozzoli. Attached to this church are two museums, one of which contains local ecclesiastical works of art, jewels and vestments, the other, the finds from nearby Etruscan sites. If you can absorb any more religious artworks, go to the **Museo Civico** (Civic Museum) in the Palazzo del Popolo adjacent to the cathedral. Here in the Pinacoteca (art gallery) are more works by Gozzoli and Filippino Lippi. From the piazza, the Via Matteo, littered with fine medieval buildings including the Church of **San Bartolo**, leads down to the Church of **Sant'Agostino** with more frescos by Gozzoli.

*Take the road via the hamlet of San Donato to Castel San Gimignano, then go west on the **SS68** to Volterra.*

Volterra, Toscana

10 Once a rival to Florence, Volterra was one of the most important centres in Italy for over 2,000 years. It was already an inhabited site in the 9th century BC, and was most favoured by the Etruscans for its defensive hilltop position. Their presence survives in the **Museo Etrusco Guarnacci**, one of the most important of all Etruscan museums, whose collection includes carved sarcophagi and a large array of funerary urns. To continue the leaps through history, you can visit the remains of the Roman occupation of the town: the ruins of an **amphitheatre** survive, as do those of the **baths**. The rest of the town is predominantly medieval. Enclosed by fearsome brooding walls (in which you can see the best preserved Etruscan gateway in Italy – the **Porta dell'Arco**), it has a large 15th-century castle, the **Fortezza Medicea**, and the oldest town hall in Tuscany, the **Palazzo dei Priori**, which dates from 1208. This contains Volterra's art gallery, the **Pinacoteca Comunale** whose prized possession is an *Annunciation* by Luca Signorelli. Other places to see are the 15th-century **cathedral**, with its fine frescos by Gozzoli, and the earlier octagonal **baptistery**.

*From Volterra, continue along the **SS68** towards the sea, then branch on to the **SS206** which goes back to Pisa.*

Pisa – Viareggio 21 (13)
Viareggio – Lucca 28 (17)
Lucca – Pistoia 43 (27)
Pistoia – Prato 18 (11)
Prato – Poggio a Caiano 10 (6)
Poggio a Caiano – Artimino 7 (4)
Artimino – Empoli 28 (17)
Empoli – Certaldo 27 (17)
Certaldo – San Gimignano 13 (8)
San Gimignano – Volterra 29 (18)
Volterra – Pisa 90 (56)

The skyscrapers of San Gimignano: once there were scores of towers

RECOMMENDED WALKS

North of Lucca (take the **SS12** going up the River Serchio) is the mountainous Garfagnano region. At Borgo a Mozzano, go left along the **SS445** to Barga – a pretty town with good views, and a good starting point for walks into the Garfagnano.

BACK TO NATURE

Parco Naturale Migliarino, San Rossore lies to the west of Pisa. It is a large area of coastal forest – mainly stone pines – together with macchia (scrub) vegetation and wetlands. It is excellent for birds, butterflies and reptiles.

SCENIC ROUTES

Particularly scenic is the steep road between Artimino and Poggio a Caiano: Artimino is on the top of the hill, Poggio a Caiano at the bottom, on a small hillock. Just before you reach Artimino, stop and look back down to Poggio a Caiano.

The **A12** between Viareggio and Lucca is a beautiful motorway in a country noted for the functionalism of its main routes. As you leave Lucca, look to the right at the rugged Apuan Alps.

3 days – 456km (282 miles)

THE CRADLE OF THE RENAISSANCE

Firenze • Colle di Val d'Elsa • Siena Montalcino • Monte San Savino • Cortona Arezzo • Bibbiena • Caprese Michelangelo Poppi • Pratovecchio • Firenze

From a flat plain in the midst of a gently hilly landscape flecked with olive groves and vineyards, cypresses and ancient terracotta-coloured villas, rises the city of Firenze (Florence). This was the cradle of the Renaissance, the brilliant new world which succeeded the murk of the Dark Ages. Throughout this city you will find evidence of a great civilised past: the Galleria degli Uffizi with its vast collection of paintings and sculpture; the medieval Palazzo Vecchio; the Cattedrale di Santa Maria del Fiore; the Battistero (baptistery), opposite, with its famous bronze doors; and countless other museums, galleries and palaces. It would take days to see the great sights of Florence properly, and even then you would still not have explored all its medieval streets, its shops and its markets. Visiting Florence first gives a foretaste of the feast of other great monuments of art and architecture to be seen in such places as Siena and Arezzo. And the landscapes on the way are among the most beautiful in Italy.

FOR HISTORY BUFFS

1 From Colle di Val d'Elsa, go to **Monteriggione** (about 8km/5 miles), a fortified hamlet that survives with its walls and 11 of its huge towers intact. It has a little church and sits on its own like an island in a sea of olive groves.

[i] Via Manzoni 16, Firenze

From Firenze, take the ***SS2*** *going south for about 43km (27 miles) to Poggibonsi. Two kilometres (1 mile) further on, branch right to Colle di Val d'Elsa.*

Colle di Val d'Elsa, Toscana

1 Colle di Val d'Elsa is a small town sloping down the side of a steep ridge. There are two parts to it: the **Colle Alto** (upper town) was always the religious and administrative centre, while the **Colle Basso** (lower town) was home to artisans and their workshops. And today, while the buildings in the former are still almost uniformly Renaissance, the latter has changed with the times and today there are factories producing excellent glassware and crystal. In the upper town, the **Castello** is still walled by grim fortifications in which is a massive castellated gate called the **Porta Volterrana** (or Porta Nuova). Beyond, crammed in among dark stone alleyways lined with brooding medieval houses, are the **Duomo** (cathedral) – go inside and see the 16th-century bronze crucifix over the altar – and ancient administrative buildings, including the **Palazzo dei Priori** (now the Civic Museum) and the **Palazzo Vescovile** (the museum of religious art). The most interesting museum is the little **Antiquarium** in the Piazza del Duomo, containing a collection of objects from the Casone Necropolis, in use from the late Iron Age to the last days of the Romans. Colle di Val d'Elsa was the birthplace of the architect Arnolfo di Cambio (died *c*1302), who designed the belltower – the Campanile – of the cathedral in Florence. His house is marked with a plaque.

Florence's glorious cathedral, one of Italy's unmissable sights

From Colle di Val d'Elsa, the road leads southeast towards Siena, about 24km (15 miles).

Siena, Toscana

2 After Florence, Siena is the most interesting city in Tuscany. Its most memorable characteristic is the **Campo**, a sloping semi-circular piazza dominated by the mighty **Palazzo Pubblico**. This late 13th-century Gothic building is topped by a 102m (335-foot) high tower, the **Torre del Mangia**, from the top of which there are amazing views of the surrounding countryside. Nearer at hand, it looks down over the Campo crammed with the tables of open-air cafés, and other important Sienese landmarks, including the **Duomo** (cathedral), sited at the city's highest point. This Romanesque building was added to over the centuries and restored in the 19th century. The most ambitious part of it is the polychrome marble façade designed in the 13th century by Giovanni Pisano. There is also a magnificent rose window in the upper façade, which was added in the next century, and the pinnacles of the gables are decorated with 19th-century mosaics. This remarkable decorative display is matched inside by black and white bands on the columns and walls. Before leaving the building look at Nicola Pisano's fantastic pulpit, 1265–8, with New Testament scenes in relief. One of Siena's greatest works of sculpture is in the **Battistero San Giovanni** (baptistery) under the cathedral. This is a baptismal font, the bronze relief panels of which are by some of the greatest exponents of Renaissance art – Ghiberti, Donatello and Della Quercia. As with Florence, it would take days to explore Siena fully. Nearly any church you see is worth entering, though **San Francesco**, with 14th-century frescos by the Lorenzettis, is among the best. For a closer look at the original works from the cathedral go to the **Museo dell'Opera del Duomo** (cathedral museum). The **Pinacoteca Nazionale** (art gallery) is in the 14th-century **Palazzo Buonsignori**; here there is an excellent survey of Sienese art from its beginnings to the 17th century. Pre-eminent here are the works of Guido da Siena, the

The 'icing sugar' fantasy of Siena's cathedral rises above the city's roofscape

best of the earliest Sienese painters, and the work of Pietro and Ambrogio Lorenzetti. Others to look out for are the works of Beccafumi, born 1484, a High Renaissance artist and contemporary of Raphael, and the works of Il Sodoma, born in 1477, the leading mannerist painter in Siena. You

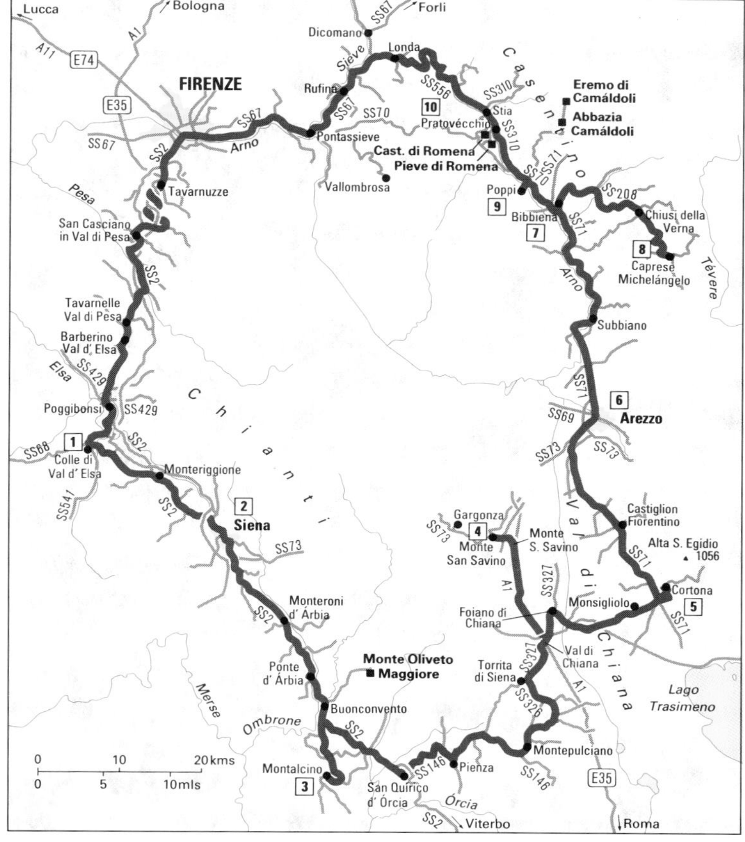

SPECIAL TO . . .

2 Siena hosts the **Palio**, a horse race between the *contrade* (districts) of the city, which takes place twice a year on 2 July and 16 August. It is preceded by parades in medieval costume and takes place in the Campo which is always filled to the brim with spectators.

6 In Arezzo the **antiques fair** happens on the first Sunday of every month. This is one of the best in Italy and has items ranging from statues to old brass beds for sale. Arezzo also has an annual medieval festival called the **Giostra del Saracino** (the Joust of the Saracen), which takes place on the first Sunday in September. It happens in Piazza Grande with the contestants all dressed in 14th-century costume.

can see other works by him in the nearby Church of **Sant'Agostino**. While in Siena make sure you wander through the back streets, away from the main tourist spots, and see its medieval houses, ancient alleyways and little churches. The Church of **San Domenico** contains the head of Saint Catherine in a golden reliquary. She, like St Francis, received the *stigmata*. Not far away is **Casa di Santa Caterina** (Saint Catherine's house), now a museum and a shrine to this mystic reformer, one of the co-patrons of Italy. Also near by is the medieval **Fonte Branda**, a fountain once an important source of water for Siena's inhabitants.

If you have time, go out of Siena on the **SS2**, south, and after about 27km (16 miles) branch right on the **SS451** to the remote Abbey of **Monte Oliveto Maggiore** which is still inhabited by monks. Chief among its treasures is the huge cloister with a fresco cycle depicting the life of St Benedict, partially by Luca Signorelli (born *c*1441), and by Il Sodoma. There is a lovely early 15th-century church here, and the entrance gate is decorated by fine della Robbia terracottas. The abbey is set in a striking position and is considered one of the chief attractions of the Sienese locality (you could go here on the way to the next town, Montalcino).

ℹ Via di Città 43

From Siena, take the ***SS2*** *south as far as Buonconvento, about 27km (17 miles) then, about 2km (1 mile) further on, branch on to the smaller country road that leads for about 12km (7 miles) on to Montalcino.*

Montalcino, Toscana

3 The most memorable thing about Montalcino is the number of wine shops scattered around what is a rather small town. They make sightseeing difficult because their attractions are hugely popular. Montalcino is the home of the famous *Brunello di Montalcino* and perhaps the best place to taste this wine is in the café housed in the old **Rocca**, the 14th-century castle at the top of the town. Montalcino is a hilltown surrounded by medieval walls. Its precipitous streets straggle up to a lovely medieval **Palazzo Comunale** in the Piazza del Popolo, while higher up is the Romanesque Church of **Sant'Agostino** with a good rose window in its façade. There are two collections of Sienese paintings in the town, one in the **Museo Civico** (Civic Museum), the other in the **Museo Diocesano** (Diocesan Museum). Montalcino is a good place from which to visit a collection of other lovely, typically Tuscan towns and villages. It should take an extra afternoon or morning. One of these, Castelnuovo dell'Abate, just 8km (5 miles) to the south, has the lovely 12th-century Benedictine **Abbazia di Sant'Antimo** which is supposed to have been founded by Charlemagne.

RECOMMENDED WALKS

4 A lovely walk is one that takes in the estate surrounding the **castle of Gargonza**, just outside Monte San Savino. It is even better if you stay in the castle hotel here. Routes are planned and laid out on paths through the woods and gardens and there are good views out over the plain to Monte San Savino.

Off the beaten track: the medieval village of Gargonza

Just to the north of Montalcino, also about 8km (5 miles), is the little town of Pienza, famous for having been the birthplace of one of the greatest popes of the early Renaissance, Pius II (Aeneas Sylvius Piccolomini). During the Pope's lifetime it became something of a centre for art – see the magnificent façade of Pius' family home, the **Palazzo Piccolomini** which was designed by Bernardo Rossellino in 1460, one of the great Renaissance architects, with significant works in Florence. He was also responsible for Pienza's cathedral. To the east of Montalcino is San Quirico d'Orcia, another well preserved town with a good Romanesque church.

*Return to the **SS2**, turn right and continue southeast for about 14km (9 miles) on this road to San Quirico d'Orcia. From here, take the **SS146** to Pienza and Montepulciano and then follow the signs to the **A1** via the **SS326** and the **SS327**. Go north on the **A1** for about 14km (9 miles) to the exit for Monte San Savino.*

Monte San Savino, Toscana

4 Monte San Savino is another of Tuscany's most characteristic hill-towns. It is a quiet, pretty place that comes alive early in the morning, the shopping hours, and late in the afternoon when everyone takes their evening stroll. The most interesting things to see here are the monuments that were either designed or restructured by Andrea Cantucci, a sculptor who was born here in 1496, and subsequently nicknamed Sansovino. His is the **Loggia dei Mercanti** in the Corso Sangallo and he was responsible for altering the 14th-century Church of **Sant'Agostino**. Some of his sculptural works can be seen in **Santa Chiara**. It was Antonio da Sangallo the elder, an architect who built some of the masterpieces of Renaissance architecture, who designed the **Palazzo Comunale** early in the 16th century. Not far from Monte San Savino (take the **SS73**), is the little walled village of Gargonza. Turned by its owners into a hotel, it was once frequented by Dante and is an interesting and beautiful spot to stay. It has a little church dedicated to the saints Tiburzio and Susanna, and the whole clutch of buildings behind their north wall is dominated by a medieval tower.

*Go back down the **A1** for 14km (9 miles) as far as Val di Chiana, then follow the signs via Foiano di Chiana and Monsigliolo to Cortona 16km (10 miles).*

The Sienese-style Palazzo Comunale in Montalcino

BACK TO NATURE

A wide variety of wild orchids grace the countryside of Tuscany from March until May. Seemingly dry and barren areas are often surprisingly good, especially if the soil is undisturbed and the bedrock is limestone. Look for numerous members of the bee orchid family – the flowers resemble small, furry insects – as well as tongue orchids, lizard orchids and giant orchids.

Cortona, Toscana

5 Cortona, one of the oldest towns in Tuscany, is also one of the highest. The views from its ramparts are among the best in the region. There is a lot to see and do here but be prepared for your calf muscles to bear the brunt of your sightseeing. Cortona is perched on the side of **Monte Egidio** and all the streets, like the medieval Via del Gesù with its overhanging houses, and the steps leading to and from the central piazza, are immensely steep. The **Duomo** (cathedral), poised above a steep drop to the valley below, is perhaps the least interesting building in this lovely medieval town. Originally Romanesque, it underwent later alterations that left it leagues behind the 13th-century Church of **Sant'Agostino** and the 14th-century **San Niccolò** which contains a *Deposition* by Luca Signorelli. More works by Signorelli, who was born in Cortona, can be found in the **Museo Diocesano** (Diocesan Museum) alongside other precious Renaissance paintings, most notably those by Fra Angelico and Pietro Lorenzetti. Relics of the Etruscans can be seen in the museum in the **Palazzo Pretorio**, while the **Etruscan walls**, nearly obliterated by the Roman and medieval ones, can be seen around the **Porta Colonia** (the Colonia Gate). At the top of the town is the forbidding **Fortezza Medicea** not far from the **Basilica di Santa Margherita da Cortona**, which contains a fine Gothic tomb. Cortona is a lovely place to be in the late afternoon when the townsfolk emerge after their siesta. They loiter in the main square eating ice-creams and gossiping, or else indulge in the universal Italian pastime – *la passeggiata*. This is the leisurely evening stroll backwards and forwards up the piazza, down the other side, then along one of the side streets and back again. Overlooked by ancient buildings, this scene can not have changed much over the centuries.

Medieval houses in Arezzo, a city originating in Etruscan times

SCENIC ROUTES

The most scenic parts of the route are:
– the road from Montalcino to Montepulciano. This is the classic Tuscany that attracts visitors, richly agricultural with wheatfields, vineyards and distant hill villages and castles;
– the **SS2** from Siena to Buonconvento, typical Chianti landscape with trails of cypresses following each other in a line up to the crest of a hill. Look out for the characteristic Tuscan farmhouses;
– the views from Cortona to the Lake of Trasimeno. These are among the highest and most far-reaching in this part of the region. Look first at the Renaissance landscapes in the art galleries, then look at the views from Cortona. The perspectives, the detail and colours are the same;
– the views from Stia across the Casentino to Poppi and Caprese Michelangelo. In this unspoilt landscape you can see each of these towns – over a distance of about 40km (25 miles).

*From Cortona, return to the **SS71**, west of Cortona, which leads to Arezzo, about 29km (18 miles) further on.*

Arezzo, Toscana

6 Arezzo, birthplace of the poet Petrarch, is another Tuscan city with a medieval air about it. **Piazza Grande** is its most magnificent square, lined with an assortment of medieval houses, some of which are attached to castellated towers. The piazza slopes downwards from Giorgio Vasari's 16th-century **loggia** – built in the style of an ancient Greek stoa or portico – of the **Palazzo delle Logge** on the right of which is the **Palazzo della Fraternità dei Laici** topped by a clocktower. Just below this building, also on the right, is the apse of the Romanesque Church of **Santa Maria della Pieve**. The entrance to this church is at the other side, by way of a most extraordinary façade consisting of a three-tiered loggia. Inside is Pietro Lorenzetti's famous polyptych (1320) of the *Madonna and Saints*. The Gothic **Duomo** (cathedral) is further up the hill past the **Palazzo Pretorio**, whose façade is decked with the coats of arms of imperial and Florentine governors of the city. The best things about the cathedral, begun in 1277, are the 16th-century stained glass, by the Frenchman Guillaume de Marcillat, and the tomb of Bishop Guido Tarlati, who died in 1327, an enormous sculpted monument set with 16 relief panels. Above all, do not miss the Church of **San Francesco** which contains one of the finest fresco cycles to have emerged from the Renaissance. The work of the great Piero della Francesca, it depicts the *Legend of the Cross*, and is generally accepted as one of the world's greatest paintings. Piero, a follower of the Florentine school of painting, produced his masterpiece between 1452 and 1466, but its drama, colour and light speak across the centuries. Other places to visit are the **Casa del Vasari**, the house of the painter and early art critic Giorgio Vasari (1511–74) which is now a museum; the remains of a **Roman amphitheatre** down near the station; and the **Museo Archeologico** next door, containing the relics of the city's more ancient past, including good Etruscan items.

[i] Piazza Risorgimento 116

*From Arezzo, take the **SS71** going north to Bibbiena, about 31km (19 miles).*

Bibbiena, Toscana

7 Bibbiena is in the heart of the Casentino area of Tuscany, the lovely wooded valley in which the River Arno rises. Bibbiena is the biggest town in the area, a typical hilltown where the pace of life is slow and easy. Here is the 15th-century Church of **San Lorenzo** which contains terracottas attributed to the school of della Robbia. The 12th-century Church of **SS Ippolito e Donato** has a triptych painted by Bicci di Lorenzo (1435) as well as the remains of some late medieval frescos. Most interesting of all is the 16th-century **Palazzo Dovizi** with a dramatic façade lining the main street in the centre of town. This was the home of Cardinal Bibbiena (1470–1520), friend of the painter Raphael. From Bibbiena (take the **SS208**) it is easy to get to the **Abbey of La Verna** high above the town, the site of which was given to St Francis in 1213; it was here that he received the *stigmata* (Christ's wounds).

*Take the **SS208** to Chiusi della Verna from where follow signs to Caprese Michelangelo, a total of 35km (22 miles).*

Caprese Michelangelo, Toscana

8 This tiny hamlet, birthplace of Michelangelo, occupies a rock site with the source of the Tevere (Tiber) river (that runs through Rome) just to the east, and the upper reaches of the Arno river to the west. Everything there is to see here has something to do with Michelagniolo di Lodovico Buonarroti – Michelangelo – perhaps the greatest artist that Italy ever produced. You can visit his birthplace among the chestnut trees; the **Casa del Podestà**, where his father was the Florentine governor, is now a museum. There are also the remains of a **castle** and the little Chapel of **San Giovanni Battista** where Michelangelo is said to have been baptised.

*From Caprese Michelangelo, return to Bibbiena. Turn right on the **SS70**, which leads after 6km (4 miles) to the turning for Poppi.*

Pieve di Romena church near Pratovecchio, a Romanesque gem

Poppi, Toscana

9 You can see Poppi from miles around. It stands high above the plain of **Campaldino**, where an important battle was fought in 1289 (at which the poet Dante was present). Dante's bust faces the piazza in front of the **Palazzo Pretorio** which dominates the town and the countryside. This was once home to the Guidi counts who, in the Middle Ages dominated the entire Casentino hill region. Today it houses some frescos from the 15th century and a chapel decorated a century earlier. Poppi is very pretty indeed. Its main street is arcaded and lined with medieval houses. Nothing stirs here, not even the cats lying in the sun when you walk past. From Poppi cross over to the **Abbey of Camaldoli**, about 8km (5 miles) to the north. Its buildings date mostly from the 17th and 18th centuries – visit the monks' old **pharmacy**, and also the little baroque **church** about 2.5km (1½ miles) above the abbey. Here, housed in cells, lived (and still live) hermit monks in complete isolation.

*From Poppi, return to and turn left on to the **SS70**. Turn right within 2km (1 mile) on to the **SS310** to Pratovecchio, a further 6km (4 miles).*

Pratovecchio, Toscana

10 Pratovecchio, like other places in the area, is associated with the poet Dante. It serves as a base from which to visit places of interest in the immediate vicinity. For example, a short way out of town is Stia, from whose lofty position you can see right over Casentino to Poppi and Caprese Michelangelo. In the centre of this village, and at its highest point, are the remains of a **castle** which also belonged to the Guidi counts and in which Dante was imprisoned for a while. Near by, and just above Pratovecchio, is the **Castello di Romena**, once a fortified village but now in ruins, and a country church called the **Pieve di Romena**, one of the most beautiful Romanesque buildings in the region. Ask for the key at the neighbouring farmhouse, go inside, and examine the carvings on the columns lining the nave.

*From Pratovecchio continue north on the **SS310**. After 2km (1 mile), branch left on to, and follow, the **SS556** via Stia until it cuts the **SS67** which leads back into Firenze.*

Firenze – Colle di Val d'Elsa 50 (31)
Colle di Val d'Elsa – Siena 24 (15)
Siena – Montalcino 41 (25)
Montalcino – Monte San Savino 89 (55)
Monte San Savino – Cortona 42 (26)
Cortona – Arezzo 34 (21)
Arezzo – Bibbiena 31 (19)
Bibbiena – Caprese Michelangelo 35 (22)
Caprese Michelangelo – Poppi 41 (25)
Poppi – Pratovecchio 8 (5)
Pratovecchio – Firenze 61 (38)

FOR CHILDREN

Show the children true Tuscan cooking. Take them to a barbecue Tuscan style (by doing so you are following the real tradition of Tuscan cuisine) and eat juicy wild boar sausages or a steak *alla Fiorentina* grilled on the open flame. The latter is a steak on the bone with a drop of olive oil added once it is cooked. Fish, too, is delicious. Follow the whole lot with the best ice-cream in Italy – from Vivoli's in Florence.

UMBRIA & THE MARCHES

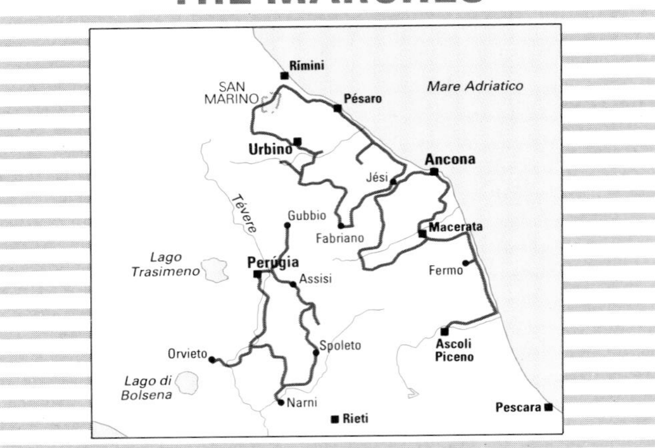

Even though it is so close to Tuscany, Umbria is remarkably under-visited. It is green and fertile, a land of saints and artists, a gentle region whose towns have on the whole been left alone by the march of progress. The Marches (so called because they were a border province of the Holy Roman Empire), lying just to the east and bordering the Adriatic Sea, are a lesser version of the same thing. But whereas Umbria has been opened up by the great central valley running through its midst from Città di Castello to Todi, the hilly landscape of The Marches has been miraculously preserved from development, since a large portion of its terrain is too difficult to negotiate with sweeping motorways. Access to The Marches is easier by way of the coastal autostrada; as a result, few visitors to the region venture beyond the easily reached coastal resorts to explore the ancient cities and treasures further inland.

It is the Apennines, the mountainous backbone of Italy, that are responsible for the region's varied scenery. They continue their southward march from Firenze towards Perugia in Umbria, becoming more and more rugged as they approach The Marches. But by the time they reach the coast the landscape has transformed itself entirely into a gently rolling coastal belt which falls away to the sandy beaches of the Adriatic shore. In both Umbria and The Marches you will find old cities tucked away on the sides of remote gorges and valleys, and see ancient fortresses and abbeys clinging to the tops of hills in positions chosen for their strategic and defensive possibilities in times of trouble.

Most of the Umbrian towns you will visit have, hidden in the gloom of a church or palace, a fresco of a dewy-eyed Madonna or a scene of the life of a local saint, on a wall or inside a niche. Surrounded by a typically Umbrian landscape, with cypresses and miniature villages scattered about, it is more than likely to be the work of some great painter of the 15th or 16th century. If you look carefully, the painted landscape may even represent the lie of the local terrain.

But if Umbria is under-visited, then The Marches region is Italy's best kept secret. Quiet, small towns, packed with magnificent art and architecture, punctuate the mountain valleys, just waiting to be discovered by the more adventurous traveller. And in the north, in Urbino, the region can boast a city on a par for beauty and interest with such towns as Lucca or Siena in Tuscany.

Perugia

Perugia, capital of Umbria, is a treasure-house of art, centre for industry and commerce, medieval hilltown, and home of two universities. As Umbria's major city – and surrounded by motorways – its old character could have been ruined, but this is not so. Indeed, the dominant face that it presents to the world is its medieval one. Perugia was a flourishing commercial centre in the Middle Ages, and its major buildings, the Duomo, the Palazzo dei Priori and the Corso Vannucci lined with fortified palaces (now shops and cafés) – date from this period or shortly after. The narrow cavernous back streets contribute to this old world character. In addition, Perugia has the region's finest paintings in the Galleria Nazionale dell'Umbria (National Gallery of Umbria) in the Palazzo dei Priori.

Ancona

Ancona, the capital of The Marches region, was the ancient Greeks'

northernmost Adriatic settlement. Its oldest quarters sit on a promontory which juts out into the Adriatic, with the half-moon of the harbour below. Although much of it was destroyed during World War II, with further damage caused by an earthquake and landslide in 1972, a large-scale restoration effort has meant that there is once again plenty to see and do here. There are one or two churches with fine Romanesque façades (Santa Maria della Piazza is one, with entertaining carvings), and the cathedral was built on the site of a very much more ancient temple of Venus.

Urbino

Urbino is dramatically placed overlooking the Metauro river. It is a perfect – and rare – example of a Renaissance city that has survived intact, complete with surrounding walls. Dominating all is the huge Palazzo Ducale (Ducal Palace) that seems, even though it was never finished, almost like a city within a city. Started in 1444, this was once home to the Montefeltro dukes of Urbino whose cultured court was the envy of the rulers of many other Italian city-states during the Renaissance. At the time, it contained an enviable art collection and, although the Montefeltro family no longer exists, a part of the collection does and you can see what survives in the palace, now, in part, an art gallery – Galleria Nazionale delle Marche. Raphael, one of the greatest artists of the later Renaissance, was born in Urbino in 1483, and you can visit his home. A quiet walk around the town, preferably after dark, through the cobbled lanes lined with ancient houses, is an evocative experience, transporting you back in time very nearly to the period of the Montefeltro family.

The medieval heart of Perugia belies the city's present day status as a busy regional capital

The little church of Santa Maria Maggiore in Assisi

3 days – 381km (237 miles)

THE GREEN HEART OF ITALY

A modern sample of Gubbio's centuries-old pottery industry

Perugia • Gubbio • Assisi • Spello • Trevi Montefalco • Spoleto • Narni • Todi • Orvieto Perugia

Umbria, 'The Green Heart of Italy', is best observed from the ramparts of the ancient hilltowns crammed into its central valley. Its hills and lower slopes are covered with olive groves, pines and grapevines and the towns in this magical region, looking very much as they did in the Middle Ages, are among the most evocative in Italy. The gentle landscape is reflected in the paintings of the 15th-century Umbrian School – which includes the work of Perugino, Raphael's teacher, and Pinturicchio – in the churches and galleries of Umbria. Perugia is an imposing city with a grand central square, Gothic cathedral and magnificent 13th-century fountain. The Galleria Nazionale dell'Umbria (National Gallery of Umbria) has an unrivalled collection of Umbrian art.

[i] Via Mazzini 21, Perugia

Take the SS298 going northeast from Perugia to Gubbio.

Gubbio, Umbria

1 Beautifully situated at the mouth of a gorge and rising up the slopes of Mont'Ingino, Gubbio has managed to preserve much of its medieval appearance. In the Middle Ages it was one of the fiercest and most warlike places in Umbria, and the 14th-century **Palazzo dei Consoli**, a massive Gothic battlemented structure of dressed stone, in Piazza della Signoria, still dominates the town. It now houses a museum and art gallery. Among its many exhibits are the famous *Tavole Eugubine* (Gubbio Tablets), seven 2nd- to 1st-century BC bronze plaques with inscriptions in Umbrian and Latin, which are the most important evidence extant of the Umbrian language. The **Palazzo Ducale**, built in 1476 for Federico da Montefeltro, Duke of Urbino, by Luciano Laurano, has a delightful Renaissance courtyard and charming rooms with unusual architectural fashions, carved doors and 16th-century fireplaces. As you wander through the town look out for the **Porte del Morto** (Doors of Death or Deadman's Gates). Many houses still have two doorways. The lower one, according to tradition, was where coffins were removed from the house after death. In the lower part of the town is the Gothic Church of **San Francesco**, whose simple façade is adorned with a great rose window, creating a striking effect. Inside is a notable fresco depicting the *Life of the Virgin*, painted by Ottaviano Nelli in the early 1400s.

Gubbio's 1st-century AD **Roman theatre** is one of the largest surviving of its kind. It is in an excellent state of preservation, and in the summer provides dramatic performances.

[i] Piazza Oderisi 6

*Return towards Perugia on the **SS298**. Just before Perugia turn south on the **SS3bis**, then on to the **SS75** eastwards for a short distance before taking the **SS147** to Assisi.*

Assisi, Umbria

2 Nestling on the slopes of Monte Subasio, Assisi has hardly changed since St Francis, born here in 1182, the son of a wealthy merchant, walked its streets, and its ancient character has helped to preserve his cult. Little winding, stone-paved streets, lined with old houses, lead from the base of the town to the various monuments. Almost everything worth seeing is in some way associated with the saint. Art-lovers should head for the **Basilica di San Francesco**, which consists of two fine 13th-century churches, one on top of the other. Here there are frescos celebrating the life of St Francis. Most important is the series of 28 by Giotto, the first major artist of the early Renaissance, in the basilica's upper church. More exquisite are the scenes from the life of St Martin by the Sienese painter Simone Martini (1322) in the Chapel of St Martin in the basilica's lower church. In addition, there are a number of relics belonging to the saint, among them his sandals and his patched grey cassock.

You cannot avoid the religious life in Assisi: the streets are full of nuns and monks and there are several other churches well worth visiting, including the 13th-century **Santa Chiara** which enshrines St Clare's body still intact. Even though she died nearly 750 years ago, her body, blackened by time, lies open to view in the crypt. One of St Francis' earliest and most enthusiastic supporters, St Clare founded the order of the

Basilica di San Francesco in Assisi, begun in 1228

Poor Clares. With your back to this church gaze out over the pinkish-brown rooftops to the Umbrian Plain below, one of the most stunning views you will ever see.

It is well worth the stiff walk up **Via San Francesco** to the **Piazza del Comune**. Here you can see the remains of the **Temple of Minerva**, a good example of Roman architecture dating from the 1st century AD and now the Church of **Santa Maria della Minerva**. There are also several fine medieval buildings: the **Palazzo del Capitano del Popolo**, and the **Torre** and **Palazzo del Comune**, the latter containing the **Pinacoteca Civica** (Civic Picture Gallery).

[i] Piazza del Commune 12

Take the road southeast from Assisi to the ***SS75****, which runs for 3km (2 miles) before the turning to Spello, about 13km (8 miles) from Assisi.*

Spello, Umbria

3 Clinging to the southern slopes of Monte Subasio, Spello has changed little since the Middle Ages. History lies all around you here, as you will find if you pick your way through its streets: if not Roman, then it is bound to be medieval or, at the very latest, Renaissance. The town was under the influence of the Romans for much of its history. Look for the **Porta Venere**, a fine old Roman gateway which survives in the town's walls. Near the station you will find another, the **Porta Consolare**, with three statues from the Roman theatre whose ruins can be seen just before entering the town. Steep winding streets lead from it and up into the town, past higgledy-piggledy medieval shops and houses to the centre and the Church of **Santa Maria Maggiore**. The church's magnificent **Cappella Baglioni** (Baglioni Chapel) contains frescos (1501) by Pinturicchio, which tell the life of the Virgin in a fresh and lively way. An important Renaissance artist, whose work can be seen in the Sistine Chapel in the Vatican, Pinturicchio was assistant to Perugino. The church itself is a hotchpotch of different periods – the front door is Renaissance, the carvings above it Roman and the interior is unexpectedly baroque.

Rejoin the ***SS75*** *heading southwest and turn right on to the* ***SS3*** *round Foligno to Trevi, about 18km (11 miles) away.*

SPECIAL TO . . .

1 In Gubbio is the **Corsa dei Ceri** (Feast of Candles), which takes place every year on 15 May and begins with a picturesque procession through the streets to the **Abbey of Sant'Ubaldo** on Mont'Ingino, just outside the town. The festival is centred round a dramatic race in which three teams of sturdy men each carry a huge, heavy, candle-shaped pillar up the hill to the abbey in honour of St Ubaldo, whose mortal remains are preserved in an urn beneath the main altar. Legend has it that the venerable saint intervened in a battle against Perugia, giving the victory to the outnumbered Gubbians. If you don't care to walk, the abbey can be reached by car or funicular.

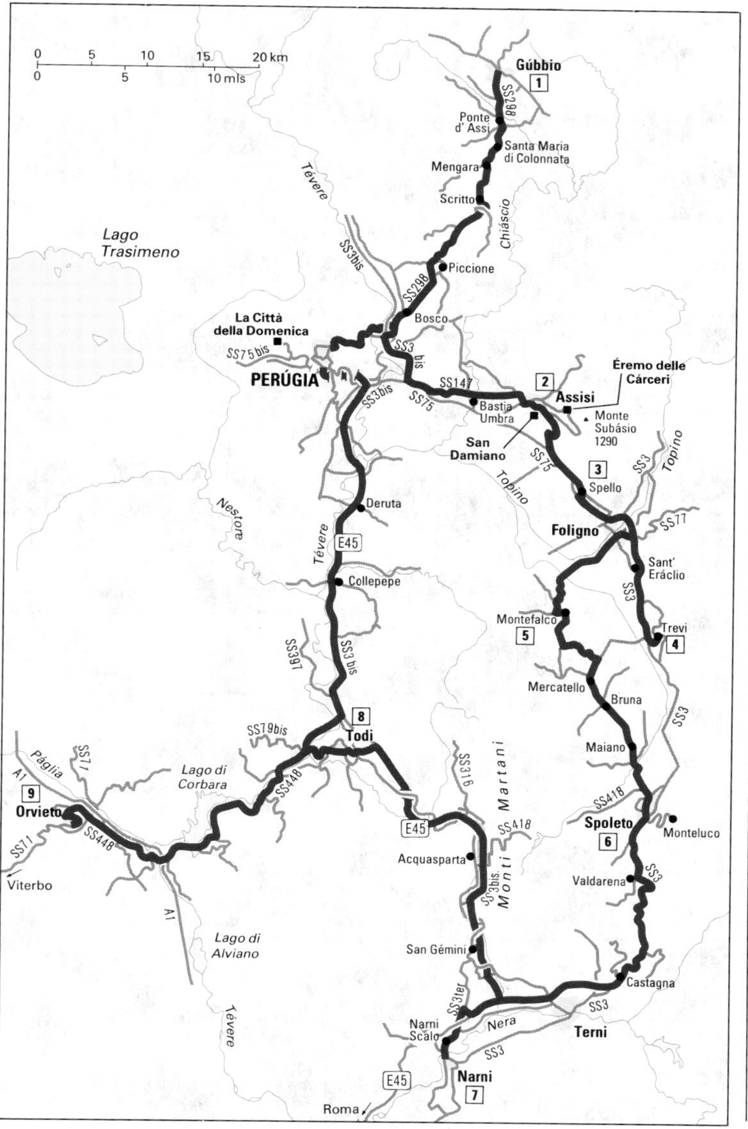

FOR HISTORY BUFFS

2 For those interested in the life of St Francis, and who have the stamina, a walk up Monte Subasio, offering magnificent panoramas of the surrounding countryside, brings you to the **Eremo delle Carceri**, the saint's favourite retreat. The hermitage, cut out of the rock, is set in the dense woodland covering the mountain, 5km (3 miles) behind Assisi. Most of the miracles recounted in St Francis' *Fioretti* ('Little Flowers') took place in these woods.

9 On the east side of Orvieto, you can descend into **Pozzo di San Patrizio** (St Patrick's Well), a vast cylinder cut through the rock on which Orvieto stands. Built in the 16th century, this 61m (200-foot) deep well, with two separate spiral staircases winding round the shaft, one for the descent and the other for the ascent of the donkeys which brought up the water, was commissioned to ensure the town's water supply in times of siege. Near by are the remains of an Etruscan temple. Take a look at the **Etruscan Museum** and the various artefacts unearthed from tombs in the area – in particular, see the 4th-century sarcophagus found near the Torre San Severo in 1912.

FOR CHILDREN

La Città della Domenica is a Disney-style playground 8km (5 miles) west of Perugia, just off the **SS75bis**. The 200-hectare (500-acre) park has a zoo, and archaeological zone, games rooms, bumper cars and a variety of buildings based on fairy-tale themes, such as 'Snow White's House' and 'The Witch Wood'.

SCENIC ROUTES

Most of the route along this tour of Umbria offers an outstanding range of scenery, but there are certain stretches of road where the views are particularly spectacular. They are:
Perugia to Gubbio – along the **SS298** between Piccione and Santa Maria di Colonnata;
Gubbio to Assisi – the last 13km (8 miles) of the **SS147** before Assisi;
The roads in and around Montefalco;
Todi to Orvieto – the **SS448** round the south shore of Lake Corbara and in to Orvieto;
Orvieto to Perugia – the **SS3bis** from Deruta to Perugia.

Trevi, Umbria

4 Magnificently situated on the slopes of a steep hill, dominating the Spoletino plain, Trevi is set so high that on approaching it you cannot see it from the car windows. It is a lovely, undiscovered place whose pavements are speckled with mosaic-like arrangements of cobbles, while a maze of winding streets and blind alleys is contained within two sets of medieval walls. The 14th-century **Palazzo Comunale** in Piazza Mazzini, the site of the town's **Pinacoteca** (art gallery), contains a mixture of Renaissance paintings by Pinturicchio and Lo Spagna, Roman remains, sculptures and ceramics. You can see Lo Spagna's fresco of the *Life of St Francis*, 1512, in the Church of **San Martino** in Via Augusto Ciufelli on the edge of town. This is thought to be his best painting and it has a contemporary view of Assisi in its background. Also worth a visit is the 12th-century Church of **Sant' Emiliano** with its richly decorated altar by Rocca da Vicenza, and if you still have time, take a walk below the town to the Church of **Santa Maria delle Lacrime**, with its beautiful doorway and fine Umbrian School pictures, including one by Perugino.

*Return to Foligno via the **SS3**, then follow signs to Montefalco.*

Narni, on Umbria's border, was once a fortress-city

Montefalco, Umbria

5 The pretty little walled hilltown of Montefalco – 'Falcon's Mount' – once boasted more saints than any other town in the region, earning itself the title of 'a little strip of heaven fallen to earth'. With a population of only 6,000, this was quite a feat! The Church of **San Francesco**, founded in 1336, contains 15th-century frescos by Benozzo Gozzoli, and work by other Umbrian painters. These frescos are considered so important that the building is no longer used as a church but has become a museum. Other churches to see are the Gothic Church of **Sant'Agostino** with its selection of Renaissance frescos by local artists, and the baroque Church of **Santa Chiara di Montefalco**. Here you can see the crumbling remains of Santa Chiara's heart. Montefalco is a tranquil, peaceful place, often called the 'Balcony of Italy'; you should sit in one of its cafés and sample the famed *Sagrantino* wine or take in the delightful views of the surrounding countryside.

Head across country, via Mercatello and Bruna, to Spoleto.

Spoleto, Umbria

6 Spoleto, shadowed by its 14th-century **Rocca** (castle), is a very old city, rich in evidence of a history that began centuries before the Roman occupation. It has survived sieges, earthquakes, plagues, a period of misrule by the notorious Lucrezia Borgia and World War II bombing. The **Duomo** (cathedral), built in 1067 but restored in the 12th century, with its splendid doorway and Renaissance porch surrounded with mosaics, is without doubt the most beautiful in Umbria, though the Spoleto churches of **San Gregorio Maggiore, Sant'Eufemia** and **San Pietro** come close. Be sure to visit them all, particularly the latter (just out of town), with its extremely early relief sculptures.

Among Spoleto's many Roman ruins is a partially restored **theatre** in the vicinity of Piazza della Libertà, which is still used for concerts, and the 1st-century AD **Arch of Drusus**, in an excellent state of preservation. The imposing **Ponte delle Torri** (Bridge of the Towers) was erected in the 13th century as an aqueduct over a river gorge (pedestrians only now), and links the town with neighbouring Monteluco. Built of stone, with 10 arches, it is 230m (755 feet) long and 81m (265 feet) high and was probably constructed on the foundations of an earlier Roman aqueduct.

Spoleto can get very busy at peak times, so it is best to plan your visit to avoid these. It is one of the liveliest towns in the region, helped by the annual **Festival dei Due Mondi** (Festival of the Two Worlds) that takes place here. The festival, in June and July, presents the latest trends in art, music, theatre, painting and sculpture against the magnificent setting of the ancient town.

[i] Piazza della Libertà 7

*Take the **SS3** south. Bypass Terni, and head for Narni, entering on the **SS3ter**.*

Narni, Umbria

7 Narni, crammed on its hilltop, is so constricted that it has hardly expanded since Roman times. This solid, stone-built town has an interesting, though ruined, 14th-century **Rocca** (castle), with fine views in most directions, and the odd-looking **Palazzo del Podestà**, which was created by joining three fortified tower houses together. Now it houses the

Duomo, Orvieto: detail from the much-admired carved façade

local art gallery whose greatest treasure is a *Coronation of the Virgin* by the 15th-century master Ghirlandaio. See the fine inlaid choir stalls and early marble screen in the Romanesque **Duomo** (cathedral), which, with the Podestà Palace, provides a splendid backdrop to the **Corso dell'Anello**, a spectacular costumed pageant enacted each May, when horsemen representing the town's rival quarters joust for a coveted prize. Just below Narni, on the line of the ancient Via Flaminia, are the ruins of the Roman **Ponte d'Augusto** (Bridge of Augustus) which was originally 120m (400 feet) long and carried the road almost 30m (100 feet) up over the River Nera.

*From Narni, head back towards Terni, turning north on **SS3bis** to Todi, about 45km (28 miles).*

Todi, Umbria

8 Todi occupies a triangular site, still partly surrounded by its rings of Etruscan, Roman and medieval walls, on a ridge above the Tevere (Tiber) valley. The **Piazza del Popolo**, at the centre of town, is the kind of place where you could sit all day in the sun at one of the cafés and do nothing but watch the world pass by. On one side of the piazza is the Romanesque **Duomo** (cathedral), on the site of a former Roman temple to Apollo, while the remaining sides are bounded by a variety of other medieval buildings, in particular the 14th-century **Palazzo del Capitano**. The sleepy charm of this place is enlivened early in the evening when the residents pour into the piazza for the daily stroll and a chat: then it seems like a drawing room with a party in progress. You should not leave Todi without visiting **Santa Maria della Consolazione**, inspired by Bramante's plan for St Peter's in Rome. This domed church on the plan of a Greek cross, is much admired as one of the finest creations of Renaissance architecture. Started in 1508, it took over 100 years to complete.

i Piazza del Popolo 38

*Leave Todi on the **SS448**, and head southwest, around the Lake of Corbara, for 38km (24 miles) to Orvieto.*

Orvieto, Umbria

9 Orvieto's commanding position on a great square rock makes it an amazing sight, visible from miles around. An ideal site for a fort, it was first settled by the Etruscans (who called it *Volsinii*), but they could not withstand the might of the rising new power, and eventually Orvieto fell to Rome. It is a dark, brooding town, dominated by its glorious Gothic-style **Duomo** (cathedral), which was started in the late 1200s, supposedly to the designs of Arnolfi di Cambio, famed for his Duomo and Palazzo Vecchio in Florence. It was built in alternate courses of black basalt and greyish-yellow limestone, and decorated by the finest artists of the day, to commemorate the Miracle of Bolsena (when the Host started to bleed during a celebration of Mass in the town of Bolsena). The façade, adorned with elaborate sculptures and coloured mosaics, was designed by Lorenzo Maitani of Siena. To appreciate fully, you should view it in bright sunlight, when the effect is quite stunning. Inside, magnificent frescos in the lovely Cappella della Madonna de San Brigio are largely the work of Fra Angelico and, later, Luca Signorelli. The town abounds in interesting monuments: the 11th-century **Palazzo Vescovile**, an old papal residence; the 12th-century **Palazzo del Capitano del Popolo**; and the churches of **San Domenico, San Lorenzo, Sant'Andrea** and **San Giovenale** are among the best buildings.

Orvieto is famous for its wine, particularly the whites. Signorelli, when painting the Duomo, is said to have asked that part of his contract be paid in wine, and the rock beneath the city is honeycombed with caves used to ferment the grapes for the Orvieto vintages.

i Piazza dell Duomo 24

*Take the **SS448** back towards Todi, then turn left on to the **SS3bis** to Perugia.*

Perugia – Gubbio 40 (25)
Gubbio – Assisi 53 (33)
Assisi – Spello 13 (8)
Spello – Trevi 18 (11)
Trevi – Montefalco 26 (16)
Montefalco – Spoleto 24 (15)
Spoleto – Narni 43 (27)
Narni – Todi 45 (28)
Todi – Orvieto 38 (24)
Orvieto – Perugia 81 (50)

RECOMMENDED WALKS

6 The countryside round Spoleto is particularly picturesque and quite accessible by foot. For spectacular views follow the road at the eastern end of the Ponte delle Torri for 1km (half a mile) to the Church of San Pietro (one of the finest achievements of Umbrian architecture and sculpture). A little further afield, for those who have the stamina, another road from the east end of the Ponte delle Torri winds its way up the hillside for 6km (3½ miles). Here, at the top of thickly wooded Monteluco, you will find a monastery founded by St Francis, with enchanting views of the valley.

BACK TO NATURE

While you are travelling in Umbria you will undoubtedly notice the kind of countryside which naturalists call *macchia* (*maquis*). This is the characteristic Mediterranean habitat of evergreen trees with a shrubby understorey.

As well as its distinctive wildflowers, including several species of orchid and the much more easily spotted, but no less pretty, rock-roses, this habitat contains such creatures as praying mantids, wall lizards and green lizards (look for them basking in the morning sunshine) and lots of snakes (don't worry, they are likely to see you a long time before you see them and beat a quiet retreat!). You probably will not see, but will almost certainly hear, Scop's owls. Their call, delivered for most of the night – usually from trees – is a quite uncanny and unnatural sound, likened by some to sonar bleeps.

3/4 days – 406km (252 miles)

ITALY'S BEST KEPT SECRET

Luigi Vanvitelli designed the campanile on the Sanctuary of the Holy House in Loreto

Ancona • Portonovo • Sirolo • Loreto • Macerata Fermo • Ascoli Piceno • Tolentino • Camerino San Severino Marche • Cingoli • Ancona

It takes hours to get through the Marches region of central Italy. This is not because of heavy traffic, but because the interior has hardly any major routes, so that the twists and turns of the little country roads make driving slow. And with so many breathtaking views between the hairpin bends as you traverse the valleys, who wants to travel quickly? Mud-coloured towns are the norm – some walled, some surrounding an ancient castle. Each contains some noteworthy work of art which might simply be a Madonna fresco fading in a forgotten chapel. Ancona is the biggest port in the region, running along a natural promontory in the shadow of Monte Conero. Severely damaged by World War II bombs and in a later earthquake, the city's charms are well hidden.

ⓘ Via Marcello Marini 14, Ancona

Take the coast road from Ancona going south for about 11km (7 miles) to Portonovo, which itself is 1km (½ mile) off the main road.

Portonovo, Marche

1 One of the most beautiful stretches of coastline along the Adriatic begins just south of Ancona. Called the **Riviera del Conero**, it is made up of sheltered beaches which alternate with cliffs dropping straight down into the ocean. The first port of call among the pines and the holm-oaks lodged into the crevices of this area, is Portonovo, a minute settlement whose major attraction, apart from its shoreline and attendant campsites, is the ancient Church of **Santa Maria di Portonovo**. Built in 1034, it sits among the olives and the scrubland not far from the shore. This Romanesque building is in very good condition and you can clearly see Byzantine influences on its design. It has always been regarded as an architectural gem – the poet Dante mentions it in his *Divina Commedia* (*Divine Comedy*). Also at Portonovo is a reconstructed Napoleonic **fortress** erected in 1808 and an early 18th-century **watchtower**, where the writer Gabriele D'Annunzio often stayed.

Return to the main road, which winds further south to Sirolo, about 10km (6 miles).

Sirolo, Marche

2 Monte Conero, 572m (1,877 feet) separates Portonovo from Sirolo which is bigger and better equipped as a holiday place. There is a handful of hotels, restaurants and one or two nightclubs and, because this is still the Riviera del Conero, there are also little coves and places to swim. Sirolo has a medieval **fortress** of the Counts Cortesi, and the local Franciscan **convent**, now a villa, has two elms planted, according to legend, by St Francis himself on a visit to the town in 1215. In the **Church of the Sacrament** you will find a lovely local painting of the *Madonna of the Misericordia*, about 1500. Not far away at Numana, about 1.5km/1 mile further south, go to the **Santuario del Crocefisso** (Sanctuary of the Cross) and see the venerated Byzantine *Crucifixion*.

*From Numana follow the signs to the **SS16**. Turn left on to the **SS77** for 5km (3 miles) before taking the turnoff for Loreto.*

Loreto, Marche

3 This town has the incredible reputation of being the point at which the Madonna's house, transported by angels from Nazareth to Italy, came down to earth late in the 13th century. This much-venerated relic, which is a simple brick building containing traces of medieval frescos inside, is the final destination of a pilgrimage undertaken by thousands of Italians each year. The **Santa Casa** (Holy

House) is kept in the **Santuario della Santa Casa** (Sanctuary of the Holy House) and is placed directly under its dome. It is worth noting that the church's baroque façade is one of Italy's finest. Nobody knows who designed the façade, but a whole host of other great names worked on the building: for instance Giuliano da Sangallo was responsible for the cupola and Bramante (one of Italy's greatest Renaissance architects) designed the side chapels. In the Piazza della Madonna in front of the building is a beautiful loggia designed by Bramante in 1510, and in the middle of the square is a large fountain by Carlo Maderna, one of the architects of St Peter's in Rome. The sanctuary is brimming over with great works of art. Look out for the frescos by Angelica Kauffmann, who was a founder member of the London Royal Academy, in the right transept chapels. Bramante designed the beautiful marble screen in front of the Santa Casa itself and there are statues by Baccio Bandinelli.

[i] Via G Solari 3

*From Loreto, take the **SS77** across country, via Recanati, to Macerata, about 29km (18 miles).*

Macerata, Marche

4 Macerata is one of the oldest university towns in Italy. It crowns a series of low hills and is a quiet place, full of bookshops and hidden restaurants, with narrow streets and stairways. Mostly medieval, everything is built of terracotta-coloured brick, and the homogeneity of its appearance is the town's most striking feature. But there are a host of monuments, mostly Renaissance and baroque. Apart from the 11th-century **Duomo** (cathedral), there is the even earlier **Santa Maria della Porta** – look for the Gothic doorway. The **Basilica della Misericordia** has an interior by Vanvitelli. The **Art Gallery** adjoining the Church of **San Giovanni** contains works by local 'Marchegiani' artists, as well as a *Madonna* by Carlo Crivelli, whose style of painting was influenced by Mantegna.

[i] Via Garibaldi 87

*From Macerata, go southeast for about 6km (4 miles) to the **SS485**, then head back towards the coast for about 21km (13 miles). Branch south again on the **SS16** for about 15km (9 miles) to Porto San Giórgio before turning right on to the **SS210**, which leads up to Fermo, about 7km (4 miles), further.*

Fermo, Marche

5 Fermo is a very pretty hilltown poised above the Adriatic. It has tremendous views over Monti Sibillini and the Gran Sasso peaks in the Abruzzo to one side, and to the sea on the other. As in Macerata, almost everything is of terracotta-coloured brick, in this case primped and cleaned in recent restoration programmes. Fermo was a relatively important town during the Roman past. In the Via degli Aceti, you can see the remains of the 1st-century **Piscina Epuratorio**, an underground reservoir designed to hold and to clarify rain water. Above ground again, the **Duomo** (cathedral) has a lovely façade of the 13th to 14th centuries – although most of the rest of the building was rebuilt in the 18th century. Look at St Thomas à Becket's chasuble, woven from Moorish silk in

Though mountainous and difficult of access, the Marche region is extremely fertile

FOR HISTORY BUFFS

4 In the Via Manzoni in Macerata is the **Palazzo Compagnoni-Marefoschi**, scene of the marriage in 1772 of the 'Young Pretender' to the British throne, Bonnie Prince Charlie, to Louise of Stolberg. Charles, at 52, was no longer 'young' or 'bonnie', and the marriage was a failure.

SCENIC ROUTES

For the loveliest coastal views, nothing in The Marches will beat the **Riviera del Conero**, its cliffs and sheltered coves contrasting with the uninteresting straightness of the east Italian seaboard elsewhere.

From Camerino, to the south of Cingoli, you will be able to see the great Gran Sasso ranges of mountains which actually lie in the south of the Abruzzo.

The most scenic part of this tour is undoubtedly to be seen from the **SS502** in and around Cingoli, about 650m (2,130 feet) above sea-level.

The 13th- to 14th-century cloisters of St Nicholas' Basilica in Tolentino

FOR CHILDREN

2 Children would enjoy playing on the beaches at Sirolo. Like many others along this shore, Sirolo's beaches fall gently down to the sea so that the water is shallow for some way out.

SPECIAL TO . . .

1 At Camerino, not far from Portonovo and Sirolo, is **Aspio Terme**, one of The Marches' important thermal springs. There are six of them on this spot – cold salt-bromo-iodic water good for the treatment of jaded livers, dodgy stomachs and biliary tract diseases.

6 In Ascoli Piceno is the festival, held in August, in which local townsfolk don the 15th-century costumes of musicians, soldiers, lords and ladies, and parade through the medieval streets of the town before the tournament known as the **Quintana**. In this jousting tournament, in which the rules go back to the 14th century, horsemen ride at a figure representing a Saracen.

1116. It was left here by a bishop of Fermo to whom à Becket presented it. In the **Palazzo Comunale** is a small gallery which contains a painting of the *Nativity* by Rubens. On this building's façade is a weird statue of Pope Sixtus V, once a bishop of Fermo. Other places of interest are the **Teatro dell'Aquila** (1780) and the Church of **San Domenico** (1233).

ℹ Piazza del Popolo 5

*From Fermo, return to the coastal **SS16** and continue south along the coast for about 32km (20 miles) until Porto d'Ascoli, at which branch inland on the **SS4** and continue for about 28km (17 miles) to Ascoli Piceno.*

Ascoli Piceno, Marche

6 Ascoli Piceno is one of the great towns of The Marches region. There is a lot to see, most of it confined to the Piazza del Popolo in the centre of town. The early 13th-century **Palazzo del Popolo** has a later façade by Ascoli Piceno's best known artist, Cola dell'Amatrice. Also in the square is the Church of **San Francesco** (about 1262) with a statue of Pope Julius II over the south door, and there is the Franciscan **Chiostro Grande** (Great Cloister) of the mid-16th century, which is now used as a market. The **Loggia dei Mercanti** was built by the Wool Corporation in the early 1500s. In the Piazza dell'Arringo you will find the **Duomo della Sant'Emidio** (cathedral), a largely 12th-century building with an unfinished façade, also by Cola dell'Amatrice. Look in the chapel on the right of the nave and you will see a beautiful painting by Carlo Crivelli – thought to be his finest work. The treasury contains a silver altar-frontal and an opulent silver reliquary by Pietro Vannini. Beyond the cathedral is the **Palazzo Comunale** gallery containing works by, among others, Titian and Crivelli.

ℹ Via Trivio 1

*Retrace your route to, and join, the **SS16** travelling northwards to Civitanova, at which take the **SS485** going inland past the turning to Macerata, continuing for about 19km (12 miles) to Tolentino.*

Tolentino, Marche

7 Tolentino's medieval centre is far more interesting than its outskirts, which are mostly modern. An ancient bridge known as **The Devil's Bridge** leads the way to the **Basilica di San Nicola da Tolentino** which has a beautiful early 15th-century portal by Nanni di Bartolo. In the crypt beneath the church is the tomb of St Nicholas of Tolentino who died in 1305. A great many miracles were attributed to him and in a large chapel on the right side of the basilica you can see his statue by Giorgio da Sebenico. In the cloisters is a small museum of majolica and silver. In the Palazzo Bezzi is the **Museum of Caricatures**, a collection of hundreds of cartoons from all over the world.

*Continue west from Tolentino via the **SS77** for about 23km (14 miles) to a turning on the right for Camerino, a further 9km (6 miles).*

Camerino, Marche

8 At Camerino is a massive **fortress** built by Cesare Borgia, one of the most hated figures of early Italian history. There are also the remains of the **Rocca Varano**, an early 13th-century castle built by the Varano family, whose fiefdom Camerino was for about 300 years until 1539. Churches to see include the **Duomo** (cathedral) **San Venanzio** with its beautifully executed Renaissance doorway, and the little **Church of the Annunziata**. The **Museo Diocesano** (Diocesan Museum), in Camerino's main square, has a *Madonna* by the Venetian artist Tiepolo, while the town's other museum, the **Museo Civico**, is filled with work by the local 15th-century painter Girolamo di Giovanni.

*The **SS256** leads northwards towards Castelraimondo. Shortly before Castelraimondo, turn right on to the **SS361** through the town and along the Potenza river, to San Severino Marche, about 22km (14 miles).*

San Severino Marche, Marche

9 The 16th-century anatomist Bartolomeo Eustachi was born in San Severino Marche. He is best known as the man after whom the Eustachian tube (in the ear) was named, but there is not much in the town to remind you of this fact. You will, however, see the work of a local painter who achieved great fame at the beginning of the 15th century – Lorenzo Salimbeni, who was also born here. You can see his work, some frescos, in the **Duomo Vecchio** (old cathedral), in the old upper town. While you are there, have a quick look into the cloister, then go back down to the Church of **San Lorenzo** and the **Duomo Nuovo** (new cathedral), in the lower town. The Duomo Nuovo contains a striking painting of the *Madonna* by one of the great Mannerist painters Pinturicchio. Look in at the art gallery in the **Palazzo Comunale** where there are works by yet another great 15th-century painter born here – Lorenzo d'Alessandro.

*The **SS502** goes north from San Severino Marche to Cingoli.*

Cingoli, Marche

10 Cingoli is a very ancient town famous for its views. Crammed on to the top of a hill, its nickname is *'The Balcony of The Marches'*. There is no single great masterpiece to be viewed here, but the little town's small early Renaissance palaces, particularly the **Palazzo Castiglione** in the Corso Garibaldi and those in the Polisena Quarter, appeal, with their carved entrance portals, their old window surrounds and their general air of antiquity. Narrow stone-paved streets, cupolas and belfries are the predominant characteristics of the town. Look into the churches of **San Francesco**, the proud possessor of a lovely 16th-century wooden crucifix, and **Sant'Esuperanzio**, an ancient vaulted structure founded in 1100 by the Benedictines. It contains frescos from the 15th and 16th centuries, and a *Flagellation* by Sebastiano del Piombo, one of the greatest of the Venetian painters and a contemporary of Michelangelo.

i Via Luigi Ferri 17

*From Cingoli, the **SS502** continues northwards (for about 20km/12 miles) towards Jesi. Turn right on to the dual carriageway, which goes back to Ancona, about 33km (20 miles).*

Ancona – Portonovo 11 (7)
Portonovo – Sirolo 10 (6)
Sirolo – Loreto 13 (8)
Loreto – Macerata 29 (18)
Macerata – Fermo 49 (30)
Fermo – Ascoli Piceno 66 (41)
Ascoli Piceno – Tolentino 100 (62)
Tolentino – Camerino 32 (20)
Camerino – San Severino Marche 22 (14)
San Severino Marche – Cingoli 21 (13)
Cingoli – Ancona 53 (33)

RECOMMENDED WALKS

6 To the north of Ascoli Piceno, beyond its walls, is the valley of the River Tronto, a pleasant area for walks and picnics – ideal for the family as the terrain is gentle.

BACK TO NATURE

Migrant birds – especially songbirds and birds of prey – pass through Italy each spring and autumn on their way to and from their breeding grounds in northern Europe and the wintering grounds in Africa. Many species follow the coast on their journeys and the Ancona headland is an excellent observation area. Unfortunately, countless millions are shot or trapped in Italy for 'sport'. Warblers and turtle doves suffer particularly badly.

San Severino Marche, a modest town but worth a halt

3/4 days – 410km (255 miles)

THE NORTHERN MARCHES

Cloisters of the church of Santa Maria Nuove in Fano

Urbino • San Leo • Gradara • Pesaro • Fano Corinaldo • Jesi • Fabriano • Arcevia • Urbania Fossombrone • Urbino

In the 15th century many of the towns in this part of The Marches were in the orbit of the powerful Federico di Montefeltre, Duke of Urbino. Monuments to his reign are scattered around the region. Luckily he was an enlightened individual and there is little from the time of his rule that is not worth visiting or contemplating. Other towns that were never grasped by the tentacles of the Montefeltre family, simply revere the work of a native painter, sculptor or architect. Urbino, the duke's headquarters, is the most important town in the area. The birthplace of Raphael, its artistic patrimony is very nearly on a par with that of Florence. The Palazzo Ducale, which houses a museum and art gallery, is magnificently preserved. If you stay in Urbino it will be a while before you tear yourself away.

BACK TO NATURE

The Adriatic Sea is not only a beautiful stretch of water popular for seaside holidays, but is also rich in wildlife. Shorelife is difficult to observe because of the poor tidal range, but out to sea, Cory's and the Mediterranean race of Manx shearwaters can be seen along with gulls, cormorants and dolphins.

SCENIC ROUTES

This is one of the most scenic tours in Italy. In particular, look out for the sudden views from the road, towards San Leo and Gradara as you approach them.

At dusk, the views from the parapets of Urbino are magical and in the half light the landscapes of local Renaissance painters are never far from the mind.

[i] Piazza del Rinascimento 1, Urbino

The best way to San Leo from Urbino (about 52km/32 miles) is to go cross-country via Sassocorvaro, Macerata Feltria and Montecopiolo.

San Leo, Marche

1 San Leo is accessible by a single road cut into the rock. It is a tiny place, poised way above the Marecchia river on a kind of rocky lump. Its castle, the **Rocca**, in its present state dating from the 15th century, is even higher, dramatically placed on the edge of a cliff overlooking the town. Remarkably well preserved, the little town confines most of its interesting monuments in and near to the central Piazza Dante. The 12th-century **Duomo** (cathedral) was erected in honour of St Leo. Its interior is dark, solid and unadorned, its mighty structure in a wonderful state of preservation. **La Pieve** (the parish church), which backs on to the main square, is the oldest church in the vicinity (9th-century possibly). San Leo has good restaurants and the seats in the square's cafés are good for a couple of hours' coffee-drinking and watching the world go by.

*From San Leo, follow the signs to San Marino, then towards Rimini on the **SS72** (about 39km/24 miles). Then take the autostrada **A14** southwards for about 16km (10 miles) leaving it at the Cattolica exit. Join the **SS16** travelling south for 5km (3 miles) before branching right on the minor road to Gradara.*

Gradara, Marche

2 You will be able to see the whole of Gradara in about two hours. The old town only contains about 25 buildings and a **fortress**, the whole lot contained within 14th-century walls which are mostly still intact. You can go inside the castle and see the rooms in which one of the great tragedies of medieval Italy was enacted. The beautiful young Francesca fell in love with her very ugly, and older

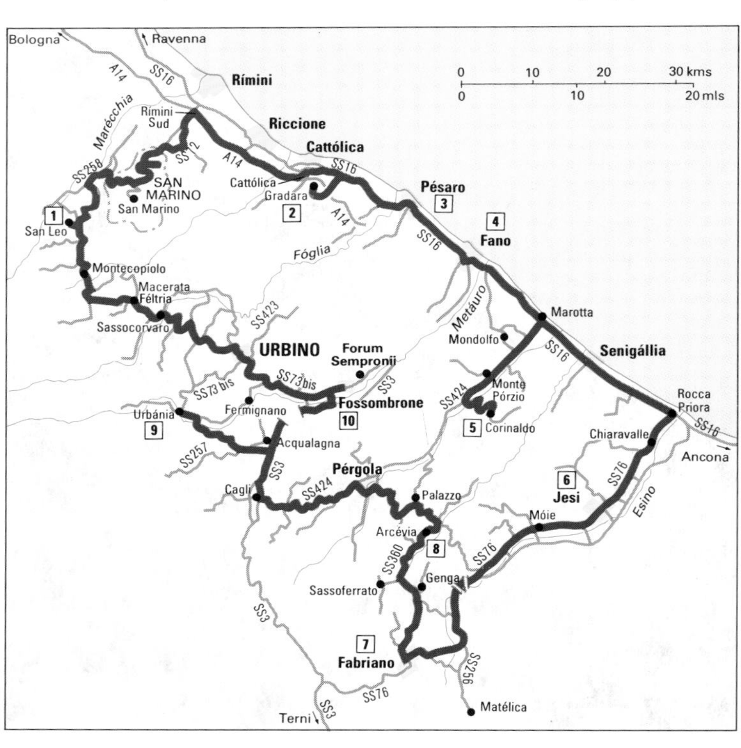

husband's younger brother, Paolo. This was almost inevitable, as Paolo had stood proxy for his older sibling at the marriage ceremony. A servant reported the two young lovers to the husband, who murdered them. You can visit the scene of the murder – an event immortalised by Dante in the *Divine Comedy* and by Tchaikovsky in his fantasy overture *Francesca da Rimini*. Once you have strolled around the castle, peered over its walls to the patchwork countryside all around, and looked in at the glazed terracotta relief by Andrea della Robbia (1435–1525) in the castle chapel, you will have seen all there is to see in Gradara.

*Return to the **SS16** and travel southeast to Pesaro.*

A massive fortress defended Gradara in medieval times

Pesaro, Marche

3 Pesaro is proud of the reputation of Rossini, the composer, who was born here in 1792. It preserves his birthplace at **Via Rossini 34**, which you can visit, and it holds a series of annual concerts and operas during the annual **Rossini festival** held towards the end of the summer. You can also go and look at his spinet and his manuscripts in the **Conservatorio** in Piazza Olivieri. Pesaro is a large, bustling city, a seaside resort brimming over with people in the summer, as well as a commercial centre. It has some quirky old streets in its older quarters but, because of heavy bombing during World War II, which laid waste large tracts of the city, its monuments are no longer very exceptional. However, the **Museo Oliveriano** contains local finds from the Etruscan and Roman periods – inscriptions, bronzes, coins; and the **Museo Civico** has some lovely majolica as well as a *Coronation of the Virgin* by Giovanni Bellini.

[i] Via Mazzolari 4

*From Pesaro, the **SS16** leads to Fano, about 12km (7 miles) away.*

Fano, Marche

4 Fano is much better preserved than its less fortunate neighbour. It was an important Roman town and you can still see the **Arco d'Augusto** (Arch of Augustus), a triumphal arch dating from the 1st century AD. Nearby buildings were constructed over the centuries using material stolen from this Roman relic. In particular, and interesting in its own right, is the 15th-century pawnshop, the **Logge di San Michele**, at the end of the street named after the arch. The old Church of **San Michele**, another structure made from recycled antique building materials, preserves a relief carved on to its façade showing what the arch looked like in the 15th century. In the Church of **Santa Maria Nuova** are fine altarpieces by Giovanni Santi, Raphael's father, and Perugino, Raphael's teacher. In fact there is also, preserved here, a little panel painting supporting the work of the young Raphael (Raffaelo Sanzio) himself. The **Museo Civico** (Civic Museum) is equally well endowed with precious works of art: apart from pieces by Santi Senior, there are works by Domenchino (1581–1641), and the 17th-century artist Mattia Preti.

*Continue along the **SS16** for about 14km (9 miles) to Marotta, at which branch inland on the **SS424** and follow the signs to Corinaldo.*

SPECIAL TO ...

The provinces of Urbino and Pesaro hold annual weekend '**gastronomia**' events, in which chosen restaurants in a variety of locations (San Leo is one) agree to produce a specific menu of local dishes on an agreed date. This keeps obscure culinary traditions going and usually results in a delicious feast. Check the details in the local tourist office.

FOR CHILDREN

When bored with the countryside and 'Great Art', youngsters can go skating at Jesi and Fabriano. Boating at Pesaro is another attraction, while places for riding can be found at Urbino, Urbania, Jesi and Fabriano.

Part of the 14th-century walls enclosing old Jesi

FOR HISTORY BUFFS

1 The **Rocca** in San Leo once housed, in its prison, the infamous Giuseppe Balsamo, better known as Count Alessandro di Cagliostro, a con-man who, in the 18th century, duped countless gullible people all over Europe into believing that he had discovered a way of turning base metals into gold. Ugly women came to him in the belief that he could make them more beautiful. He was eventually condemned for freemasonry and ended up in San Leo where he died in 1795.

Corinaldo, Marche

5 Corinaldo is a walled medieval village famous as the centre of production of the *Verdicchio* wine, one of the most popular Italian white wines. Behind its 15th-century walls, in which you can still see massive bastions, towers and old gateways – such as the Porta Nuova and the Porta di Sotto – the village is intact and compact, hardly spreading down the hillside at all. From the Porta di Sotto a massive stairway takes you into the village, ascending steeply between the little houses and lateral alleys. It is a quiet place whose churches **Sant'Agostino** and **San Francesco** are the most interesting. The latter dates from the 17th century and contains paintings by Claudio Ridolfi.

*The quickest way to Jesi is to go back to the **SS16** and continue along it for about 24km (15 miles) as far as Rocca Priora, at which branch inland on the **SS76** and continue to Jesi.*

Jesi, Marche

6 Jesi sits on the plain by the River Esino. Another walled town, it has houses built outside the walls. It is a picturesque place, best known as the birthplace of the Emperor Frederick II (1194–1250) whose empire included Germany and Sicily. If you look on the external façade of the **Palazzo Comunale**, you will see, carved on a piece of stone, the text of a letter Frederick wrote to the townspeople confirming Jesi's ancient privileges. This old curiosity is not Jesi's only treasure, however. In the **Palazzo Pianetti**, which contains the local Pinacoteca (art gallery), you will see a set of paintings by Lorenzo Lotto (1480–1556), which are some of this artist's finest works. While you are in Jesi, you should look at the 14th-century frescos in the Church of **San Marco**, just outside the town walls.

*Follow the **SS76** for about 42km (26 miles) to Fabriano.*

Fabriano, Marche

7 The paper watermark was invented in Fabriano and this little town has been an important centre for paper-making since the Renaissance. Today banknotes are manufactured here. In a small local **museum**, housed in the old **Convent of San Domenico**, you can see how the watermarks are made and also examine a variety of equipment used for doing it over the centuries. The town was the home of Gentile da Fabriano (1370–1427), whose paintings were important examples of the International Gothic style that was to influence the Florentine Renaissance. You can examine some of his work in the art gallery in the **Palazzo Vescovile** (Episcopal Palace), which also contains the more precious pieces from local churches. The baroque Church of **San Benedetto** has an extravagant gilt and stucco interior comparable to the elaborate decoration of the nearby **Oratorio del Gonfalone** (Oratory of the Gonfalone). In particular, this building has a deeply coffered ceiling of the 17th century, with figures of gilded saints and tiny figures of the Apostles. There is gold everywhere – quite out of proportion with the building's very tiny scale.

*From Fabriano, a country road leads northeast to join the **SS360** after 15km (9 miles). Continue northeast on the **SS360** for a further 10km (6 miles) to Arcevia.*

Arcevia, Marche

8 Arcevia sits on a spur of land about 535m (1,755 feet) above sea-level. The site has been inhabited since prehistory, though the oldest remains in evidence today are those from the late Middle Ages to the Renaissance. As usual, the town is fortified, and its 15th-century walls are mostly intact. Walk down the Via Ramazzani and take in the façades of a range of small country palaces – in particular the **Palazzi Anselmi**, **Pianetti** and **Manneli-Pianetti**. The parish Church of the **San Medardo**, rebuilt in 1644, can be regarded as the local art gallery, so precious are its contents. Here you can see works by Signorelli, della Robbia and Ridolfi, as well as a variety of works by minor local artists. Giovanni della Robbia's glazed terracotta altar (1513) is the most stunning piece. Sitting on it is the Madonna crowned beneath

glazed fruit and flowers. Behind her is the blue glaze, so typical of the Della Robbia family's work.

*Make your way from Arcevia via Pergola, about 27km (17 miles), to the **SS424** and follow the signs to Cagli, about 19km (12 miles). Here, take the **SS3** as far as Acqualagna, about 9km (6 miles), then follow the signs to Urbania, a further 17km (11 miles).*

Urbania, Marche

9 About the size of Arcevia, Urbania is a centre for the production of blue jeans – which seems an unlikely activity for this small walled medieval town. Its other activity is the production of majolica, a craft for which it has always been famous. However, it is for neither of these that people tend to come to Urbania. For here, in the old **Palazzo Ducale** (Ducal Palace), is the famous **library** of the dukes of Urbino, which is full of drawings and engravings. The palace also contains an art gallery and a small museum. Look in also at the **Chiesetta dei Morti** (the Little Church of the Dead) where rows of mummies lie embalmed in the shadows.

*Retrace your steps to the **SS3**, joining it once again at Acqualagna, and continue north-east for about 16km (10 miles) to Fossombrone.*

Fossombrone, Marche

10 Fossombrone lies on the lower slopes of a hill near a crumbling fortress and the River Metauro. For a town of its size, it has a remarkable number of things to visit and admire. First of all there are the ruins of the old Roman town. Called *Forum Sempronii* (which, corrupted, gives 'Fossombrone'), they lie about 3km (2 miles) downstream in San Marino. Until World War II, there were also two Roman bridges but these were destroyed by bombs. There are five churches including the **Duomo** (cathedral) and there is an elegant **Palazzo Vescovile** (Bishop's palace) dating from the 15th century, as well as a **museum** housed in a mansion which once belonged to the dukes of Urbino.

*From Fossombrone, the **SS73bis** leads directly to Urbino, about 19km (12 miles).*

Urbino – San Leo 52 (32)
San Leo – Gradara 63 (39)
Gradara – Pesaro 15 (9)
Pesaro – Fano 12 (7)
Fano – Corinaldo 35 (22)
Corinaldo – Jesi 43 (27)
Jesi – Fabriano 42 (26)
Fabriano – Arcevia 25 (15)
Arcevia – Urbania 72 (46)
Urbania – Fossombrone 32 (20)
Fossombrone – Urbino 19 (12)

RECOMMENDED WALKS

One very pleasant walk from Urbino – go west for about half and hour – is to the little Church of **San Bernardino** which is thought to have been designed by Bramante. Inside are the black marble tombs of the Montefeltro dukes.

The countryside around Urbania could be the background to a Renaissance painting

LAZIO, CAMPANIA, ABRUZZO

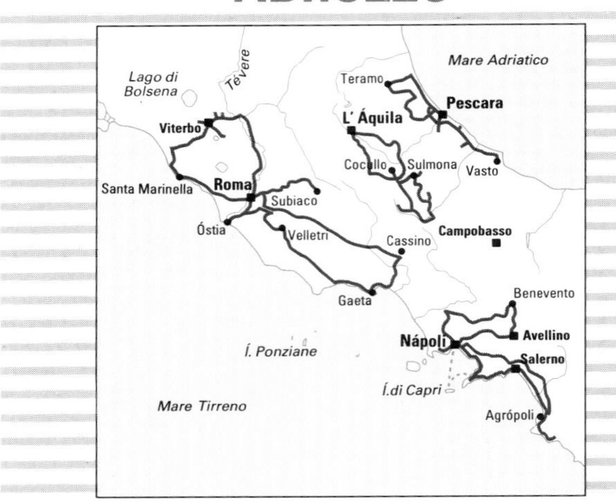

Lazio is centred on Italy's capital, Roma (Rome), home to half the region's population. The landscape surrounding this ancient metropolis is hugely varied, ranging from the hills and mountains of the Apennines to the most important lakes in the southern half of Italy – Bolsena, Bracciano, Vico and Nemi. Each of these was once a volcanic crater and the countryside all around them shows signs of turbulence. To the west of Rome is a plain which extends southwards along the Tyrrhenian Sea and here are Lazio's sandiest beaches.

The ancient origins of Italy are closely linked with the history and fortunes of Lazio. Those mysterious early Italians, the Etruscans, had important settlements in the area, and here, too, was the cradle of the Roman civilisation. Abutting Lazio on the east side is the Abruzzo region, another hilly and mountainous area where the Apennine peaks reach as high as 2,000m (6,500 feet) above sea-level. This is an essentially rustic zone, a large chunk of which is protected by legislation as a National Park. Much of Abruzzo is territory unseen by conventional travellers to Italy. Close to Rome and easily accessible (there are two motorways), it has none of the star attractions of a Florence or a Milan. Yet hidden in the hills of its awe-inspiring landscape, the region offers glimpses into a fascinating, if rather rustic, version of normal Italian life. Simple food and wine and great tracts of sandy beaches along the Adriatic shore are its other attractions.

Campania, Lazio's neighbour to the south, is often known simply as 'the Naples countryside'. Centred on this sprawling city, the region presents two distinct faces to the world – an idyllic coastal belt along the Tyrrhenian Sea and, inland, rough mountain terrain.

The Romans considered the Bay of Napoli one of their country's most beautiful spots. The emperors had their villas on its coast and scattered among its islands, and some of the principle attractions of Campania today – particularly of the areas bordering the Tyrrhenian Sea – are those left behind by the Romans. In the brooding shadow of Mount Vesuvius, coastal Campania is still a stunning part of Italy.

A few kilometres inland, however, the contrasts are enormous. Here the mountains and valleys are less visited; travellers, spoiled by the coastal luxuries, never make it to the ancient cities of the Campanian countryside, well worth the effort of the trek inland.

Napoli by night, one of the great romantic sights of Italy

Roma

The ancient capital of the Roman Empire (and now the capital of Italy) was built on seven hills – the Palatine, Capitoline, Esquiline, Viminal, Caelian, Aventine and Quirinal. Much of its ancient construction survives; you could easily spend a week just visiting the ruins of such imperial splendours as the Colosseum, the Forum and the Baths of Caracallá. In fact you could divide Rome up into historical periods, spending a week investigating each one. The city centre is full of baroque churches and convents of great magnificence, and countless palaces. Renaissance and baroque, some of them are now galleries or museums; and then there is the Vatican City with Bernini's magnificent Piazza San Pietro (St Peter's Square) and the huge and sumptuous Basilica di San Pietro. The Vatican museums give access to Michelangelo's Sistine Chapel, but they include many other museums and galleries with paintings and sculpture from all periods. Visitors will also find that Rome is a noisy, breathlessly busy city.

Napoli

Napoli (Naples) has one of the most important archaeological collections in the world housed in the Museo Archeologico Nazionale (National Museum). Here are displayed treasures and everyday items – silver and gold objects, household utensils and gladiator's weapons – from Pompeii, Ercolano and all the other ancient sites which proliferate throughout the Campania region. But Napoli is also a great seething metropolis where daily life takes place against an ever-present background cacophony of car horns and revving engines. Anarchic traffic jams, headily scented vegetable markets, a vast royal palace (Palazzo Reale) from the 17th century, overdecorated baroque churches the like of which you will never see anywhere else on the Italian mainland – all are facets of this unforgettable city. And here you can dine at pavement cafés on the best pizzas you will taste anywhere – this now universal fast-food dish was Naples' most important gastronomic contribution to the world. WARNING: Naples is an unruly city as far as traffic is concerned. Buy a detailed map of the city but do not try to be clever and take short cuts: you are bound to find yourself hopelessly lost after a very short time.

Pescara

Pescara is the Abruzzo's biggest resort. It is also its most popular watering hole, partly because it has a very good July jazz festival. Gabriele D'Annunzio, poet and dramatist, was born here in 1863, and you can visit his birthplace – Casa Natale. But apart from this and the very odd Fish Museum, Pescara's principle attractions are down on the beach and the promenades, beyond the 19th-century holiday villas and the pine trees.

L'Áquila

L'Áquila, capital of Abruzzo, was founded by the Hohenstaufen Emperor Frederick II, and the city took the name of the imperial symbol – the eagle. It is well endowed with fine buildings, and the more precious items from its history and from the region have been gathered together in the Museo Nazionale d'Abruzzo (National Museum of the Abruzzo), housed in the Castello. From L'Áquila you get the finest views of the Gran Sasso peak of the Apennines which is over 2,000m (6,562 feet) high.

The Colosseum in Rome

4 days – 483km (300 miles)

ROMAN COUNTRY RETREATS

Roma • Tivoli • Anticoli Corrado • Subiaco Gaeta • Sperlonga • Castel Gandolfo • Frascati Ostia • Roma

The upper echelons of Roman society have always relaxed in villas and secluded countryside retreats just outside Roma (Rome). There are all kinds of villas and castles, some ruined, others in perfect condition, to be visited and enjoyed, from Emperor Hadrian's ruined country palace at Tivoli to the villas of the 17th-century aristocracy at Frascati, to Pope John Paul II's country house at Castel Gandolfo But there are also more 20th-century forms of relaxation available on the beaches at Ostia, Gaeta and Sperlonga. Rome itself has a variety of palaces and villas that can be visited. Some are based on antique Roman originals, others are still occupied.

FOR HISTORY BUFFS

4 Near Gaeta (about 20km/12 miles going south on the **SS213**) are the remains of *Minturnae*, a Roman town founded in 295BC. You can visit the excavations which include an aqueduct, theatre and forum, and the **Antiquarium** which contains memorable sculptures. Closer to Gaeta, just before Formia, is the so-called **Tomb of Cicero**. The great orator and writer was killed in 43BC near his villa at Formia. Both of these monuments have the added attraction of being very near to beaches.

[i] Via Parigi II, Roma

*From the centre of Roma, the **SS5** goes east for about 32km (20 miles) to Tivoli.*

Tivoli, Lazio

1 Tivoli sits on a wide spur of Monte Ripoli just before Lazio becomes really mountainous. The town grew up as a strategic point on an ancient route from the east to Rome. Today it is largely associated with the **Villa Adriano** (Hadrian's Villa), built by the Emperor Hadrian. Construction began at his accession to the imperial throne and continued until AD134. Here the Emperor set about reconstructing buildings he had seen on his foreign travels, such as the Canopic Temple at Alexandria and Plato's Academy in Athens. But this huge villa, the biggest ever in Italy, also contained libraries, baths, temples, theatres, and there was even a little private palace built on an island in a huge pool and surrounded by a colonnade. The richness of the complex is demonstrated by the enormous quantity and excellent quality of the sculpture which has been

Ceiling fresco from St Benedict's monastery church at Subiaco, where the saint himself lived

found on this site over the centuries. Most of it has ended up in the Vatican Museum in Rome. During the Renaissance other villas were built at Tivoli by rich cardinals. The most sumptuous is the **Villa d'Este**, built by Ippolito d'Este. The gardens here are more elaborate than the actual buildings; a river was diverted to provide water for countless fountains and a huge variety of cascades and pools. The **Villa Gregoriana** is another place worth a visit, with a fine waterfall by the great architect and sculptor Bernini, formed by the diversion of the River Aniene.

[i] Largo Garibaldi

*Continue along the **SS5** from Tivoli for about 23km (14 miles) until the turning on the right to Anticoli Corrado.*

Anticoli Corrado, Lazio

2 This is a lovely hilltown poised dramatically on an eminence dominating the countryside all around, It has remained completely unspoilt by the passage of time and has for years been the destination of painters in search of sublime landscape scenes. Anticoli Corrado's houses are mostly medieval with small windows and outside staircases. The Church of **San Pietro** preserves fragments of its early mosaic floor.

*From Anticoli Corrado return to the **SS5** and turn right. Shortly after, branch right and follow the winding country road (**SS411**) southeast, past the hamlet of Agosta to Subiaco.*

Subiaco, Lazio

3 One of an isolated group of interesting little places on the edge of the Simbruini mountains, Subiaco has some very ancient buildings, most of which have something to do with St Benedict. This saint retired here late in the 5th century to write his *Rule* which was to heavily influence Christian monasticism. Subiaco originally had 12 monasteries organised by Benedict. Much later, in the atmosphere of piety and learning that these engendered, the first printed books in Italy were made (1464). While not much remains from the early illustrious period of St Benedict himself, there is the Monastery of **Santa Scolastica** (Benedict's sister) which has three cloisters. Of St Benedict's own monastery, **San Benedetto**, high upon a rocky site, all that remains are two churches, one carved out of the rock, with frescos of varying ages. Subiaco is a quiet, interesting place and well worth the visit. While you are there, you could visit the nearby gorge of the River Aniene, where there is a lake with a waterfall that might have been the work of the infamous Emperor Nero who once had a villa at Subiaco (*Sublaqueum*).

*Retrace the route via the **SS411** to the **SS5**. Head for Roma, but after 9km (6 miles) join the **A24** at the Vicovaro-Mandela junction,*

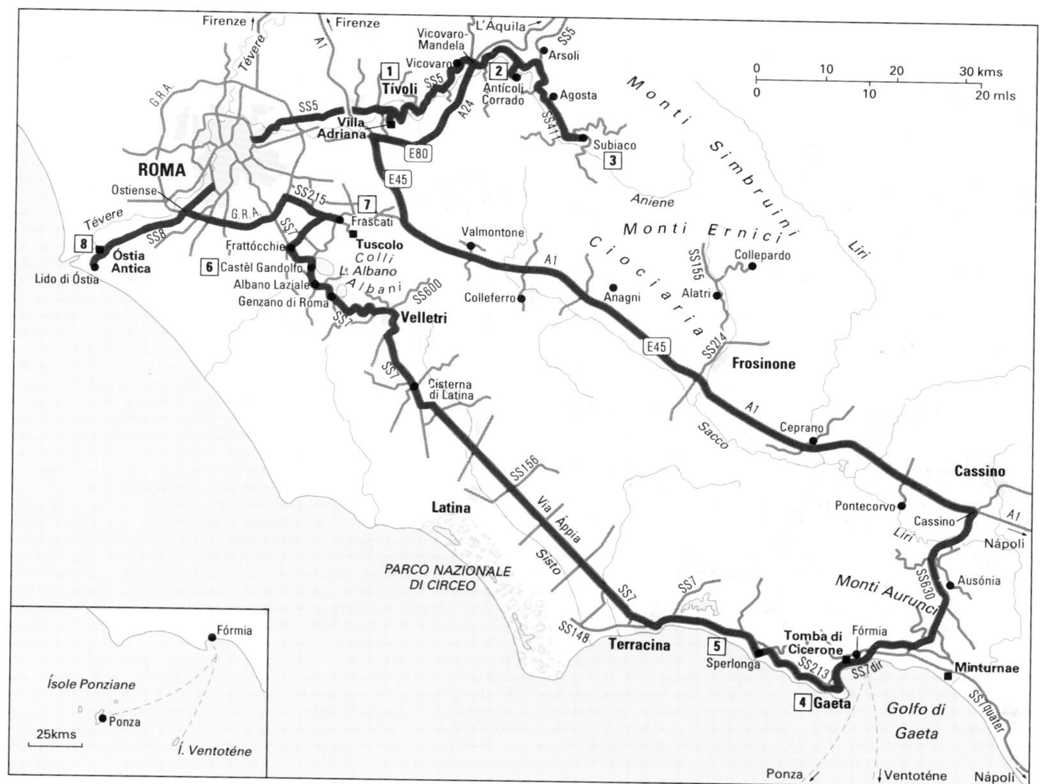

*continuing towards Roma. About 22km (14 miles) along the autostrada, turn on to the **A1** heading towards Naples. Continue on the **A1** for about 106km (66 miles) until the Cassino turning. Follow the signs to Gaeta via the **SS630**.*

One of 500 fountains in the sumptuous gardens of the Villa d'Este at Tivoli

Gaeta, Lazio

4 The old town of Gaeta sits at the very end of a promontory jutting out into the Tyrrhenian Sea. This ancient centre still stands behind its old walls and is still largely medieval. There is plenty to see here, and it might be an idea to stay, as the beaches, the restaurants and the daily life of this seaside town are lively and varied. Apart from the **Duomo** (Sant'Erasmo), there is a 13th-century

Few towns are more magnificently situated than Anticoli Corrado

RECOMMENDED WALKS

Take the boat from Formia to the Pontine Islands of which **Ponza** and **Ventoténe** are the most interesting. Ponza has some lovely beaches. You could walk along these, visiting the little isolated coves on the way, and lunching perhaps in the main town there. Ventoténe is much smaller. It has only a small beach but you can walk to the remains of the villa built by Augustus' daughter, Julia, in the 1st century AD.

SPECIAL TO ...

The area around Frascati and Castel Gandolfo has a favourite snack often consumed out in the piazza. This is *porchetta*, pig roast on a spit and eaten in huge chunks. It is very salty and delicious, especially the crackling. Wash this down with ice-cold, white Frascati wine.

fortress and a maze of little ancient alleys and streets harbouring churches, old doorways and quirky little squares full of cats. The cathedral itself has been rebuilt at various times but its **campanile** (belltower), with its decorative upper parts, is of about 1148. A great rock known as Torre d'Orlando (the Tower of Orlando) dominates Gaeta and on it is the circular mausoleum of the Roman consul Lucius Munatius Plancus, who died at Gaeta in 22BC. Mount Orlando divides ancient Gaeta, called *Sezione Erasmo*, from the newer part of town. This is the **Porto Salvo**, consisting of a series of narrow, straight streets of brightly painted houses and lots of wrought-iron balconies.

[i] Piazza Traniello

*Take the **SS213** from Gaeta to Sperlonga, about 16km (10 miles).*

Sperlonga, Lazio

5 The coastline from Gaeta to Sperlonga is beautiful, with many coves and promontories. Like Gaeta, Sperlonga sits on a spur of land that juts out into the Tyrrhenian Sea. Its centre is consistently medieval. Near by is the **Grotta di Tiberio** (Tiberius' Cave), where the emperor is said to have made merry in his own particular way. There is also the emperor's villa, and some good classical sculpture in the **Museo Archeologico Nazionale di Sperlonga**.

*From Sperlonga, continue along the **SS213** to Terracina, then take the **SS7** for 80km (50 miles) to Castel Gandolfo, leaving the **SS7** and following the signs from Albano Laziale.*

Castel Gandolfo, Lazio

6 Castel Gandolfo is where the Pope has his summer residence. Both town and **papal palace** are poised on a ridge above Lago (Lake) Albano and both come alive each year from July to September when the papal court transfers itself there from the Vatican City. All year round, however, the **Swiss Guards** are pacing up and down at the palace entrance, which faces a large square full of cafés and little shops. Entry to Castel Gandolfo, which takes its name from the castle built on the site of the present papal palace by the Gandolfi dukes in the 12th century, is via a magnificent 16th-century doorway. After resting in the square by the palace, visit the Church of **San Tommaso di Villanova** by Bernini, inside which are frescos by Pietro da Cortona. Both Bernini and da Cortona were among the founders of the Roman high baroque style. From any number of points around the town you can look down over Lago Albano, a lake of volcanic origin that was chosen in the 1960s as the venue for the Olympic Games' rowing competitions. The installations built at the time are still in use and it is a lovely place to swim. All around are thick woodlands of oaks and chestnuts and there are also some ancient remains in the form of the **Bagni di**

Diana (Baths of Diana) and the **Villa dell'Imperatore Domiziano** (Villa of the Emperor Domitian) – follow the yellow signs from the centre of town to find these.

ℹ Piazza Libertà 10

*From Castel Gandolfo, rejoin and continue along the **SS7** to Frattócchie (about 4km/2½ miles) then branch right across country for about 9km (5½ miles), past the **SS511**, to the **SS215**, turning right for Frascati.*

Frascati, Lazio

7 This little country town is famous not for the buildings in its centre, but for the country retreats in the hills surrounding it. Although Frascati itself is medieval, the existing villas are much later. However, villa retreats have been a part of Frascati's landscape since ancient Republican times when wealthy Romans settled at nearby *Tusculo*, an even more ancient city, now ruined, some distance up the slope behind modern Frascati. The villas at Frascati date mostly from the 16th and 17th centuries. Most are still private and are not normally accessible, but some, like the **Villa Falconieri**, can be visited with prior permission. One of the greatest late baroque architects, Borromini, was responsible for parts of its design, though it was unfinished at the time of his death. The **Villa Aldobrandini** is the most spectacular here. Around 1,600 plans were made to bring water to the villa and a large cascade and water theatre were constructed. You can see the villa from the road and at odd times it is open to the public. The town itself has a pretty **cathedral** (**San Pietro**) built in 1598.

ℹ Piazza G Marconi 1

*From Frascati, return on the **SS215** to the GRA encircling Roma and continue clockwise on it for 18km (11 miles) until the turning left to the **SS8**, bound for Ostia and the sea.*

Ostia, Lazio

8 Ostia, the port of Roma, offers two contrasting attractions: Ostia Antica archaeological site and Lido di Ostia. The old port was established in about 338BC when Rome needed to establish a settlement to supervise naval traffic and protect the mouth of the Tevere (Tiber) from raids by Tyrrhenian pirates. But old Ostia saw further construction right up to the 4th century AD, when it was abandoned. A visit should start perhaps at the **Porta Romana** (the Roman Gate), past the statue of Minerva Victoria and the **forum**. There are some re-erected columns of temples in the forum and a little further on are the **Terme di Nettuno** (Baths of Neptune) with their installations for heating. There is also a small restored **theatre** capable of holding 3,000 spectators. Some of the houses have lovely mosaic floors – see the **Casa di Apuleio** (House of Apuleius) – and there is one, the **Casa di Diana** (House of Diana), which still has its first floor intact. This is very unusual. You could spend hours in Ostia Antica. There is a lot to see but make sure you pick up a map of the city before you go and plan a route around it. The **Museo Ostiense** contains the portable artefacts from the site. The **Lido di Ostia** has a hugely long beach, very popular in the summer. Most people tend to rush past the old city in their haste to get to the sea. This is a mistake.

*From Ostia, the **SS8** goes directly back to the centre of Roma.*

Country villa near Frascati, an area favoured in the past for rural retreats

Roma – Tivoli 32 (20)
Tivoli – Anticoli Corrado 28 (17)
Anticoli Corrado – Subiaco 21 (13)
Subiaco – Gaeta 201 (125)
Gaeta – Sperlonga 16 (10)
Sperlonga – Castel Gandolfo 98 (61)
Castel Gandolfo – Frascati 19 (12)
Frascati – Ostia 40 (25)
Ostia – Roma 28 (17)

BACK TO NATURE

The **Parco Nazionale del Circeo** is well worth a visit. This area lies less than 100km (60 miles) south of Rome on the Italian coast. It is a calcareous promontory with unspoilt beaches and dunes. The evergreen oak forests and *macchia* are good for flowers, insects and birds.

SCENIC ROUTES

The road from Anticoli to Subiaco goes through one of the most mountainous parts of Lazio. Look at the views, up to the left, to Monte Simbruini. Particularly fine is the approach to, and views from, Anticoli Corrado. From here you can see over the artists' landscape to the village of Saracinesco and Marano Equo.

FOR CHILDREN

8 At **Lido di Ostia**, an extensive, well-organised resort, there are shallow beaches and some of the hotels have swimming pools. Also there are fine beaches both east and west of Sperlonga.

3 days – 362km (226 miles)

THE ROMAN COUNTRYSIDE

Etruscan tombs in Cerveteri's 'city of the dead'

Roma • Cerveteri • Santa Marinella • Tarquinia Tuscania • Caprarola • Viterbo • Bagnaia Vitorchiano • Bomarzo • Roma

North of Roma (Rome) the countryside is bizarrely twisted and contorted into weird shapes by the prehistoric upheavals that took place beneath the earth's surface. Rocky and pitted with deep lakes, it has a dour brooding aspect which is heightened by the fact that the ancient towns in this area are built of local purple-black volcanic rock. Glowering down over this savage landscape, these medieval towns are in sharp contrast to the handful of lyrical Renaissance gardens that some of them have, positioned on the outskirts. The tour also meanders through towns like Tarquinia and Tuscania, once important to the Etruscans, the mysterious people whose civilisation in the area predated the Romans: there are ancient sites to explore and museums containing astonishingly old 'finds' to be visited. None are very far from Rome.

FOR HISTORY BUFFS

3 On the way from Tarquinia to Tuscania, drop in on the tombs and catacombs cut out of the rock at Blera, about 12km (7½ miles) south of Vertralla. Nearby San Giuliano has one of the most important rock necropolises in the area; one tomb has a chamber decorated with reproductions of the wooden beams of a genuine habitation. Some of the tombs date back to the 8th century BC. The town to which the necropolis belonged was connected to Blera in Etruscan times by roads, cut into the soft rock. Magnificent rock-cut tombs can also be seen at Norchia, north of Blera, characterised by great façades with false entrances.

BACK TO NATURE

5 Lying to the north of Lago di Vico, the **Riserva Naturale del Lago di Vico** comprises wooded hills and mountains. In this region to the west of Caprarola, birds of prey soar overhead and wild boar and other forest animals haunt the slopes. Most of the reserve's creatures are rather shy of people, and patience and luck are needed to get good views.

[i] Via Parigi II, Roma

*From Roma, take the **SS1** going west towards the coast for 28km (17 miles) until the turning inland for Cerveteri.*

Cerveteri, Lazio

1 Under the name of *Caere*, Cerveteri was one of the richest Etruscan towns as long ago as the 7th century BC. Today, however, what you see is largely medieval. Its old walls still exist as does the **Rocca** (castle) of the Orsini, later altered for the Ruspoli family. But it is for the Etruscan remains that Cerveteri is important. A great deal survives here from the period including an extensive necropolis, the **Banditaccia Necropolis**, that has yielded important treasures – jewellery and other elegant gold objects. The Banditaccia Necropolis was laid out like a town and if you get a map on entering the site, you can walk down its principal streets and visit a great number of old family burial chambers including the **Tomba dei Rilievi** (Tomb of the Reliefs) which is covered in painted bas-reliefs of cooking utensils and other household objects. Another, called the **Tomba degli Scudi e delle Sedie** (Tomb of the Shields and Chairs) reflects the appearance of an Etruscan house. This is a rare find. You will never see the actual remains of an Etruscan house anywhere because they were built of wood, plaster or terracotta, and they never survived. Look out for the **Castello Odescalchi** at Ladispoli. The Odescalchi family were a prominent Roman family whose castles litter the countryside around Rome.

*From Cerveteri, return to, and turn right on to the **SS1** which hugs the coast for about 20km (12½ miles) until Santa Marinella.*

Santa Marinella, Lazio

2 Santa Marinella is a pleasant beach resort that provides a very welcome diversion off the exhausting

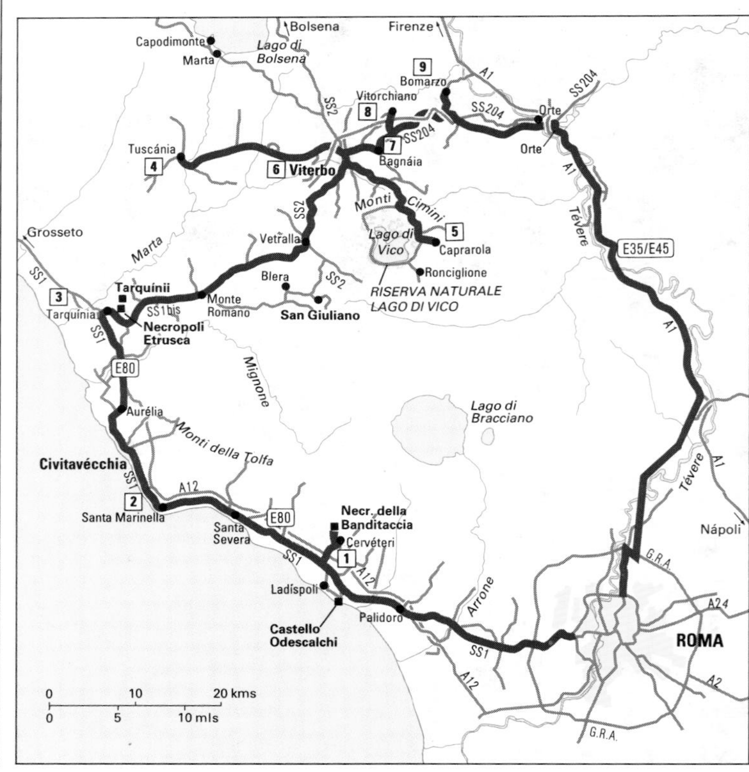

trail of the area's history. But even this place is located on Roman foundations, though there is a big **castle** here which was built by the Odescalchi family during the late Renaissance period.

Continue along the ***SS1*** *for about 30km (19 miles) to Tarquinia.*

Tarquinia, Lazio

3 Modern Tarquinia stands on a hill not far from Etruscan *Tarquinii*, which was built on another hill to the east. There is a lot to see in both places. Perhaps you could visit the newer town first: there are some pretty churches and picturesque medieval streets, particularly around the Church of **San Pancrazio**. The Romanesque Church of **Santa Maria Castello** (begun in 1121) has a lovely façade by Pietro di Ranuccio. The **Museo Nazionale Tarquiniese**, housed in the 15th-century Gothic **Palazzo Vitelleschi**, contains an extraordinary collection of objects, including sarcophagi from the Etruscan and Roman periods as well as the celebrated terracotta winged horses from a temple frieze dating from the end of the 4th century BC. The best of the 5th-century BC tomb paintings from the Etruscan period are also kept here: these include 'the Chariots', 'the Ship' and 'the Sofa'. No visit would be complete, however, without seeing at least some of the old tombs themselves. The necropolis is all that has survived from the old city, and on the walls of the tombs you will see some of the best art ever produced by these mysterious people. If time is short, make for the tombs of 'the Lionesses', 'the Augurs', and 'the Leopards'.

[i] Piazza Cavour 1

It is 5km (3 miles) southeast to the ***SS1bis****. Follow this to Vetralla, 32km (20 miles), then change to the* ***SS2*** *for about 13km (8 miles) to Viterbo. Follow the signs to Tuscania, 26km (16 miles) westwards.*

Tuscania, Lazio

4 Tuscania is another town of great antiquity, though the visible remains of its past are confined, for the most part, to the medieval period. Here you can view the Etruscan past in the **Museo Archeologico** (Archaeological Museum). You can also see a section of the ancient road, the **Via Clodia**, that once connected Rome with the Etruscan cities further north, in Tuscany. But the real treasures of the town are the little churches of **San Pietro** and **Santa Maria Maggiore**. Both are very ancient foundations, added to in the 11th, 12th and 13th centuries. San Pietro is one of the most important churches of its age in Italy and is especially noteworthy for its unusual sculpted façade – look at the shallow relief figures and plants around the rose window above the central door. There are early sculpted panels on the interior and a crypt constructed using columns, some of which are Roman. Santa Maria Maggiore also has some excellent, early sculpture, including the work on its entrance portal, and a lovely rose window.

Go back to Viterbo, then follow the signs south, in the direction of Lago di Vico (Lake Vico), to Caprarola – from Viterbo, about 19km (12 miles).

Villa Farnese, status symbol of Cardinal Alessandro Farnese

SPECIAL TO . . .

The menus of this area include great plates of wild boar, dishes using offal, and lamb scented with rosemary. Try *Saltimbocca alla Romana*, which is slices of veal cooked with *prosciutto, mozzarella* cheese and sage. The whole lot is dunked in Marsala. Its name means 'jump in the mouth'. Most of the wines from this region are white, and by far the most common is one called *Est Est Est* from Montefiascone.

SCENIC ROUTES

On the approach to Tuscania, the landscape is unusual – flat and with bamboo – quite unlike any other part of Lazio. The views from the ramparts of Bomarzo are spectacular. Look for Vitorchiano to the southwest.

On the stretch of the A1 from Orte to Rome, look back and see the characteristic Lazio hilltowns littering the landscape.

FOR CHILDREN

9 The **Parco dei Mostri** (Monster Park) at Bomarzo is an extraordinary park filled with enormous fantastical creatures, beasts, grotesques and monsters hewn from the local rock by Turkish prisoners of war in the 16th century. Among these is a huge elephant squeezing a helpless Roman soldier in its trunk and a figure tearing its adversary in half. The sheer madness exhibited could frighten children and can only be fully appreciated by adults. Children would enjoy another grotesquerie – a little house with a steeply inclined floor, which gives the impression of walking across the deck of a ship at very rough sea. There is a small park adjacent offering tamer delights – swings and a herd of deer, as well as a café and shop.

Caprarola, Lazio

5 The main reason for coming to Caprarola is to visit the vast **Villa Farnese**, built for the Farnese family (Pope Paul II, who was a member of this important family, was for a while Michelangelo's patron). It dominates the little town spread out beneath it as well as the countryside for miles around. The palace, more like a vast pentagonal fortress, was built by Giacomo Barozzi da Vignola, the influential 16th-century architect, on the foundations of an earlier fortress. Inside there is a massive circular staircase that spirals up to the centre of the building, and all around it are frescos glorifying aspects of the Farnese family's sudden rise to power. The sheer vulgarity of these is the early equivalent of a modern billionaire's tendency to display his new-found wealth. The main rooms are no longer furnished, decoration being provided by the frescos. The **gardens** behind the palace are still well kept (by the state – the family is now extinct), and they make much use of water, with fountains and a 'water chain'. There is also an elegant little summer house, the **Palazzina**. If you stand in the forecourt of the palace and look to the right you can see the 17th-century Church of **Santa Teresa**, designed by the important baroque architect Girolamo Rainaldi.

From Caprarola, return to Viterbo by the same route.

Viterbo, Lazio

6 The biggest town in this northern corner of Lazio, Viterbo is an impressive walled city, full of medieval buildings and fountains and with a lovely Romanesque **cathedral** with Gothic campanile. Viterbo once rivalled Rome as the place of residence of the popes. The 13th-century **Palazzo dei Papi** (Papal Palace), a battlemented pile more like a city hall than a palace, was where the Viterbo popes were elected. These elections were never easy and on one occasion, after the death of Clement IV, the cardinals were locked into the building and not allowed out until they had done their duty and elected a new pope. It took two years, during which the people of Viterbo tried to hurry the unfortunate cardinals by starving them out and then taking the roof off the building. There is a variety of churches, including the rebuilt **Santa Rosa**, where you can see the remains of Viterbo's patron saint. Santa Rosa's preaching is supposed to have helped the people of Viterbo defeat Emperor Frederick II in 1243 when he laid siege to the town. **Santa Maria Nuova**, the cathedral, is a good example of the local Romanesque style, altered during the Renaissance. **San Sisto** dates in part from the 9th century. Throughout the old centre of Viterbo, there are little medieval alleys, flights of steps and carved balconies hanging on to the ancient buildings. Some of the houses have little stone towers.

Formal beauty in the garden of the Villa Lante at Bagnaia

[i] Piazza dei Caduti 14

Bagnaia lies on the eastern outskirts of Viterbo, about 5km (3 miles) from the centre.

Bagnaia, Lazio

7 This hill village juts out on a spur overlooking the surrounding countryside. It is part medieval and part Renaissance. In the older section, crammed behind the old walls and overlooked by a **watchtower**, the houses line dark stone alleys and there are splendid views out to the surrounding countryside. In the newer part of town, built around the square that faces the watchtower and the old town gate, the streets are more regular. In this quarter is one of the most beautiful gardens to have emerged from the Italian Renaissance, and what it more, it is mostly still intact. The **Villa Lante** was built by Giacomo Barozzi da Vignola, in the late 1560s, for Cardinal Gambera, whose family emblem, the crayfish (in Italian *gambero*), is scattered around the garden carved in stone. The gardens are more important than the buildings: there are fountains linked by an underground stream, a water chain, formal parterres and a series of *giocchi d'acqua*, water jokes. The Cardinal enjoyed entertaining his guests (and himself) with these mechanical practical jokes. A servant would trigger a secret mechanism somewhere behind the fountain, and the guests would be sprayed with water from some hidden source. The keeper of the garden might be persuaded to show you these – some of them still work.

From Bagnaia to Vitorchiano, take the cross-country route that leaves the main square in the centre of Bagnaia. Vitorchiano is only about 7km (4 miles) away.

Vitorchiano, Lazio

8 Vitorchiano is very similar to Bagnaia. Both are built of *peperino*, the local volcanic stone, purplish in colour. They also have the same medieval aspect. Vitorchiano is fortified only on one side. The rest of the town sits on a huge impregnable rock that provided a natural defence. Walking through the little dark streets, look out for the SPQR ('Senatus Populusque Romanus') symbol of Vitorchiano's allegiance to Rome. Traditionally this goes back to when an ancient Roman is said to have run from Vitorchiano to Rome to warn the city that it was about to be attacked by the Etruscans. The man died soon afterwards but the City of Rome rewarded the people of Vitorchiano calling it the 'faithful city', and giving it special powers. This relationship persisted, hence the little medieval wall plaques showing the wolf suckling Romulus and Remus, symbol of Rome. Have lunch at Vitorchiano and wander slowly around the town. It has no special art treasures or monuments. Quite simply it is an enchanting, if strange, place, full of young people restoring their old family houses.

From Vitorchiano, follow the signs to Bomarzo via the ***SS204****.*

Bomarzo, Lazio

9 Bomarzo is another town built out of *peperino* stone. Very small, it has a forbidding military look about it. Most of its houses are crammed around a large fortress traditionally belonging to the Orsini family, though now partially divided into flats. After wandering through the slightly damp streets, and paying a quick visit to the brightly painted but tiny main **church**, you should spend some time at the **Parco dei Mostri** (Monster Park) on the edge of town.

Return to the ***SS204****. Turn left and take this road to the* ***A1*** *autostrada which leads to Roma (from the nearby Orte junction). Follow the signs.*

Roma – Cerveteri 45 (28)
Cerveteri – Santa Marinella 24 (15)
Santa Marinella – Tarquinia 30 (19)
Tarquinia – Tuscania 76 (47)
Tuscania – Caprarola 46 (29)
Caprarola – Viterbo 19 (12)
Viterbo – Bagnaia 5 (3)
Bagnaia – Vitorchiano 7 (4)
Vitorchiano – Bomarzo 15 (9)
Bomarzo – Roma 95 (60)

RECOMMENDED TRIPS

Instead of driving or walking, why not take a boat trip? On the lake of Bolsena, in the crater of a volcano just north of Viterbo, boat trips are organised from the towns of Bolsena or Capodimonte. Trips are to Martana, a rocky island covered in woodland, and to Bisentina, another island which has a lovely church, **SS Giacomo e Cristoforo**. There is also the Chapel of **Santa Caterina** with, below it, an artificial grotto and gardens created by the Farnese family. This island is a must.

Grotesquerie in the extraordinary Monster Park at Bomarzo

5 days – 323km (199 miles)

IN THE SHADOW OF VESUVIUS

Napoli • Pozzuoli • Ercolano • Pompeii • Capri Positano • Amalfi • Ravello • Salerno • Paestum Agrópoli • Napoli

Campania divides neatly into two areas – a coastal region and an inland landscape of mountains and valleys. This tour covers the coast which, after Liguria, is one of the most popular in Italy. The difference between the two rivieras is that, in addition to the idyllic seaside resorts, Campania's coast also has a series of rich historical sites to be visited. Sites such as Pompeii and Ercolano have made the Museo Nazionale (National Museum) of Napoli (Naples) one of the most important archaeological collections in the world. There are lots of other museums and galleries in Napoli but it is really the lively, vivacious character of the city, situated on the lower slopes of the still-active volcano Monte Vesuvio (Mount Vesuvius), that is unforgettable.

RECOMMENDED WALKS

4 It is possible to see the whole of Capri on foot. The walks from Capri town itself are most enjoyable. One, from the Via Tragara, leads to Faraglioni – the three enormous rocks that stick up out of the sea off the southeast coast of the island. You could have a swim a little way beyond, off the Punta di Tragara.

6 Another good walk is from Ravello to the little village of Scala, about 1.5km (1 mile) away. It has a pretty miniature cathedral.

[i] Piazza dei Martini 58

From Naples, take the autostrada or the coastal road to Pozzuoli – it is only about 12km (7 miles) from the centre of Naples going in the direction of Gaeta.

Pozzuoli, Campania

1 Pozzuoli was once a city in its own right, though nowadays it seems more like an extension of Napoli itself. Its claim to fame is that from among its aged villas and the clutter of houses around the Roman ruins, emerged the sultry film actress Sophia Loren. This, her birthplace, was once a Roman city, named *Puteoli*. It has the remains of the third largest amphitheatre in Italy – the **Anfiteatro Flavio**. You can see the well preserved dens for wild animals beneath it, but earthquakes as well as intermittent eruptions of Mount Vesuvius have otherwise destroyed much of its ancient character. What was once thought to be a **Serapeum** (Temple of Serapis – an Egyptian god), survives from the 1st century AD, though it is partially submerged beneath the water near the harbour.

Cetara, the Saracens' first settlement on the Amalfi coast

It is now believed to be the remains of a market building. You can visit other parts of the archaeological park in which it is situated. Back in the centre of town is the **Duomo** (cathedral) dedicated to St Procolo. Nowadays it is a rather tumbledown building, most of it destroyed in 1964 in a fire; after the fire, its baroque additions were removed revealing a Roman structure in marble beneath.

[i] Via Campi Flegrei 3

Go back through the centre of Napoli and follow the signs to Ercolano (Herculaneum) which lies on the other side of the city beyond Portici.

Ercolano, Campania

2 Ercolano is an important Roman site. Not as big or important as Pompeii, the city was once a residential enclave for wealthy Romans. A great many villas have survived, some with their furnishings, the whole lot having been buried beneath the mud and lava from the eruption of Vesuvius in AD79. You can see the excavations in just a couple of hours, time enough to appreciate this fossil of everyday Roman life, eerily preserved by the catastrophe of nearly 2,000 years ago. The **Casa del Tramezzo Carbonizzato** (House of the Wooden Partition) gives some idea of an early double-storeyed house, while in the **Casa del Mobilio Carbonizzato** (House of the Carbonised Furniture) you can examine ancient furniture left in the positions in which it was found. In the **Casa dell'Atrio a Mosaico** (House of the Mosaic Atrium) are some splendid mosaic floors, while the **House of the Gem** still preserves, in its kitchen, an ancient kettle. Public places such as the **palaestra** (the gym) and the **baths** survive; access around the town is by way of streets paved with original limestone slabs.

*From Ercolano, the **SS18** continues to Pompeii, about 15km (9 miles) – follow the signs.*

Pompeii, Campania

3 Pompeii was a large commercial city also destroyed by the eruption of Vesuvius in AD79, but, in this case, covered by layers of volcanic ash rather than mud. The site is huge and would take at least a morning to complete successfully. Buy a map or a guide before you enter: villas, shops, temples – there is much to see and the extent of it is confusing without some kind of guide. There are human ones only too willing to offer their services; agree a price in advance. One of the most sumptuous villas is the **Casa dei Vettii** (House of the Vettii), a large house with a decorated interior. Much of it has been reconstructed and in addition to the lavish frescos there are fountains and statues. In the Via di Nola is a **tavern** in which were found three trumpets dumped by gladiators as they fled from the nearby **amphitheatre** and in the **shop of Verus the Blacksmith** you will see a lamp and other objects either under repair or being made at the time of the eruption. Of the public buildings, the **basilica** (law courts) was the most monumental; in the **Antiquarium** you will see casts taken from the impressions left by original bodies found among the ruins. Pompeii is an extraordinary and evocative place. To see many of the movable treasures found here you will have to visit the museum in Napoli.

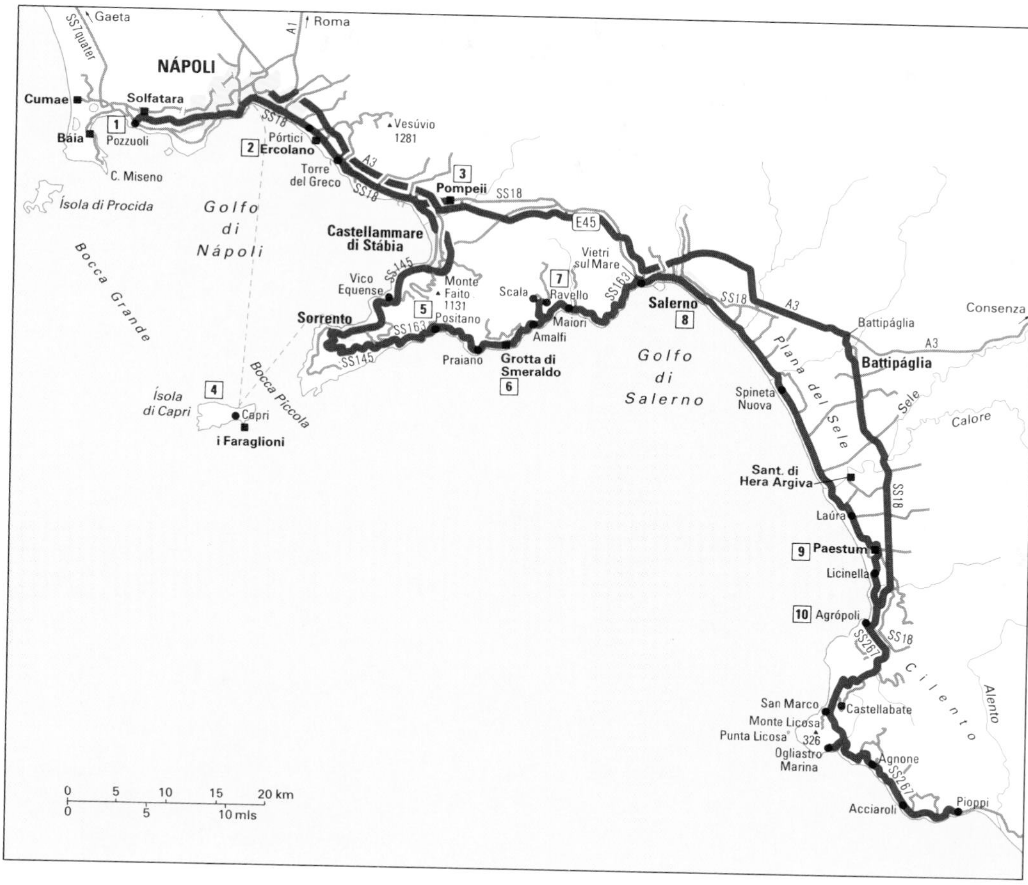

Pompeii: a look at life in a 1st-century AD Roman city

i Via Sacra 1

To get to the island of Capri, you could either go back to the port of Naples or go to Sorrento via the ***SS145*** *about 28km (17 miles) further along the coast. If you choose the latter it will add about 5km (3 miles) to the total road mileage of the tour. Either way, both ports have regular island ferry services. From Napoli the trip takes one hour and 10 minutes; from Sorrento 35 minutes.*

FOR HISTORY BUFFS

1 Near Pozzuoli are the ancient sites of Cumae (about 5km/3 miles) and Baia (about 4km/2½ miles). At *Cumae*, thought to be the oldest Greek colony in Italy, visit the **Antro della Sibilla** (Cave of the Cumaean Sibyl) just below the summit of the Acropolis. The hero Aenaes consults the Sybil in Virgil's great poem the *Aeneid*. At Baia, there are the remains of an imperial villa and at Capo (Cape) Miseno, about 5km (3 miles) further on, are the tumble-down remains of what was the greatest naval base of the Roman Empire.

SCENIC ROUTES

The most scenic route on this tour is the journey from Positano to Salerno on the **SS163**. On the way look out for the ceramic-covered domes of the churches in the midst of the hamlets that cling to the side of the steep hillsides just above the sea.

Capri, Campania

4 Capri is a good place to avoid in the middle of the summer when it is absolutely packed with tourists. Just before or just after the season you will have the benefit of pleasant rocky coves in which to swim and tan unmolested by the hordes. There is plenty to see and do on the island. Capri town is bursting with designer shops but if you are not interested in these, you can visit the **Duomo** built in the 17th century and the **Giardini di Augusto** (Gardens of Augustus), founded by Augustus himself. The **Villa Jovis**, a 45-minute walk from the town, was the home of the Emperor Tiberius towards the end of his reign. Combine a visit to the ruins with the grim **Salto di Tiberio**, the cliffs from which the emperor was supposed to have flung his enemies. The little town of Anacapri is known for the **Villa San Michele**, immortalised by Axel Munthe in *The Story of San Michele*. Near by are the remains of the **Villa Imperiale**, Augustus' villa (not as well preserved as the Villa Jovis). You could walk to here as well as to the ruined **Castello di Barbarossa**, but buses do the rounds and there are a great many other places to visit. Of great natural beauty are the **Grotta Azzurra** (Blue Grotto) – take a boat from Capri port – and the **Grotta Verde** (Green Grotto), reached from Anacapri.

ⓘ Piazza Cerio II

*From Capri, the quickest way to Positano is to take the boat back to Sorrento. From Sorrento take the **SS145** (which joins and becomes the **SS163**) to Positano, about 23km (14 miles).*

Positano, Campania

5 The town of Positano falls almost vertically into the sea. From the high cliff road above it, it seems as though the characteristic white-washed houses have been tipped over the edge to the water. There are no great monuments to be seen in Positano; the little town is simply a picturesque coastal resort, full of restaurants and cafés in which to while away the days. Within easy reach of Positano are a number of other tiny ports. One of these, Praiano, has a fine beach while at Conca dei Marini are the remains of a Norman watchtower. Just before Conca dei Marini is the **Grotta dello Smeraldo** (Emerald Cave), a large cavern to which you can descend in a lift from the roadside. It gets its name from the colour of the light filling its interior. If you look carefully, you can see, now under water, stalagmites formed when the cave was above sea-level.

ⓘ Via del Saracino 2

*The **SS163** continues to Amalfi, about 16km (10 miles).*

Amalfi, Campania

6 In the early Middle Ages, Amalfi was an important trading post, possibly the most important in Italy. This seems surprising at first glance, because the town today is so small. But its monuments reveal the truth. The **Duomo** (cathedral), in a mixture of styles, is one of the loveliest south of Napoli. You approach it up a long, steep flight of steps and enter via a set of bronze doors made in Constantinople in 1066. Next door to the cathedral is the 13th-century **Chiostro del Paradiso** (Cloisters of Paradise), with beautiful double columns, the pair intertwining voluptuously. This cloister would perhaps be more at home in Sicily where this style of Saracenic (oriental) decoration is more common. Climbing up the steep hillside outside Amalfi are villas and small hotels. One of the latter – the biggest – was at one time a **Capuchin convent**. Access is via a lift that rushes up the side of the mountain; the views from its terrace are spectacular, while the characterful interior is filled with antique furnishings.

ⓘ Corso Roma 19

There is a Moorish look to Positano, clinging to the cliffs

The beautiful stretch of coast around Amalfi

From Amalfi, branch off the ***SS163*** *on to a minor road which winds up the hillside to Ravello, about 6km (4 miles).*

Ravello, Campania

7 The beautiful village of Ravello is isolated at the top of the hill directly above Amalfi at about 350m (1,150 feet) above sea-level. It has two historic villas, Villa Cimbrone and Villa Rufolo, both of which have splendid gardens. The **Villa Rufolo** was begun in the 11th century and its remarkable Saracenic-Norman character has survived. The composer Richard Wagner was its most illustrious guest; in fact its gardens were the inspiration for the magic garden of Klingsor in the opera *Parsifal*. The villa, once the residence of popes, has a fine view of the coastline from its terrace. But the gardens of the **Villa Cimbrone** are more spectacular. These rather wild and surprisingly lush gardens with their arbours and old lichen-covered terraces, end in a long terrace from which you have an unrivalled view of the Amalfi coastline. Ravello's **Duomo** (cathedral) contains some very early art: 12th- and 13th-century pulpits, with inlaid marble and mosaic, and fine bronze doors, dating from 1179 and modelled on the more famous Amalfi cathedral doors. There is a small museum in the cathedral.

[i] Piazza Vescovado 13

From Ravello, go back to the ***SS163****, then continue eastwards along it for about 24km (15 miles) to Salerno.*

Salerno, Campania

8 The name of Salerno is familiar as the site of the Allied invasion of Italy in September 1943. Today it is a town that people tend to ignore on a tour of Campania. It is a working town with a busy port and industries. Its treasures are eclipsed by those of the other more popular towns along the coast, but it has a **Duomo** (Cathedral of St Matthew), consecrated in 1085, but much altered. This cathedral follows the local fashion in having a pair of bronze doors (from Constantinople) and another set of 12th-century mosaic-inlaid pulpits of the kind found in Ravello. Leading off the cathedral's sacristy is the **Museo del Duomo**, containing various fragments from the cathedral building as well as some of its greatest treasures. Of the latter, the early medieval altar front, with 54 ivory panels showing Biblical scenes, is the most interesting. Try to get to the **Provincial Museum**, which contains finds from excavations from all over the province of Salerno.

[i] Via Velia 15

From Salerno, follow the long straight coastal road for about 36km (22 miles) to Paestum.

SPECIAL TO . . .

4 Capri celebrates New Year festivities. Performing musicians play the *putipù*, a characteristic folk instrument, in the piazzas of Capri and Anacapri. If you are here over Christmas and New Year, then try Campania's traditional Christmas Eve dish – *capitone marinato* – eel cooked in vinegar with bay leaves and garlic, then left to marinate in its own sauce for a few days. You should also try the more usual *insalata caprese* – a salad of *mozzarella* cheese, tomatoes, basil and olive oil. It originated here.

FOR CHILDREN

If you are here towards the end of the year, the children will be fascinated by the *presepi* (Christmas cribs). Churches and private homes begin preparing to display their *presepi* in November. You find the best ones in Napoli itself, but all over Campania – even in little country churches – you will find the tradition adhered to. They usually have miniature Roman ruins, animals, beggars, musicians and many other figures, quite apart from the Holy Family.

Paestum, Campania

9 There was once a great city at Paestum. All that remains is a handful of ancient buildings in a remarkable state of preservation – the **Basilica** (dedicated to the queen goddess Hera), the **Tempio di Nettuno** (the Temple of Neptune), the **Tempio di Cerere** (Temple of Ceres) and about 4km (2½ miles) of walls that once surrounded the old city. Paestum was abandoned around the 9th century because of the threat of malaria from surrounding marshes and attacks by invading Saracens, and the temples lay hidden for centuries in a kind of subtropical forest, now converted, into a dry plain. The Temple of Neptune, dating from about 450BC, is the best preserved building here. Huge and solid, it is in the unadorned, Doric style. The **museum** contains some of the sculptural fragments from the temples here as well as finds from the Sanctuary of Hera, about 10km (6 miles) to the north of Paestum. But the prize exhibits in the museum are the tomb paintings – in particular those from the **Tomba del Tuffatore** (Tomb of the Diver), thought to be the only surviving examples of Greek funerary mural painting anywhere.

Temple of Neptune at Paestum, a city founded by Greek colonists in the 7th century BC

ⓘ Via Magna Grecia 151

From Paestum, it is only a short run to the beginning of the Cilento Coast. Go south for about 9km (6 miles) and begin at Agrópoli.

Agrópoli, Campania

10 The coastline changes completely after Paestum; if you follow the sea all the way to Pioppi you encounter miniature bays, long white beaches and a series of small ports with nothing more than a fine position to recommend them. Agrópoli is perhaps the most popular. Its core is medieval and you can visit the Convent of **San Francesco**. At San Marco there are ancient Roman remains including the breakwater carved out of the rock. From here the road leads to Agnone, bypassing Monte Licosa which drops down into the sea. You should not miss this part of the coast, so take the smaller road – or track – to Ogliastro Marina, park the car, then walk around to the **Punta Licosa** (Licosa Point), named after a siren, Leucosia, said to have jumped into the sea from the promontory after failing to enchant Odysseus as he sailed past.

*From Agrópoli, make for the **SS18** going north across the Sele Plain to Battipaglia, about 31km (19 miles), at which join the **A3** going back to Napoli, a further 76km (47 miles).*

Napoli – Pozzuoli 12 (7)
Pozzuoli – Ercolano 20 (12)
Ercolano – Pompeii 15 (9)
Pompeii – Napoli (Capri ferry) 23 (14)
Pompeii – Sorrento (Capri ferry) 28 (17)
Sorrento – Positano 23 (14)
Positano – Amalfi 16 (10)
Amalfi – Ravello 6 (4)
Ravello – Salerno 28 (17)
Salerno – Paestum 36 (22)
Paestum – Agrópoli (Cilento coast) 9 (6)
Agrópoli – Napoli 107 (67)

BACK TO NATURE

Because it is effectively landlocked, the Mediterranean has a small tidal range and so relatively few marine creatures can be seen on its shores. However, the coastal vegetation is impressive in unspoilt areas. For birdwatchers, colourful *macchia* vegetation may grow almost to the shoreline and this harbours a wide variety of warblers. Blue rock thrushes sing from exposed rocky outcrops.

4 days – 176km (110 miles)

BEYOND NAPLES: SMALL CITIES OF CAMPANIA

Galleria Umberto I, Naples' elegant glass and iron arcade

Napoli • Aversa • Capua • Caserta • Benevento Avellino • Napoli

Away from the coastal resort, Campania is a quiet rural region, mountainous in parts, with a sprinkling of old cities. Great tracts of countryside are empty but even the loneliest parts are within reach of Napoli (Naples). Here you will find good restaurants representative of the great variety of cooking from the provinces. Napoli is Campania's melting pot. As in the provincial towns surrounding it, many people have left their mark on this great metropolis, and you will find Roman and Greek remains as well as buildings with Byzantine or Spanish influences.

[i] Piazza dei Martini 58

*From Naples, take the **SS7bis** north to Aversa, about 17km (11 miles).*

Aversa, Campania

1 This small town was founded by the Normans in 1029 – in fact it was their very first settlement in this part of Italy. Although the **castle** was originally their work, it was rebuilt in the 18th century and later turned into a hospital. King Andrew of Hungary was murdered here in 1345 and here, too, his death was avenged by his brother Louis of Hungary. The **Duomo** (cathedral of San Paolo) was also founded by the Normans. Though it was altered later, you can see some original Norman work inside. If you are not reeling from the effects of the potent local brew, a white wine called *Asprinio* which is generally considered a 'thirst-quenching' wine for hot summer days, then be sure to visit the Church of **San Lorenzo** which has a beautiful cloister.

*The **SS7bis** continues for 16km (10 miles) to Capua.*

Capua, Campania

2 Capua was the greatest town in Campania during the Roman period. Its small size today makes this hard to believe, but enough survives from its heyday to give some idea of its early importance. At Santa Maria di Capua Vetere, the old city that was utterly destroyed in about AD830 by the Arabs, and about 2km (1 mile) from newer Capua, are the remains of a large **amphitheatre**, second in size only to the Colosseum in Rome. Great blocks of stone and a hefty arched construction survive among the cypresses. Here, too, is the **Arco di Adriano** (Hadrian's Arch – also

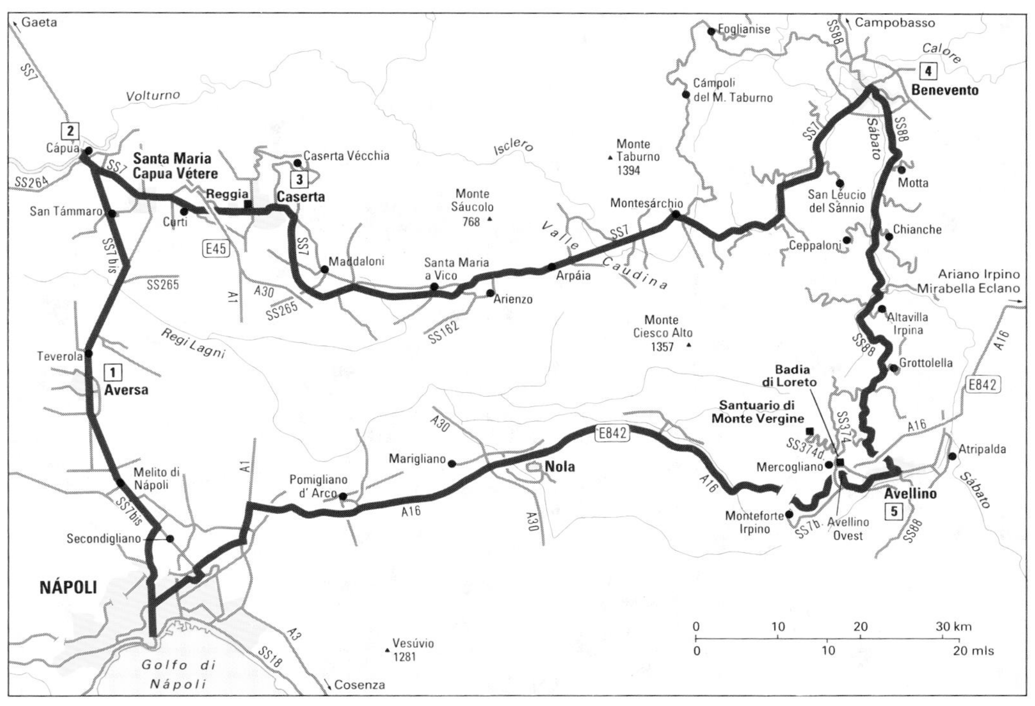

Fountains and cascades are the main feature of the gardens of the Reggia at Caserta

FOR HISTORY BUFFS

5 About 22km (15 miles) from Avellino up in the heart of the Partenio massif is the **Santuario di Monte Vergine** (Sanctuary of Monte Vergine), a church dedicated to the Mother of God, founded in the 12th century. Preserved here, in this very beautiful spot on the mountainside, is a painting of a head of the Virgin, supposed to have been done by St Luke. Visit the museum and the basilica. If this is not enough, further down the hill is the **Convent of Loreto** which was built on the site of a pagan laurel grove. Here you will find an 18th-century pharmacy with a collection of majolica apothecary's jars, important 16th-century Flemish tapestries and a vast archive.

RECOMMENDED WALKS

3 The best walks on this tour would, perhaps surprisingly, be in the vast grounds of **La Reggia**, the royal palace at Caserta. They are amazingly big and full of little surprises, such as hidden fountains among the undergrowth.

called the Arch of Capua) built in honour of the emperor who restored the amphitheatre in AD119. One of the best preserved ancient monuments here is the **Mithraeum**, an underground hall dedicated to the worship of the Persian Sun-god Mithras – a cult very popular with Roman soldiers. It dates from about the 2nd century AD and is probably the best example of a rectangular underground area with a vault painted with stars. The rites of the cult included the slaying of a bull and here there is a fresco of Mithras killing a large white bull – a very rare survival. New Capua contains the most interesting finds from these ancient sites in the **Museo Campano**, including an array of ancient sculpture. The **Duomo** (cathedral), founded in AD835, was destroyed in 1942 and completely rebuilt, though its beautiful campanile (bell tower) dates from 861.

From Capua, follow the signs to Caserta, only about 11km (7 miles) away.

Caserta, Campania

3 The only reason to come to Caserta is to see the biggest palace in Italy, started in 1752 by Vanvitelli for the Bourbon King of Naples, Charles III, and intended to rival Versailles. Known as **La Reggia**, or the **Palazzo Reale**, its interior, in which there are some 1,200 rooms, is extremely richly decorated (in particular the State Apartments) with gilding, different types of marble, tapestries, paintings and frescos. The park and the gardens, famous for their water gardens, cascades and fountains, are as elaborate as the interior is extravagant. They are also huge. One of the focal points, the statue group of *Diana and Actaeon*, is about 3km (2 miles) from the palace itself. If, for some reason, you cannot get into the building, there is plenty to see and do in the garden. Look out for the 18th-century **English Garden**. King Vittorio Emanuele III presented the palace to the State in 1921. Not far from the palace, which is situated in the newer town, is Caserta Vecchia, a medieval town which was all but abandoned when the newer one was built along with the palace. There is an interesting Norman and Sicilian-style **cathedral**. Its interior is a hotch-potch of fascinating details: particularly noteworthy are the 18 antique columns and the early mosaic details.

ⓘ Piazza Dante 35

The **SS7** *leads to Benevento, about 50km (31 miles).*

Benevento, Campania

4 Benevento is possibly the most interesting town on the tour of Campania's hinterland. The old streets in its centre preserve monuments ranging from a Roman theatre to an early medieval gate, the **Port'Arsa**. Benevento was badly bombed in World War II with the near total loss of its **cathedral**, a 13th-century Romanesque building of which only the richly sculpted façade and campanile (bell tower) are original. The rest has been rebuilt. The Roman **theatre** was begun in the 2nd century AD, in the reign of Hadrian; its most remarkable features are three monumental gates. The **triggio** quarter of town contains more visible remains of Benevento's Roman past. You will see bits of ancient stonework built into the walls of the houses, and on the outskirts of town is the **Ponte Leproso** (Leproso Bridge), a Roman construction carrying the Via Appia (Appian Way) over the Sabato river. A particularly fine Roman monument is the **Porta Aurea** (Arch of Trajan), a marble triumphal arch 15m (50 feet) high with bas-reliefs of the life of Trajan and a variety of mythological subjects.

ⓘ Via Giustiniani 36

From Benevento, take the **SS88** *to Avellino, a cross-country route of about 33km (21 miles).*

Avellino, Campania

5 Like many of the cities in this region, 'modern' Avellino occupies a site just a few kilometres from its original position. In this case, ancient *Abellinum* was situated near to the present-day village of Atripalda, just 4km (2½ miles) to the east of Avellino. The **Museo Provinciale** in Avellino (Corso Europa) houses the finds from the old town as well as archaeological collections from the necropolises of **Mirabella Eclano** (take the **A16** going north from Avellino about 40km/25 miles) and **Ariano Irpino** (about 12km/7½ miles further on, just off the **A16** on the

On the way to Naples, visit the grim landscape of Vesuvius

SS90). Also in the town are a medieval **castle** and a 17th-century customs house, the **Palazzo della Dogana**, with a sculpted façade. Avellino's **art gallery** displays a magnificent 18th-century crib (*presepio*) a very popular element of southern Italian religious culture.

From Avellino, take the **A16** *going west for about 41km (25 miles) to the junction with the* **A1**. *Take the latter back to Napoli (south), about 8km (5 miles).*

Napoli – Aversa 17 (11)
Aversa – Capua 16 (10)
Capua – Caserta 11 (7)
Caserta – Benevento 50 (31)
Benevento – Avellino 33 (21)
Avellino – Napoli 49 (30)

The Porta Aurea in Benevento, built in AD*114, is one of the finest existing Roman arches*

SPECIAL TO . . .

5 The province of Avellino has a wide variety of arts and crafts including inlaid and carved woodwork. In Avellino you will also find lots of shops selling the local brands of *mozzarella, pecorino* and *treccia cheeses – mozzarella* is made from buffalo's milk, *pecorino* from the local ewe's milk, while *treccia* (which means 'plait') is a mixture of cheese from cow's milk and *mozzarella*.

4 Special to Benevento is *Strega*, a sweet liqueur made from a variety of herbs. Bright yellow in colour, it is named after the witches of Benevento (*strega* means witch).

BACK TO NATURE

Although built up to a large extent, the outskirts of Naples still support areas of woodland, with associated wildlife. Look and listen for firecrest, golden orioles and spotted flycatchers in the trees. It can also be rewarding to look down, as orchids often grow in the leaf litter on the ground below in early spring.

FOR CHILDREN

4 Just outside Benevento (about 16km/10 miles to the east) is the town of Foglianise where every year, on 16 August, the villagers celebrate with a wheat festival. Children would probably like to see this: tractors decorated with straw are paraded through the streets followed by young girls in traditional costume with baskets of wheat on their heads. In the evening there is a display of coloured lights.

SCENIC ROUTES

The most scenic parts of this particular tour are the following:

the last 20km (12½ miles) on the **SS88** from Benevento to Avellino, which wind through the mountains past Altavilla Irpina and a scattering of small hilltowns. There is nothing in particular to look out for; it is simply a lovely scenic route;

the trip to the **Sanctuary of Monte Vergine** from Avellino looks back over the valley to Altavilla Irpina.

4 days – 373km (231 miles)

THE APENNINES & THE ADRIATIC

Pescara • Pineto • Teramo • Atri • Penne Loreto Aprutino • Ortona • Lanciano • Vasto Chieti • Pescara

This tour takes in maritime Abruzzo, which consists of a coastal plain fringed by thick pinewoods and long sunny beaches. The resorts along the Adriatic are very popular in the summer, though you won't have to fight for beach space. Pescara, for example, has 16km (10 miles) of sandy shoreline. Just inland, beyond the fertile valleys close to the sea, are the rugged mountains of the region – you can see the vast Gran Sasso range to the west. While seafood is available by the shore, dishes with lamb, mutton and kid are the staple inland, traditionally too barren to produce anything else.

BACK TO NATURE

From Chieti and Lanciano it is not far into the mountains of Abruzzo. The area is rich in woodlands, including the pinewoods of **Piana delle Mele** and **Valle delle Monache**. Here, look for birds of prey, including perhaps even a red kite or a golden eagle soaring overhead, and warblers, nightingales and other songbirds among the trees themselves.

FOR CHILDREN

2 About 29km (18 miles) south of Teramo, just off the motorway, is the village of **Castelli** in whose **Institute of Ceramic Art** you can see a 100-figure ceramic **crib**. Highly detailed, this is a remarkable example of the art of crib-making, popular all over the south of Italy, and is fascinating for children.

ⓘ Corso Umberto 44, Pescara

*From Pescara, take the coastal **SS16** to Pineto, about 21km (13 miles).*

Pineto, Abruzzo

1 Pineto is one of the prettiest resorts on the Abruzzo coast. Its wide, sandy beach is lined with pines about five trees deep, so that in the heat of summer you can be near the sea without boiling on the sand all day. Many people come here for the camp sites, though if you cannot find places in these there are a great many others to choose from, lining the coastline practically all the way from Pescara to Martinsicuro, about 35km (22 miles) further north from Pineto. There are seafront hotels, some with swimming pools, nightclubs and restaurants where the speciality is *brodetto alla pescarese*, an extremely hot, peppery fish stew. Otherwise, Pineto's chief attraction is the **Torre di Cerrano**, a tower built by the Emperor Charles V as defence against the threat of the Ottoman Turks in the 16th century.

ⓘ Gabriele D'Annunzio 123

*From Pineto, continue along the **SS16** for about 16km (10 miles) as far as Giulianova, at which branch inland on the **SS80** in the direction of Teramo, about 25km (15 miles).*

Teramo, Abruzzo

2 Teramo is the capital of the northern chunk of the Abruzzo. Its special attractions, apart from the amazing views to the Gran Sasso, are its two cathedrals. The earlier **Duomo di Santa Maria Aprutiensis** is full of assorted decorative bits and pieces – such as the ancient frescos of angels and some splendid Lombard carvings. The 'newer' (12th-century) **cathedral** has a lovely Romanesque entrance portal, which incorporates sculpture, a rose window and mosaics. Its chief interior attractions are the 15th-century altarpiece by Jacobello del Fiore and a silver altar frontal of the same date by a local artist Nicola da Guardiagrele, which depicts scenes from the New Testament. This artist was obviously much in favour at the time: his work can also be seen on the façade of the building, in the statues of the Archangel Gabriel and the Virgin Annunziata balancing on the tops of columns borne by lions. Teramo was originally a Roman city: bits of its ancient past pop up everywhere. You might have noticed the remains of a **Roman house** (*domus*) incorporated within Santa Maria, but near the 'new' cathedral are the more modern buildings that grace Teramo's streets these days. Look out for the **Casa dei Melatini**, a well-preserved 14th-century house, and the old Franciscan Church of the **Madonna delle Grazie** which houses a painted wooden *Madonna and Child* by Silvestro dall'Aquila, one of the region's most important 15th-century sculptors. The **Museo Civico** (Civic Museum) in the Villa Comunale contains more works by local artists of the 15th century.

An impressive entrée to Penne, the elegant Porta San Nicola

ⓘ Via del Castello 10

*From Teramo, take the **SS81** going southeast for about 14km (9 miles) until it cuts the **SS150**. Continue east along this for about 13km (8 miles) until a turning on the right for Atri, a further 12km (7 miles).*

Atri, Abruzzo

3 Still in the shadow of the Gran Sasso massif, Atri is another ancient place that was once a Roman colony. You can survey relics of this era of its past among the **excavations** in the piazza and in the crypt of the **Cattedrale dell'Assunta** (Cathedral of the Assumption). In the gloom beneath this building are the remains of a **Roman piscina** (pool). The cathedral itself contains some excellent 15th-century frescos of the *Lives of the Virgin and Jesus* by Andrea Delitio, one of the most renowned local painters, and there is an interesting 16th-century tabernacle. But the real treasures of this town are to be found in the **cathedral museum** – ivories, statues, majolicas and an interesting array of fragments from the much more ancient church that preceded the cathedral. A wander around Atri should also take in the churches of **Sant'Agostino** and **Sant'Andrea** and the courtyard of the **Palazzo Acquaviva**, once the home of the Dukes of Acquaviva, which dates from the 14th century.

From Atri, the best way to get to Penne is to go across country. Leave the town the way you entered, and after about 1.5km (1

Pineto's beautiful beach is typical of the Abruzzo coast

*mile), follow the signs on the left to Villa Bozza from which follow the signs to the **SS81** and Penne, about 36km (22 miles) in all.*

Penne, Abruzzo

4 Penne is a small town that sits on a low rise not far from the Lake of Penne. Surprisingly for its size it is full of miniature but majestic palaces and mansions, some baroque, others Renaissance. Just by the **Porta San Francesco**, the town's main gate, is the **Palazzo Castiglione** with two tiers of balconies wrapped around with wrought iron. Further up among the old brick-paved streets and alleys is the **Palazzo del Bono** (in the Via Pansa), a lovely two-storeyed Renaissance palace. There is a homogeneity about Penne: churches, houses, palaces and streets are all built of the same material, a reddish

FOR HISTORY BUFFS

7 A few kilometres beyond Lanciano is Guardiagrele, whose most famous inhabitant, Nicola da Guardiagrele, produced some of the region's finest works in gold and silver in the 15th century. In the church here is a silver crucifix by this artist.

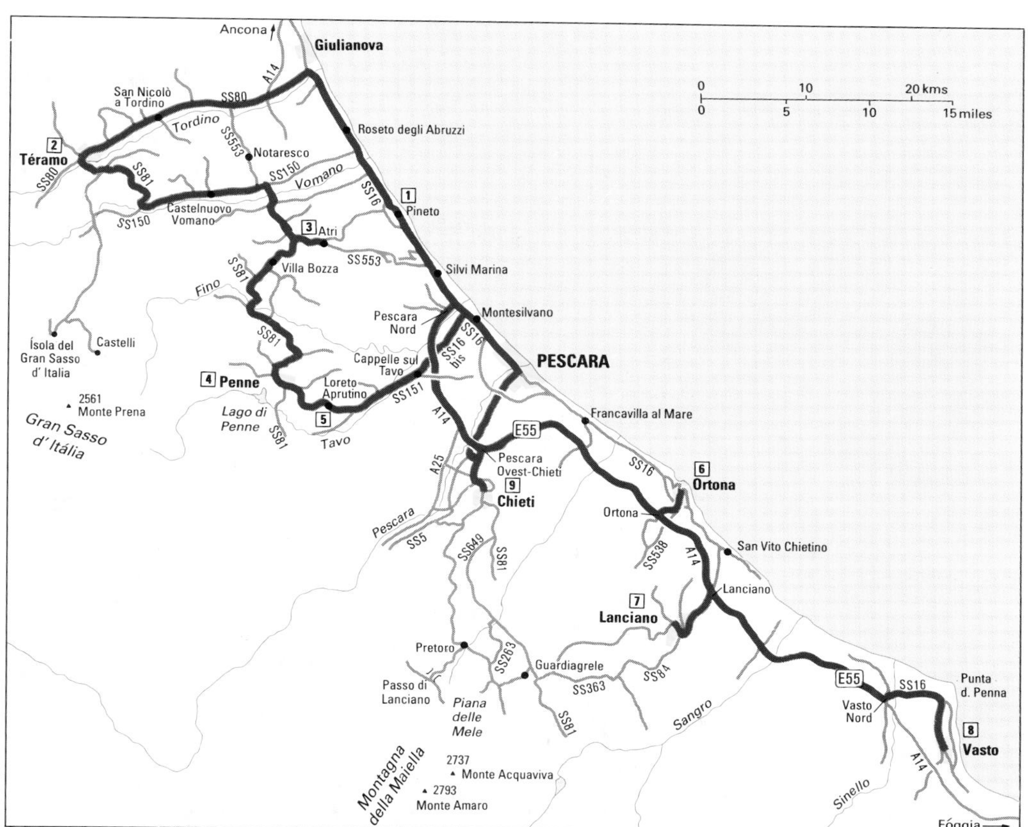

One for the connoisseur of hilltowns: Loreto Aprutino

SCENIC ROUTES

Fine views can be seen on the route via Orsogna from Lanciano to Guardiagrele and the approach to Loreto Aprutino from the Penne side.

SPECIAL TO . . .

3 In Atri is the **Parade of Carts**, when traditional carts are drawn through town carrying singers and dancers in costume.

5 Special to Loreto Aprutino, are the celebrations of the **Feast of St Zopito**. An elaborately dressed ox carrying a child dressed as an angel is led to the statue of the saint. The ox is made to kneel and receive the abbot's benediction. Strange but true.

9 Chieti's **Good Friday Procession** is one of Italy's oldest Easter ceremonies. Participants in the torchlight procession wear the black tunic and grey mantle of penitents.

brick, which gives the town a warm glow. Penne's **cathedral** is perhaps the town's least interesting building. It was destroyed in World War II, then rebuilt, but it does have an interesting crypt which has survived from the earlier building. The 18th-century Church of the **Annunziata** is far more interesting; with its columned façade it is considered to be the most perfect church of its period anywhere in the region.

Loreto Aprutino is about 8km (5 miles) to the southeast.

Loreto Aprutino, Abruzzo

5 Everybody who comes to Loreto Aprutino comes to see the *Last Judgement* fresco in the Church of **Santa Maria in Piano**. Here the dead are seen heaving themselves out of their graves, some to end in Hell, the others in Paradise. A centre for the production of olive oil, this is one of the region's prettiest hilltowns; the cottages that make up the bulk of the town are squeezed among churches, whose belltowers can be seen from afar. At the summit of the town is **San Pietro Apostolo** with a good Renaissance portal. Near by is the **Palazzo Acerbo** in which is a small museum housing a stunning collection of antique Abruzzesi ceramics with examples from the very early Middle Ages to the 18th century.

*Take the **SS151** towards the coast, branching left on to the **SS16bis** at Capelle sul Tavo. Join the **A14** north of Montesilvano at the Pescara Nord junction and follow the autostrada south to the exit for Ortona.*

Ortona, Abruzzo

6 Most of Ortona was reconstructed after two of the most horrific battles fought during World War II – the battles of the Sangro and Moro rivers in November–December 1943. The **Duomo** (Cathedral) has been partially rebuilt since, but its lovely 14th-century portal was unscathed. The **Palazzo Farnese**, begun in 1584 for a visit to the town by Margaret of Parma, also survived. Although unfinished, it is the town's best building, its architect having been Giacomo della Porta, notable as a follower of Michelangelo. Ortona is now the region's largest port with the usual kind of raffish, tangy character to match, particularly in the **Terravecchia** quarter beside the remains of the Aragonese **castle**. While the restaurants here are good, you will probably find it more pleasant at the resort of **Francavilla a Mare**, just 6km (4 miles) to the north, a more popular place to stay and to relax.

*Rejoin the **A14** travelling south to the next exit (Lanciano). Lanciano is 7km (4 miles) to the southwest along a minor road.*

Lanciano, Abruzzo

7 Lanciano was an important market town with international trade in the Middle Ages. Its medieval nucleus survives, known as **Lanciano Vecchia**, at the centre of which are the churches of **Sant'Agostino** and

San Biagio. However, in the Città Nuova, the 16th-century 'new town', the Church of Santa Maria Maggiore is far more interesting. Dating mostly from the early 14th century, it has two perfect rose windows and a huge Gothic portal lined with highly decorative columns. Its most spectacular interior fitting is a 15th-century crucifix. The **Duomo** (cathedral), with its 17th-century belfry, actually sits on the remains of a Roman bridge, dating from the time of the Emperor Diocletian and restored in the 11th century. The only town gate to survive from medieval times is the **Porta San Biagio**.

*From Lanciano return to the **A14** and travel south to the Vasto Nord turn-off. Take the **SS16** and follow the signs to Vasto.*

Vasto, Abruzzo

8 The town of Vasto is dominated by a huge 13th-century **fortress** which looks on to the Piazza Rossetti, site of a former Roman amphitheatre. It sits on the edge of the medieval town whose limits are still marked out in part by walls, punctured occasionally by old gates. The aspect of the town changes as you pass from the newer part to the old: whereas the streets are wider and more elegant outside the **Porta Santa Maria** or **Porta Nuova**, inside the walls, beyond these gates, they are narrow and tortuous, full of strange little squares and old doorways. The older precincts contain the more interesting churches, particularly **San Giuseppe** (the cathedral) and **Santa Maria Maggiore**. The 13th-century cathedral has a good Gothic portal. The remains of another church, **San Pietro**, can be found not far from the **Palazzo d'Avalos**. In the lunette of the entrance portal – all that remains of the church – is an interesting sculpture of the crucified Christ wearing a regal crown rather than the usual crown of thorns. Vasto has a **Museo Civico** (Civic Museum) whose section on the Roman antecedents of the town is the most interesting. One last fact about the town – in the Piazza Diomede is a statue of the English Pre-Raphaelite poet and painter Dante Gabriel Rossetti, whose family originated in Vasto.

*Rejoin and travel north on the **A14** until the Pescara Ovest-Chieti turn-off.*

Chieti, Abruzzo

9 Chieti has a number of star attractions which make it an indispensable part of the tour. You should set aside two hours to see the excellent **Museo Archeologico degli Abruzzi** (Archaeological Museum), whose chief exhibit, the peculiar-looking *Warrior of Capestrano*, is an over-life-size figure probably dating from the 6th century BC, accompanied by an as yet undeciphered inscription. Substantial parts of the town's **Roman baths** have survived, including a room which retains its mosaic pavement. The Roman theme continues throughout the town with the ruins of three small **temples**, a **cistern** (the former reservoir) and the intact original early town layout (of the Civitella district, the oldest section of Chieti). If you examine these then look at the Roman artefacts in the museum, you should be able to build up a good picture of ancient Chieti. Another important period of Chieti's history is represented by the Gothic Cathedral of **San Giustino**, which contains a silver statue of St Justin.

[i] Via Spaventa 29

*Return towards the **A14** and follow the signs to Pescara, about 21km (13 miles).*

Pescara – Pineto 21 (13)
Pineto – Teramo 41 (25)
Teramo – Atri 39 (24)
Atri – Penne 36 (22)
Penne – Loreto Aprutino 8 (5)
Loreto Aprutino – Ortona 65 (40)
Ortona – Lanciano 20 (12)
Lanciano – Vasto 44 (27)
Vasto – Chieti 78 (48)
Chieti – Pescara 21 (13)

The Aragonese castle at Ortona dates from the 15th century

RECOMMENDED WALKS

3 Near Atri, on the outskirts of the town, in fact, and within easy walking distance from it, are the strange *calanchi* rock formations – you cannot miss them. The odd geology of the area has also given rise to caves which were once inhabited by human beings.

9 From Passo di Lanciano, a small resort in the Abruzzo massif between Chieti and Lanciano, it is possible to enjoy mountain walking in the Maiella range, which reaches over 2,700m (9,000 feet).

3 days – 362km (226 miles)

ABRUZZO – THE REMOTE INTERIOR

L'Áquila • Cocullo • Scanno • Pescasséroli Pescocostanzo • Sulmona • Pacentro • Celano L'Áquila

Although geographically not very far from some of Italy's biggest cities, the Abruzzo is a largely untamed region. This tour gives you the best of this aspect of it, introducing you to places where Italy's natural environment is at its wildest. Centred on the area between southern Italy's highest mountain, the Gran Sasso (2,912m/9,554 feet above sea-level), and the Abruzzo National Park, most of the smaller towns on this tour, in particular Cocullo and Pescocostanzo, have managed to escape the march of progress. Some are situated on upland plains, others are isolated high above deep valleys. Some may only have one church to see, or a good view, but each has a friendly atmosphere and perhaps a small local-style restaurant where you can eat traditional food. L'Áquila has plenty to keep sightseers happy – notably a cathedral, fortress (now a museum) and fine fountain. At 600m (2,000 feet), it is a good stopping-off point for this journey into the hilly interior.

SPECIAL TO . . .

1 Cocullo holds the **Processione dei Serpari** which takes place in the town every year on the first Thursday in May. Snakes (non-poisonous) are collected from the surrounding countryside then flung at the statue of San Domenico Abate. Those that cling on are carried around the town entwined around the statue – the aim is to touch one. If you do, claim the villagers, you will have a longer life.

2 In Scanno, the women's costumes are little different from medieval garb. They take the form of long patterned dresses and turban-like headdresses. The older women often still wear them for everyday work, but many younger ones bring them out of wraps only for special occasions.

[i] Piazza Santa Maria di Paganica 5, L'Áquila

*From L'Áquila, take the **SS17** for about 34km (21 miles) until Navelli, at which bear left via the **SS153** to the **SS5**. Turn left and after 2km (1 mile) join the **A25** at the Bussi junction. Travel in the direction of Roma for about 30km (18 miles) until Cocullo, which lies just 3km (2 miles) off the autostrada.*

Cocullo, Abruzzo

1 Cocullo is a small rural town full of ancient mud-coloured houses clinging to the side of a hill beneath the spire of a church. It has one main street, a single piazza and an important sanctuary dedicated to **San Domenico Abate**. The town's patron saint and a hermit who, like St Francis, made 'friends' with animals, he used to live in a cave that still exists beneath the sanctuary. The sanctuary itself contained the painted wooden statue of the hermit which, in 1981, following an earthquake, was transferred further up the hill, to an ancient chapel whose miniature pilastered façade faces the main piazza.

*Cross over the **A25** and go south, following the little country road via Anversa degli Abruzzi to Scanno, about 20km (13 miles).*

Scanno successfully combines the medieval and the modern

Scanno, Abruzzi

2 Scanno, which overlooks the attractive Lago (Lake) di Scanno, is one of the most popular places in the region, especially for summer holidays. There are hotels, places to swim, eat and relax. At the same time, Scanno itself is a perfectly preserved medieval hilltown. The old town sits apart from the modern outskirts, partly because it crowns the pinnacle of a low rise on the side of a hill. A map on a signboard as you enter the town suggests a route through its centre (very small). This will take you past **Santa Maria della Valle**, a medieval church built on the remains of a pagan temple, the 16th-century **Fontana di Saracco** (Saracco Fountain) and the little Church of **Santa Maria di Constantinopoli**, which contains a fresco of the *Madonna Enthroned*, signed 'De Ciollis AD1478'. There are other churches squeezed into oddly-shaped little squares as well as Renaissance and baroque houses and small noble palaces. There are also ancient mansions in whose windows you sometimes catch glimpses of old women in costume mending clothes or embroidering. Other characteristic features are the external staircases on to steep streets, arches and dark passages. Scanno has much else to offer: superb landscape views; folklore; local arts and handicrafts, such as lace-making and the production of gold and silver jewellery (beautiful filigree earrings for example); and a handful of delicatessen which cater for tourists, selling local wine, bottled peppers, sausages and local cheeses.

*From Scanno, follow the **SS479** south for about 7km (6½ miles) to Villetta Barrea at which turn right on to the **SS83**, following the signs to Pescasséroli, about 16km (10 miles).*

Pescasséroli, Abruzzo

3 Pescasséroli lies within the confines of the **Parco Nazionale d'Abruzzo** (Abruzzo National Park). Although its principle attraction is as the starting point for walks and expeditions into the mountains and valleys of the park, it does also have a handful of interesting buildings. The **parish church** has been added to over the years, having started life in the 8th century AD as part of a monastery. It has a simple Gothic entrance portal and inside, in the **Cappella della Madonna Nera** (Chapel of the Black Madonna), is a very early wooden statue of the Madonna carved from black wood. In the Strada Valle del Fiume is one of the town's earliest remaining houses and one or two slightly later characteristic baronial palaces. In the Piazza Benedetto Croce is the **Palazzo Sipari**, birthplace of Pescasséroli's most famous inhabitant, the philosopher Benedetto Croce, who was born here in 1866. The **Casa Comunale** preserves his manuscripts. As you wander through the town, look out for old, carved stone doorways and windows – in particular notice the Gothic mullioned window in the Piazza Umberto I which is thought to have come from Pescasséroli's castle. For winter visitors there are ski runs in the nearby mountains – on Monte Ceraso and Monte Vitelle.

[i] Via Piave

*Go back via Villetta Barrea, continuing on the **SS83** to its junction with the **SS17**. Follow this road northwards for about 15km (9 miles), at which branch off on the **SS84** and follow the signs to Pescocostanzo, about 5km (3 miles).*

Pescocostanzo, Abruzzo

4 The collegiate Church of **Santa Maria del Colle** (or Collegiata) in Pescocostanzo, is one of the most beautiful churches in the Abruzzo – even though it was badly damaged

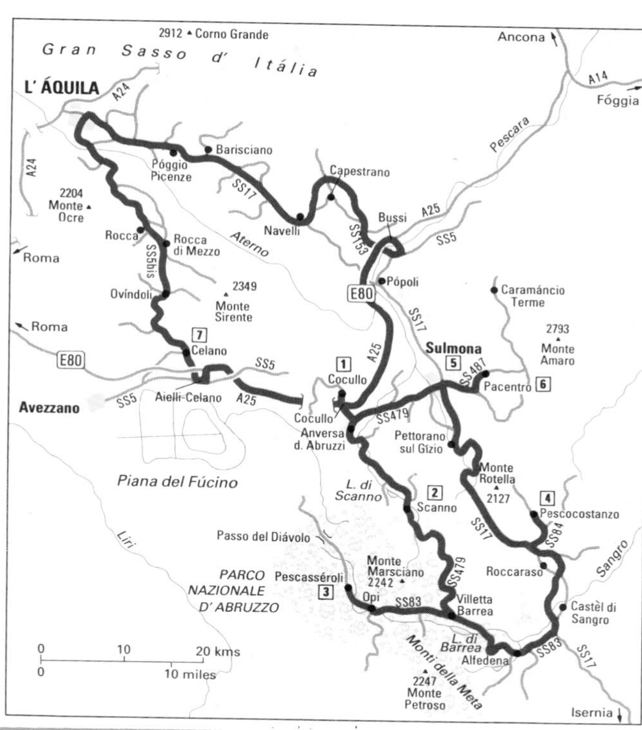

Autostrada viaduct near Scanno. The mountains of the Abruzzo are no longer so remote

SCENIC ROUTES

Perhaps the most scenic parts of this tour are the following:
– the first 10km (6 miles) of the road by which you leave Scanno, going south. You might be forgiven for thinking yourself in Scotland;
– the famous **Passo del Diavolo** (the Devil's Pass), just north of Pescasséroli. Although this is not strictly part of the tour route, it is worth a detour to drive at least a section of it. The pass takes you through part of the Parco Nazionale d'Abruzzo (Abruzzo National Park).

Corso Ovidio in Sulmona: the Roman poet Ovid was born here

BACK TO NATURE

3 Accessible from Pescasséroli via the Sangro Valley, the **Parco Nazionale d'Abruzzo** is a region of wooded slopes and mountains offering a last refuge for the Italian race of the European brown bear and chamois as well as the European wolf. The alpine meadows are a riot of colour in the spring and summer and golden eagles, goshawks and peregrines are regularly seen. Mountain birds are well represented at high altitudes.

FOR CHILDREN

3 Organised riding lessons can be had at equitation centres in and around Pescasséroli in the Abruzzo National Park. Also available are guided rides on horseback through the countryside – for adults and children.

during World War II. Having been started in the 13th century, it was rebuilt after an earthquake 200 years later. Nowadays its most beautiful components are the late 17th-century wrought-iron gates to the Chapel of the Sacrament, and the gilded and painted wooden ceiling of the nave. Look out for the medieval wooden statue of Santa Maria del Colle incorporated in a niche of the high altar. Pescocostanzo is an unusual place: it seems bland, even uninteresting at first, but it has a surprising number of worthwhile buildings. The principal *piazza* has a 16th-century **Palazzo Comunale** and there is an array of mansions in the Corso Roma – **Palazzo Grilli** and **Palazzo Mansi** in particular – and in the Via della Fontana are **Palazzo Colecchi**, **Palazzo Ricciardelli** and **Palazzo Mosca**. You sometimes see local women wearing the town's traditional costume – bright red skirts, lace aprons and dark bodices in brown, blue or black, decorated with gold thread. Local handicrafts here are the same as those in Scanno. Once a wealthy town, Pescocostanzo was at one time controlled by Vittoria Colonna, patroness of Michelangelo and a member of the great Roman Colonna family.

ⓘ Piazza Umberto 1

*Return to the **SS17**, then continue northwards via Pettorano to Sulmona.*

Sulmona, Abruzzo

5 Sulmona is the biggest town (apart from L'Áquila) on the tour. Its situation at the centre of a small plain surrounded by high mountains is perhaps what visitors find most attractive about it. As the birthplace of the Roman poet Ovid (43BC–AD17), however, and with its complement of old buildings, it has a decidedly antique air. The church and palace of **Santa Maria Annunziata** are perhaps the finest buildings. Originally a mixture of Gothic and Renaissance styles, the exteriors were rebuilt in baroque style early in the 18th century. The palace is the finer. Its façade has richly carved elements, statues – in particular the lunette fig-

ures of the *Madonna and Child*, once gilded and painted – and delicate tracery (see the first-floor windows). Today the palace houses the town's **museum** with local paintings and goldsmith's work. Running through the centre of town is the old **aqueduct**, constructed in the mid-13th century. It wends its way through Piazza Garibaldi on Gothic arches, adjacent to the Church of **San Francesco della Scarpa**. Sulmona's best-known product is confetti, not coloured paper but sugared almonds which are handed out at weddings and christenings.

[i] Via Roma 21

*Take the **SS487**, going east to Pacentro, about 9km (6 miles).*

Pacentro, Abruzzo

6 Pacentro is just one of a clutch of pretty hilltowns in the vicinity of Sulmona. Its ancient centre focuses on the **Castello Cantelmo** with its handful of surviving towers. Beneath these and the church steeple, the rustic houses, a collection of sandy-coloured blocks, sit crammed together, linked by tiny weaving passages and alleys. Further north is Caramancio Terme, a hilltown resort with sulphur baths. It lies at the very heart of the Maiella mountains. Caramancio has a lovely parish church, **Santa Maria Maggiore**, with a fine late 15th-century portal and reliquary by local master Nicola da Guardiagrele.

*From Pacentro, return to Sulmona, then take the **SS479** via Anversa degli Abruzzi in the direction of Roma for 20km (12½ miles), exiting at the Aielli-Celano turn-off, and follow the signs to Celano.*

Celano, Abruzzo

7 Celano is another lovely hilltown, this time overlooking the Fucino Basin, the most fertile piece of Abruzzo countryside, in antiquity a lake. The little town clusters beneath the **Castello Piccolomini**, which was begun in 1392. This imposing building was restored after an earthquake (along with Celano's churches) earlier this century and today has regained its appearance as a formidable example of a feudal power base, in this case of the Piccolomini family. Not far from Celano is the **Gole di Celano**, a spectacular, narrow and very deep gorge – or canyon – containing a torrent. It runs down from the direction of Monte Sirente towards the town.

*From Celano, take the **SS5bis** back to L'Áquila, about 48km (30 miles).*

L'Áquila – Cocullo 92 (57)
Cocullo – Scanno 20 (13)
Scanno – Pescasséroli 43 (27)
Pescasséroli – Pescocostanzo 58 (36)
Pescocostanzo – Sulmona 37 (23)
Sulmona – Pacentro 9 (6)
Pacentro – Celano 55 (34)
Celano – L'Áquila 48 (30)

The hilltop above Celano is crowned by the massive castle of the Piccolomini family

FOR HISTORY BUFFS

4 At Alfedana, on the way to Pescocostanzo are the ruins of the ancient Samnite town of *Aufidena* – you can see the cyclopean walls (built with enormous stone blocks) above the river and the ancient necropolis. The Samnites were an ancient Italian people who flourished in the 4th century BC. They came into conflict with the Romans, who eventually crushed them in 82BC.

RECOMMENDED WALKS

The best walks on this tour are to be had in the **Parco Nazionale d'Abruzzo** (Abruzzo National Park). Pick up trail maps at Pescasséroli – there are special trails as well as refuge huts should you want to stay overnight.

CALABRIA, BASILICATA, PUGLIA

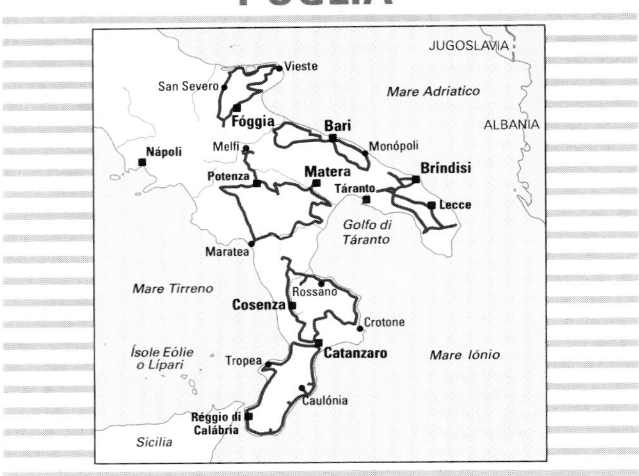

The far south is perhaps the most intriguing and dramatic part of Italy. Wild, uncontrollable territory alternates with dense woodland and gentle, cultivated plains. For many people, Italy stops at Roma or, at a push, Napoli. Beyond, there is nothing but an unfamiliar, mountainous land mass, full of strange rustics with peculiar customs and leading backward lives.

Nothing could be further from the truth; the attractions of the south are merely less obvious and altogether extraordinary. Who would have thought that some of the strangest customs and dialects in Calabria had their origins in 15th-century Albania; or that some of the inhabitants of Matera in Basilicata are quite happy to live underground; or even stranger – that people in parts of Puglia live in prehistoric-type houses that look like beehives? Most of Calabria and Basilicata is mountainous, with craggy outcrops of rock blanketed with thick forests. Shut away in the hinterland of both regions are remote whitewashed hill villages, cities and castles. Ancient buildings, medieval city centres, and traditional customs, dress and dialect have survived in Calabria and Basilicata as a result of the lie of the land and its inaccessibility.

But these areas are fascinating, especially to anyone interested in archaeology and history. Much of the south was once a part of Magna Graecia – the name given to the ancient Greek colonies founded in southern Italy and Sicily from the 8th century BC – and the archaeological sites of the region have yielded important finds from that period, the time of their greatest prosperity. In these areas, and in Puglia too, there are Roman remains as well as Byzantine and Norman architecture and a variety of other evidence of the trail left behind by the conquerors of the south over the centuries.

In Puglia, which forms the spur and heel of the boot of Italy, the terrain is mostly gentler – flatter, with greater areas of cultivation (wheat, tobacco, vegetables, grapes and olives are all grown). Some of the region's ports are the busiest in Italy, with regular ferries to Greece and Croatia. It bustles with life, where Calabria and Basilicata seem to brood on their past. The southern Italian coastline is attractive, often dramatic, with sheer cliffs plunging into the sea. It is little geared towards tourism, though the Tyrrhenian coast of Calabria has undergone some holiday development.

Catanzaro
Catanzaro is a lively town. It sits on a stony peak with deep gorges on either side, surrounded by a wonderful panorama. Just a few kilometres away is the sea. Although it might not be obvious behind the results of Catanzaro's rapid modern development, the city has ancient Byzantine origins and a rich cultural tradition, some traces of which can be seen in the Museo Provinciale (Provincial Museum).

Cosenza
Cosenza had an eventful history giving it a varied cultural background – at different times it fell under the sway of the Romans, Normans, Swabians, Angevins and Aragonese. All these have left their mark, though the old city has a predominantly medieval aspect, dominated by a huge Norman castle. Cosenza is a thriving market town, and can boast some of Calabria's best restaurants.

Matera
The different periods of Matera's history are clearly defined as you walk through the city centre and around its outskirts. The town's main attraction is the fascinating Sassi, with rockcut dwellings gouged from the city's foundations along with tunnels and labyrinthine grottoes; there are also rock chapels, some of whose walls are covered with frescos. Just outside town there are many more small churches cut into the hills. But more normal buildings are in plentiful supply – the Duomo is 13th-century Romanesque, with much of interest to be seen both inside and out

Green and rolling Puglian countryside near Bovino

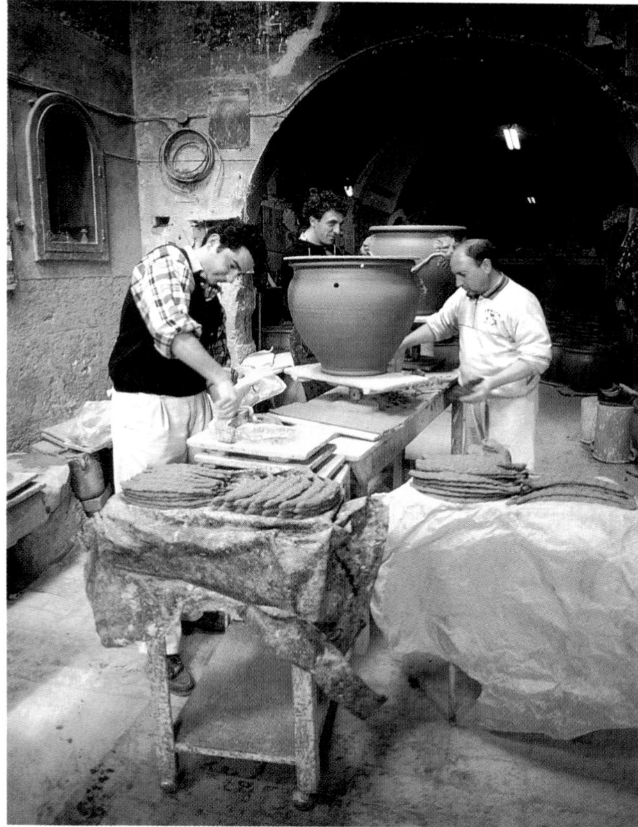

Pottery-making in Grottaglie, Puglia, is an old tradition

Bari

Bari, Puglia's capital consists of an old quarter – the Città Vecchia – which lies nearest the sea and has medieval buildings in its streets; the newer Città Nuova, with a neat grid-plan of streets; and the industrial area further inland. The city contains some of the most magnificent buildings in the region: the Romanesque cathedral, the castle and the great Basilica of San Nicola, founded in the 11th century by the Normans – their first major church in Puglia. The Museo Archeologico, with its fine ceramics, and the Pinacoteca Provinciale, full of southern Italian art from the 11th to the 18th century, are also worth seeing.

Brindisi

Both Bari and Brindisi are important Adriatic ports. The latter sits on a peninsula between two arms of land, forming a natural harbour. Strangely, for a city whose claim to fame is as the major point of embarkation for Greece, the centre of Brindisi has the air of a small provincial town. Cafés line the main street and there is a pretty promenade at the town centre overlooking the water. Brindisi's archaeological museum (Museo Archeologico Provinciale) preserves the best of the finds from nearby Roman sites. Be sure to visit the colourful Church of Santa Maria del Casale with its impressive Byzantine *Last Judgement*, a few kilometres north, near the airport.

Foggia

Foggia is Puglia's third city. Not much of its ancient aspect survives. Today it is a city of wide avenues and mostly low-rise, modern buildings. However, the cathedral survives, a strange mixture of Romanesque and baroque. The Museo Civico (Civic Museum) contains archaeological finds from the area as well as an exhibition of Puglian traditional crafts.

Below right: the lovely hilltop town of Rivello, Basilicata

5 days – 478km (296 miles)

THE TOE OF THE BOOT

The wild landscape of the River Lao in northwest Calabria

Catanzaro • Stilo • Caulonia • Gerace • Bova Reggio di Calabria • Palmi • Tropea • Pizzo Catanzaro

Southern Calabria consists mostly of the Aspromonte mountain range. Its valleys, gorges and massive craggy peaks dwarf the little towns lodged on its slopes and along its coastline. While the latter is largely built up, the interior, being more difficult to access, has been left relatively untouched, the only additions being the concrete infill where an earthquake shattered some older structure – perhaps ancient Greek, Norman, Renaissance or baroque. Catanzaro is the exception. Big, lively and modern, it engulfs the outcrop on which it stands. Legends of brigands, communities where the people still speak a version of ancient Greek in their dialects, and towns with bloodthirsty histories, are the norm here in the far south of Italy.

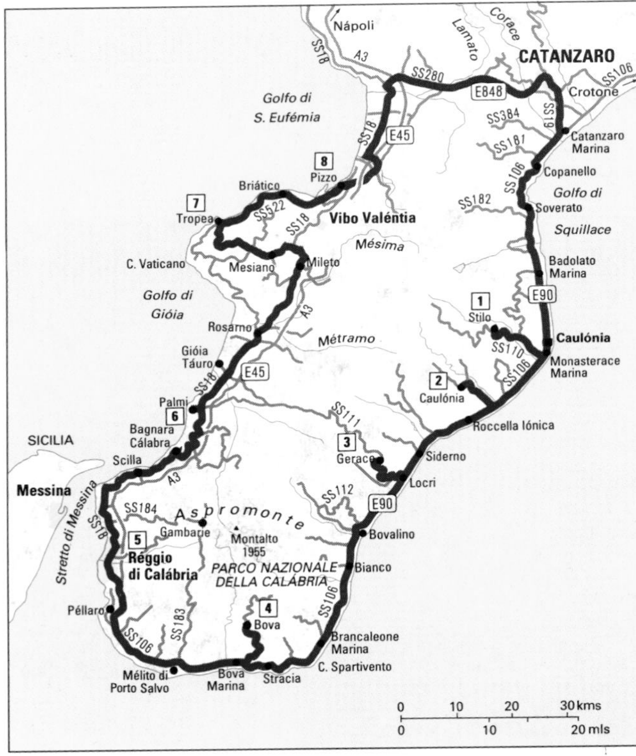

🛈 Galleria Mancuso, Catanzaro

*Take the **SS19** south to the coast, then branch southwest on the coastal **SS106** for about 48km (30 miles) until Monasterace Marina, at which follow the **SS110** to Stilo, about 15km (9 miles).*

Stilo, Calabria

1 Stilo, halfway down the Monte Consolino, contains one of the most exquisite buildings in Calabria. Called **La Cattolica**, it is a terracotta-coloured Byzantine chapel. Inside, one of its antique columns has been placed upside down as a symbol of the defeat of paganism by Christianity. On a ledge above the town, La Cattolica looks out over the rocky valley at the head of which Stilo stands. The best time to come to Stilo would be at Easter, when Holy Week is celebrated with religious processions which meander through the town from church to church. In one of these the inhabitants start at the parish church, the **Chiesa Madre**, following the statue of the Madonna Addolorata, weaving through the ancient and narrow stone-walled streets, on their way to the Church of **San Giovanni Jeresti** where, before a large cross they pray, listen to music and sing hymns in dialect. Special cakes with names like *nzulle* and *cuzzepe* are prepared for the occasion. Shaped like hearts and fishes, they are made of nuts, eggs, dried figs and sugar. In addition to this all the town's churches (there are five) are open for the event. Try to see the Church of **San Francesco**, founded in 1400, with its ornately carved wooden altar. On the edge of town the **Porta Stefanina**, one of Stilo's ancient gateways, still has an intact defensive tower.

*Go back to Monasterace Marina and continue southwards on the **SS106** for about 14km (9 miles) until the turning west for Caulonia, about 8km (5 miles).*

Caulonia, Calabria

2 This little clay-coloured town, situated between the rivers Assi and Amusa, was founded by refugees from the ancient city of Caulonia which was destroyed by Dionysius I of Syracuse in 389BC. There is little to be seen here except for a notable tomb in the **Chiesa Madre** (parish church). By a Tuscan sculptor, it belongs to one of the members of the Carafa family and is dated 1488. There is also the **Chiesetta Zaccaria**, a little church filled with Byzantine frescos. Nonetheless, Caulonia is interesting as a country town where not much has changed for centuries.

*Returning to the **SS106**, continue south for 23km (14 miles) as far as Locri at which follow the signs west to Gerace on the **SS111**.*

Gerace, Calabria

3 You could spend hours in Gerace simply sitting in the sun in the piazza in front of the cathedral. Wild flowers poke up between the old battered cobbles; goats wander by; widows in black and old men in grey peaked hats slowly pass, while the odd tiny Fiat 500 might squeeze into sight from some narrow adjacent alley. Gerace, sitting on an impregnable crag above the Gerace river on one side and the great dried-up bed of the

The market in Scilla between Reggio di Calabria and Palmi

Novita river on the other, is an ancient place, originally founded by refugees from Locri who fled there in the 10th century to escape the continual stream of Saracen attacks. It is full of little churches and houses ranging from the Norman period to the baroque. The **Cattedrale**, the largest cathedral in Calabria, dominates the town. It is a strange building containing additions from a variety of centuries. Consecrated in 1045, it was rebuilt in the 13th century and restored in the 18th. Worth studying are the columns supporting the vault of the crypt – which you will not want to leave in summer because it is cool and dark – and those dividing the nave from the aisle in the upper church. Some of red and white marble, others of granite, they are believed to have come from ancient Locri down on the coast where they would have adorned an antique temple. Do not miss the cathedral treasury with its exquisite Renaissance ivory crucifix. Picking your way over the cobbles to the right of the cathedral, through the elaborate baroque archway you come to the Church of **San Giovanello**, part Byzantine and part Norman in style. At the back of the town is the old ruined **fortress** of Gerace, which still bears traces of its Roman origins. Before leaving Gerace you should consider buying some of the local ceramic vases and jugs. The origins of their decoration can often be traced back to the period when southern Italy was part of Magna Graecia (ancient Greek colonies in the west) – long before the Romans. You will see the ceramics spilling out of shops in the piazza by the cathedral.

*Returning once again to the coastal **SS106**, continue still further south for about 53km (33 miles) until Bova Marina at which branch inland for 14km (9 miles) to Bova.*

Bova, Calabria

4 The most extraordinary thing about Bova is that the dialect spoken by its inhabitants is a version of ancient Greek. The little mountain town is of great antiquity, shut away at a height of 820m (2,690 feet) on a remote peak of the Aspromonte. But the oldest visible remains – part of the **cathedral** and the ruins of the **castle** – date only from the Norman period, and the cathedral was rebuilt in 1783 after a tremendous earthquake. Also worthy of a visit is the Church of **San Leo** which, along with the cathedral, is the town's most prominent building. It dates from the 16th century, and is a later reconstruction of a

FOR HISTORY BUFFS

3 For those interested in clambering over the ruins of ancient Calabria, **Locri** (near Gerace) has the most visible remains – temples, a theatre, and both Greek and Roman tombs. Though most of the artefacts from the site are now in the museum at Reggio di Calabria, on site is an **Antiquarium** with a small collection of vases, votive statues and sculpture as well as a diagram of the site which, for the uninitiated, is a must. The ruins of old ***Caulonia*** (on the coast near Stilo) are more fragmentary. If you haven't time for both, go to Locri.

BACK TO NATURE

5 Visiting nature-lovers should not miss the **Parco Nazionale della Calabria**. To the east of Reggio di Calabria lies the southernmost of the 10 zones of this fragmented national park. It is an area of granite mountains with forests, rivers and meadows among the many scenic attractions. The wildlife includes birds of prey, wild cats and deer.

SPECIAL TO ...

1 The Stilo district is *Bivongi*, a red wine best drunk with *salamis*, very sour cheese and red meat.

3 The district around Gerace is noted for *Kalipea*, another local red wine, best drunk with piquant dishes and with roast meat, and for the locally produced ceramics.

much earlier church. The countryside around Bova, which you can observe from the ramparts of the town, gives a wild, rugged and desolate impression. However, it is also full of gnarled old olive trees and in spring glows with masses of wild flowers. You might perhaps be tempted to go for a walk along the rocky, dried-up bed of the Palizzi river.

*Back to the coast, the **SS106** continues to Reggio di Calabria, 43km (27 miles) further on.*

Reggio di Calabria, Calabria

5 From Reggio di Calabria, the regional capital, you can see across the Straits of Messina to Sicily – one of the most stunning views in southern Italy. This city is a big, lively town, straddling the coastline beneath the great peaks of the Aspromonte. It was shattered by an earthquake in 1908 and subsequently rebuilt, mostly of concrete. However, older fragments of its past have survived and, apart from viewing them in the important **Museo Nazionale della Magna Grecia** (see below), you can see one or two of them still *in situ* in the town. Apart from the mid-15th-century **Castello Aragonese** (Aragonese fortress), of which two massive circular bastions remain, there are the remains of the old **Greek city walls** and the **Roman baths** – both near the cathedral. But not to be missed on a visit to Reggio di Calabria is the **Museo Nazionale** (National Museum). It contains a fascinating array of treasures – jewellery, statuary, sarcophagi, vases, glassware and mosaics – from classical sites like Locri and ancient Caulonia, but its most celebrated exhibits are the **Bronzi di Riace** (the Riace Warriors), two sculptures dredged from the sea in 1972. Of ancient Greek origin, one dates from about 460BC, the other from about 430BC. The later figure is thought to be by the greatest of ancient Greek sculptors, Phidias, and to have come from the temple at Delphi in Greece. What they were doing at the bottom of the sea off the coast of Italy is anyone's guess.

Olive grove near Palmi. Most Calabrians live off the land

[i] Via D Tripepi 72

*The route continues out the other side of Reggio di Calabria and is now called the **SS18**. After about 49km (30 miles) it comes to Palmi.*

Palmi, Calabria

6 Palmi is the best place in which to examine the minutiae of rural Calabrian life. Its **Museo Calabrese di Etnografia e Folclore** (Ethnographic and Folklore Museum of Calabria) displays all kinds of everyday tools and household equipment that went out of use long ago in the mountains and valleys of the region. It also has an exhibition of ritual sweets handed out on religious occasions (some of which you might still find in the remoter areas of Calabria), allegorical masks relating to popular superstitions and legends, fascinating in an area noted in the past for Saracen raids and brigands, and traditional costumes. Palmi is also the first place after Reggio di Calabria where the coastline is pleasant enough to swim. Palmi was first developed in the 10th century by the inhabitants of ancient *Taurianum*. Of this old settlement, there are only the barest remains about 4km (2½ miles) further up the coast. Palmi was devastated in the 18th century and again in 1908 by violent earthquakes. Today, while its regular squares, some with centrally placed fountains and African-style palms, and its wide streets, are pleasant enough to stroll through, the attractions of the coastline are greater. Just off the coast there is an odd clump of rock with a single olive tree, known as Isola d'Olive (Isle of the Olive), to which you can swim (if you have the energy on one of Calabria's scorching summer days).

*From Palmi continue northwards on the **SS18** for about 37km (23 miles) to Mileto. After about 6km (4 miles) branch left and take the small country road towards the sea to Tropea.*

The little church of Santa Maria dell'Isola in Tropea

Tropea, Calabria

7 Tropea is a fishing town with the prettiest stretch of beach on Calabria's western coastline. The town, clamped to the cliff above the sea, is faced by a great lump of rock out in the sea, joined to the mainland by a stretch of sand. The islet is known as **Santa Maria dell'Isola**, after the old Benedictine sanctuary there. Since everything closes in the afternoon in Italy – churches, shops and most museums – you should spend the morning in the old town, whose most impressive monument, the **Duomo** (cathedral), is of pre-Norman origin. Try not to miss the very curious *Madonna of Romania*, in a silver frame, supposed to have been painted by St Luke himself, and the even stranger 15th-century black crucifix with wood inlay. There are numerous little old palaces scattered about the town: **Casa Trampo**, in Vicolo Manco has an elaborate doorway, and further down the same alley you will find the **Palazzo Cesareo**, whose balcony has lovely carved corbels. Further on there are others – some with carved doorways, others sporting the occupants' defence against the evil eye. Most often this takes the form of a grotesque face but sometimes it is a single eye in a circle. Other sights include the 18th-century Church of **San Giuseppe** and, of course, the startling views out over the sea that suddenly meet you as you turn a corner in one of the town's alleys. You can sometimes see as far as the Lipari Islands, out over the bright roofs of the fishermen's cottages.

Continue northwards along the coast road, the SS522 to Pizzo.

Pizzo, Calabria

8 While Tropea has generous expanses of white sandy beaches, the country around Pizzo plunges dramatically into the sea. The medieval origins of this little fishing town are obvious when you wander through its narrow streets full of ancient houses crammed into the confined space. Ferdinand of Aragon's stout, impregnable **Castello di Pizzo** greets your arrival at one side of the town. Built in 1486, and since restored, it is famous for having been the scene of the execution in 1815 of Joachim Murat (or Il Re Gioacchino, as locals called him), ex-king of Naples. Not far from this unhappy place you can visit the **Collegiata di San Giorgio** with a lovely baroque façade and, inside, some 16th-century sculpture.

Take the SS18 north until it joins the SS280. Follow the latter for about 33km (20 miles) until Catanzaro.

Catanzaro – Stilo 66 (41)
Stilo – Caulonia 37 (23)
Caulonia – Gerace 39 (24)
Gerace – Bova 76 (47)
Bova – Reggio di Calabria 57 (35)
Reggio di Calabria – Palmi 49 (30)
Palmi – Tropea 67 (42)
Tropea – Pizzo 27 (17)
Pizzo – Catanzaro 60 (37)

FOR CHILDREN

Apart from private facilities at individual hotels around the Calabrian coast, this region is not noted for facilities provided for the amusement of children.

RECOMMENDED WALKS

5 Above Reggio di Calabria is the little town of **Gambarie**, on the side of the Aspromonte mountain. Here you can walk among the pinewoods and admire the views out over the Straits of Messina to Sicily.

SCENIC ROUTES

To get to the sea at Copanello, about 6km (3½ miles) on the **SS106** south of Catanzaro, you drive through the flat lands between the sea and the mountains, an area characterised by clumps of umbrella pines and 2m (6-foot) high reeds. From here, right down the coast of Calabria, the scenery is the same.

The whole of the **SS18** going north is a panoramic route: to one side are the famous white Palmi sands and the beautiful beaches right up to Nicotera (about 22km/13 miles from Tropea), and on the other high mountains which drop sharply down to sea-level.

4 days – 556km (345 miles)

THE HIGHLANDS OF CALABRIA

Cosenza • Morano Calabro • Spezzano Albanese • San Demetrio Corone • Rossano Santa Severina • San Giovanni in Fiore • Tiriolo Nicastro • Rogliano • Cosenza

Little known, unexplored towns where some of the inhabitants speak ancient Albanian are common in this more northerly part of Calabria. Known as La Sila, it is only slightly less mountainous than its southern counterpart. In these parts you have to search hard for traces of the 20th century. Though the area is essentially rural, many of the bigger towns have the remains of a more glorious past scattered about their precincts. Cosenza, while the proud possessor of a cathedral, the consecration of which in 1222 was attended by Frederick II (Holy Roman Emperor and King of Sicily), is now mostly modern. Frequently damaged by earthquakes as well as a victim of World War II bombs, the city does not really prepare you for the remote and ancient places you will see on a tour into the mountains. The towns of this tour are mostly scattered on the highest peaks – generally for their own defence in a warring past – and have panoramic views over the wild landscape.

BACK TO NATURE

In the northern part of the Sila, in the Sila Greca, is another part of the **Parco Nazionale della Calabria**. Easy to reach from either Cosenza, Rossano or San Giovanni in Fiore, the national park comprises mostly forest of ancient larch, beech, chestnut and Hungarian oak. In the spring there are clearings of asphodels and wild violets. The greatest wild population of wolves left in Italy survives in this park and in another just south of San Giovanni in Fiore. There are also wild cats and fallow deer, kept in enclosures which can be visited. Walks in the parks are recommended – the best way to see the goshawks, buzzards and eagle owls of the region.

i Piazza P Rossi, Cosenza

*Take the Autostrada **A3** north from Cosenza until the Morano Calabro turning. Then follow the signposted country road.*

Morano Calabro, Calabria

1 From afar Morano Calabro looks like a part of the rock on which it was built. Although constructed on the pinnacle of a conical mountain 694m (2,277 feet) above sea-level, it is dwarfed by the huge Pollino mountain range all around it. The approach from the autostrada is enchanting: as you wind through the valleys at its feet, the town appears and vanishes with equal consistency as the car dips and turns. At dawn it is shrouded in mist, only the tips of the highest buildings visible from below. At dusk it is a murky silhouette enlivened by flickering lights and the sound of hooters and radios which echo across the valley in front of it. Close inspection reveals little square houses piled one on top of the other beneath the gaze of the Church of **Santi Pietro e Paolo** and the derelict remains of a Norman **castle**, partly rebuilt in the 16th century. The town was once an important centre of the local rural economy and some of the houses lining the steep streets have a prosperous air about them. Some have carved doorways. Many still have barns for livestock in use on the ground floors; while cattle were taken to the fields during the day to graze, they were brought home for the night for their own protection against thieves. A steep walk to the top of the town's hill will be rewarded in Santi Pietro e Paolo by statues of Santa Caterina and Santa Lucia thought to be by Pietro Bernini, father of the more famous Gianlorenzo Bernini, architect of St Peter's in Rome. Others in the church are by Bernini Senior's followers. Other churches include the 15th-century **San Bernardino**, with a fine portal and the baroque **Collegiata della Maddalena** which has a very pretty cupola. The little town is an excellent base for excursions into the **Pollino massif**, in particular the **Serra del Prete** and the **Serra Dolcedorme** which, at its highest point, is 2,271m (7,451 feet) above sea-level.

A quiet corner of old Cosenza, flourishing provincial capital

*Back to the **A3**, return southwards for about 23km (14 miles) until the Spezzano Albanese turning. Follow the **SS534** east-*

Cascading down the hillside, the unspoiled town of Morano Calabro

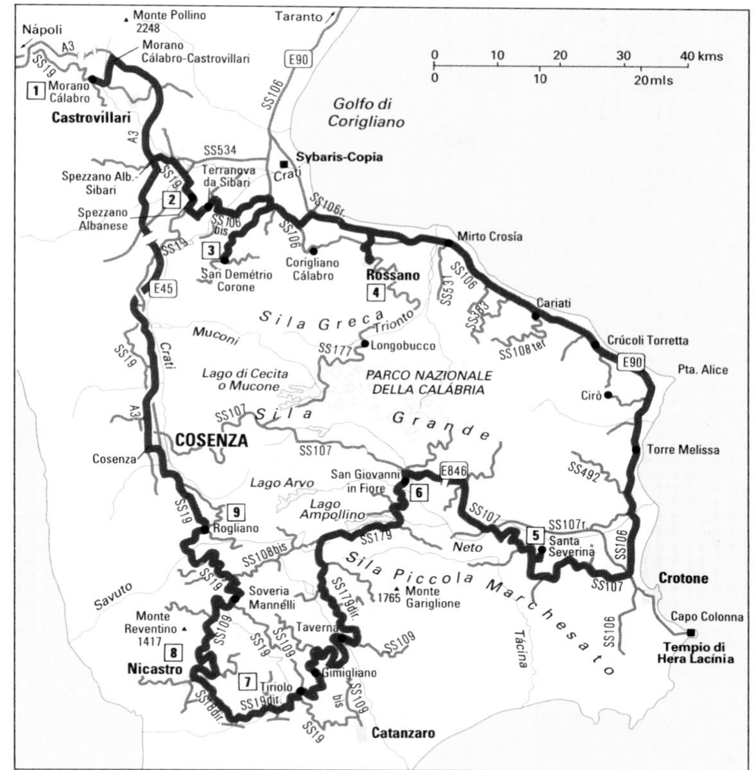

wards for 4km (2½ miles), then branch right along the ***SS19*** *until Spezzano Albanese.*

Spezzano Albanese, Calabria

2 This little town has a very un-Italian aspect. In the height of summer, as the bleached, whitewashed walls of the buildings hurt your eyes in the glare of sunlight, visions of Greece are never far from the mind's eye. The flat-roofed houses in the old quarter, with their small, square windows and their outside staircases, abut a warren of old passages and alleyways stacked with firewood. Adding to the strangely foreign character is the fact that most of the inhabitants of Spezzano speak Albanian – not the modern version

FOR HISTORY BUFFS

4 The site of the ancient Greek city of *Sybaris*, once with nearly 300,000 inhabitants, lies on the plain about 20km (12½ miles) along the **SS106** northwest of Rossano. Destroyed in 510BC, it disappeared for millennia under the swamps of the Crati river and its ruins have been excavated only in the past 30 years. There are remains of houses, some of which have surviving mosaic floors. Some of the artefacts found here have been deposited in a museum on the site. Otherwise you have to go to Crotone (on the way to Santa Severina) to see items from Sybaris in the museum there. It was once the richest city in Magna Graecia, and its luxury and decadence – as well as its corruption – were legendary (giving rise to the word 'sybaritic'). Don't miss the site of the **Tempio** (Sanctuary) **di Hera Lacinia** at Capo Colonna, 11km (7 miles) south of Crotone. It has a single huge remaining column near the beach.

Santa Severina, once a Byzantine stronghold, now dreams peacefully of its days of glory

but a dialect going back to the 15th century when their ancestors fled here from the Turks. You hear it in the bars, in the market, in the pastry shops, in the streets – everywhere. Some older women wear antique-looking costume; the everyday version is simple and rustic with floral-printed long skirts and wide lace collars. A more elaborate outfit is kept for festive occasions such as the Easter celebrations during Holy Week. For these events the women often wear costumes of great antiquity and deck themselves with gold jewellery. The **Sanctuary of the Madonna delle Grazie** on the outskirts of town is the focal point of the Easter celebrations during which its resident Madonna is covered in jewellery matching that of the local girls. Perhaps this is the best time to come to Spezzano Albanese. Everyone flocks here from the surrounding countryside; cakes and drinks are sold and most people make an effort to wear their traditional costumes. Spezzano is also a spa town, its installations dating from the 1920s and 1930s.

*Leave by the **SS19** travelling south, branching left within 2km (1 mile) on to the **SS106bis**, passing through Terranova da Sibari, and continue until you join the **SS106**, turning right. One kilometre (½ mile) further is the turning for San Demetrio Corone, just by the River Mizofato. Continue along this small country road for about 15km (9 miles) until San Demetrio Corone.*

San Demetrio Corone, Calabria

3 While Spezzano Albanese is sometimes called the capital of 'Little Albania', as this district is known, San Demetrio Corone is perhaps its most picturesque town – and its most uncompromisingly Albanian one. Here the street signs are in two languages and there is an **Italo-Albanian college** which trains young men as priests for the Orthodox church. The college stands next to the 12th-century Church of **Sant'Adriano** where you will see antique columns incorporated into the building work and a Byzantine tessellated pavement decorated with pictures of leopards, birds and snakes. In the main square is a statue of Skanderbeg, the Albanian hero who died in the fight against the Turks in the 15th century.

*Return to the **SS106**. Turn right and continue along it for 7km (4 miles) then turn left at Corigliano station. After 2km (1 mile) you reach the **SS106r**. Join this and continue south for about 10km (6 miles) until you reach the turning for Rossano, which is 7km (4 miles) further.*

SCENIC ROUTES

Stretches of this tour that are particularly scenic are the countryside around Morano Calabro, excellent for walks and drives, and the views from Tiriolo to the sea on either side of the Calabrian peninsula. The approach roads to the town (**SS109** and **SS19**) are spectacular.

Rossano, Calabria

4 This is one of the most important and picturesque hilltowns in the Sila Greca (so called because the Albanians were formerly thought of as Greeks by the locals). It has had a colourful history and was an important settlement during the Roman period and again during the 9th and 10th centuries. The single most important monument to the great past is the **Codex Purpureus**, the 6th-century Greek 'Rossano Gospels', now kept in the cathedral's treasury, the **Museo Diocesano**. This early Christian illuminated manuscript is extremely rare. Scenes from the New Testament are jewel-like with brilliant colour and fine detailed drawing. There is more to see in the town. A walk around the upper part will take in the Church of **San Bernardino** and the **cathedral**, which contains early sculpture. Perhaps more worthwhile are the small Byzantine churches of **Santa Maria del Pilerio** and the **Panaghia**, the latter with pretty frescos, while **San Marco** is not to be missed. Standing on high above the Celati river, this Byzantine church is not unlike the Cattolica at Stilo, with five little domes covered in terracotta tiles.

*Return to and continue along the coastal **SS106r** (which becomes the **SS106**) for about 84km (52 miles) until the junction with the **SS107**, 5km (3 miles) before Crotone. Take the **SS107** to Santa Severina, about 28km (17 miles) further on.*

Santa Severina, Calabria

5 From its much eroded rocky pinnacle, Santa Severina dominates a now deforested, hot, dry landscape. It was denuded of its trees by the ancient Greeks and the Normans, who needed wood for their ships. This particular area of the Sila is called the Marchesato and is characterised by *calanchi* – strange other-worldly rock formations scattered about among the huge old, gnarled olive trees – and by *timpe*, other strange conical formations of clay. Santa Severina's situation on its table-like rock means that it has always been provided with natural defences, made use of first by the Byzantines then by the Normans. Part of the town was abandoned after an earthquake in 1783. This is the **Grecia** quarter, in which you can still wander and see the remains of buildings which cannot have changed much since the first Byzantine settlement of the town. Do not miss the adjacent **Iudea** (Jewish) quarter either – this is still inhabited. There is enough up here to keep you busy for a good few hours. As so often, it is the churches that are full of the more interesting items of the town's history, in particular the **Addolorata**, the Norman cathedral with its 13th-century entrance portal. While the cathedral has largely been rebuilt, the adjacent **Battistero** (Baptistery) is still very largely Byzantine, dating mostly from the 8th century. Its construction is reminiscent of the buildings of Ravenna. The little 11th-century Church of **Santa Filomena**, with the Church of the **Pozzolio** underneath, looks like something from Armenia or Anatolia, its construction very un-Italian. It is a remarkable survivor in this part of the world. The old **Castello** may have been rebuilt on top of an earlier Byzantine one. In its present form it dates from the Norman period; from here there are incredible views out over the Neto valley.

*Continue on the **SS107** in a northwesterly direction for 34km (21 miles) until you reach the turning for the town of San Giovanni in Fiore.*

San Giovanni in Fiore, Calabria

6 From San Giovanni in Fiore, 1,049m (3,442 feet) above sea level, there are fine views of the surrounding countryside. This hilltown grew up around the old *Badia Florense*; in fact, the town's community land today corresponds to the former territories of the *Badia* (abbey), which was founded by the Abbot Gioacchino in 1189. The abbey itself was suppressed at the beginning of the 19th century and its buildings are currently being restored. You

Vineyard in the Santa Severina region: characterful red, white and rosé wines are produced here

SPECIAL TO . . .

In certain areas of this region are individual wines which you will not find outside Italy.

5 *Val di Neto Bianco* (best with antipasti and fish), *Rosso* (good with local cheese) and *Rosato* (drunk with any local dishes), are wines from the **Santa Severina** district; *Melissa Bianco* (best with antipasti and fish) and *Rosato* (best with soups, dishes using offal and light sweet cheese), originate from around Santa Severina and Crotone; *Ciro Bianco DOC* (best with antipasti and fish) and *Rosso DOC* (best with any sort of local dish) are both excellent and well known wines from Ciro, just off the **SS106** about 32km (20 miles) from Crotone.

9 *Savuto DOC*, a red wine best with more piquant dishes and with roast meat, comes from the province of Cosenza, in particular from the countryside near Rogliano.

FOR CHILDREN

The hilly interior of Calabria is not particularly suitable for families travelling with young children. Local colour, particularly during religious festivals, would interest older children, and their are special sweetmeats made from nougat, chocolate and walnuts or dried figs made for festivals.

RECOMMENDED WALKS

Continue from Rossano to the town of Longobucco (take the **SS177** via Cropalati – 23km/14 miles to Longobucco – 18km/11 miles) at the edge of a section of Parco Nazionale della Calabria. Here in the national park there are walks, wonderful scenery, rivers and excellent places for picnics.

can see its original buildings near the base of the town. Older townswomen still wear the traditional costume (the *rituartu*) of black velvet skirt, bodice, white lacy blouse and jewellery. All the town's traditional crafts are flourishing, including its wrought-iron workshops. It is also an important textile centre, as well as one of the few places where you will find craftsmen working with inlaid wood.

Go directly south from San Giovanni in Fiore for about 15km (9 miles) until you reach the ***SS179****. Turn right and follow this west for a further 15km (9 miles) at which point turn left on to the* ***SS179dir*** *heading south. On reaching the* ***SS109*** *after a further 27km (16½ miles) turn right and follow this road through Taverna and (remaining on the* ***SS109*** *where the* ***SS109bis*** *branches off to Catanzaro) follow the signs to Gimigliano to Tiriolo.*

Tiriolo, Calabria

7 The views of the surrounding countryside from Tiriolo are legendary. It stands high above the narrow ridge of mountains that divides the Tyrrhenian Sea from the Ionian Sea. If you venture about 200m (650 feet) further up the mountain from Tiriolo, you can see both seas – one of the great views of Calabria. In summer it is far cooler up in Tiriolo than at the bottom of the valleys – a good place to stop for lunch. Some of the women, usually the older ones, still wear their antique traditional costumes.

Take the ***SS19*** *from Tiriolo going south but almost immediately turn right on to the* ***SS19dir*** *for 17km (11 miles) until the* ***SS18dir*** *turning for Nicastro.*

Nicastro, Calabria

8 Nicastro is another Calabrian town of Byzantine origin. Hanging precariously from the side of Monte Reventino, it is dominated by what remains of the Norman **castle**, mostly demolished in an earthquake in 1638. The Emperor Frederick II rebuilt the fortress and imprisoned his son Henry there. Scattered up and down the precipitous streets of this little town are a number of churches worth looking at. Apart from the 18th-century **cathedral** and Church of **San Domenico**, there is the Church of **Santa Caterina** and the even more interesting Church of the Cappuccini dedicated to **Sant'Antonio**.

The ***SS109*** *wends its way north to Rogliano, becoming the* ***SS19*** *at Soveria Mannelli after 27km (16½ miles).*

Rogliano, Calabria

9 A town has existed on this site since before the Romans ever came here. An earthquake destroyed the medieval town in 1638 so that much of what survives today dates from the later 17th century. The Church of **San Giorgio**, built from the local tufa stone and dating from 1544, has a mixed interior with items from various periods. It was restored in 1924. Other churches include the **Cappuccini** with a good wooden altar, and the Church of **Santa Maria delle Grazie** with a wonderful inlaid and gilded wooden ceiling. Wooden artefacts in the churches seem to be a speciality of this town – you will see more in the little **Chiesetta dell'Annunziata**.

Continue north on the ***SS19*** *to Cosenza.*

Cosenza – Morano Calabro 81 (50)
Morano Calabro – Spezzano Albanese 42 (26)
Spezzano Albanese – San Demetrio Corone 37 (23)
San Demetrio Corone – Rossano 41 (25)
Rossano – Santa Severina 120 (75)
Santa Severina – San Giovanni in Fiore 34 (21)
San Giovanni in Fiore – Tiriolo 96 (60)
Tiriolo – Nicastro 28 (17)
Nicastro – Rogliano 59 (37)
Rogliano – Cosenza 18 (11)

Red-roofed Rogliano in its green setting is largely 17th-century

4/5 days – 710km (442 miles)

FORGOTTEN BASILICATA

'Real' food, like these cheeses on sale near Rivello, can still be tasted in remote Basilicata

Matera • Metaponto • Pisticci • Maratea Rivello • Melfi • Venosa • Pietrapertosa Tricárico • Miglionico • Matera

The towns of this region are the least discovered in southern Italy. The countryside is possibly also the most unspoilt in the south, perhaps because it is so unyielding and so impenetrable. Here the towns are cut off from the rest of the world and nowhere in Italy do you find anything quite like them. From the troglodytic old city of Matera – an astonishing labyrinth of subterranean houses adjacent to the newer centre – to the great castle of Melfi, the Norman tombs at Venosa and the Greek-looking, whitewashed town of Pisticci, Basilicata is a world all on its own.

ℹ Viti de Marco 9, Matera

Leave Matera going south on the main road to Ferrandina, the ***SS7****, and after 12km (7½ miles) branch left on the* ***SS380*** *(which, after about 12km/7½ miles becomes the* ***SS175****) and continue for 38km (23½ miles) to Metaponto*

Metaponto, Basilicata

1 The countryside on the way to Metaponto has a North African look. The eucalyptus and the maritime pines lining the route are strangely out of place. The ancient city of *Metapontum* was founded in the 7th century BC by Greek colonists and today is one of the better known sites of Magna Graecia (the Greek colonies in southern Italy). By contrast, the modern town is no more than a small resort by the sea. Beaches, hotels and restaurants make it a good place to stay and a convenient base from which to explore the ruins of the old city. Much of the latter survives including the remains of four large **temples**, a **theatre**, a **forum** and a **Roman camp**. *Metapontum* is famous for having been the town in which the mathematician and philosopher Pythagoras chose to live (at the end of the 6th century BC). He taught here and you can still see the 15 surviving columns (out of a total of 30 plus) of the **Tavole Palatine**, once his home and school, later transformed into the **Temple of Hera**. The **antiquarium** on the site provides welcome relief in its cool dark rooms from the hot sun.

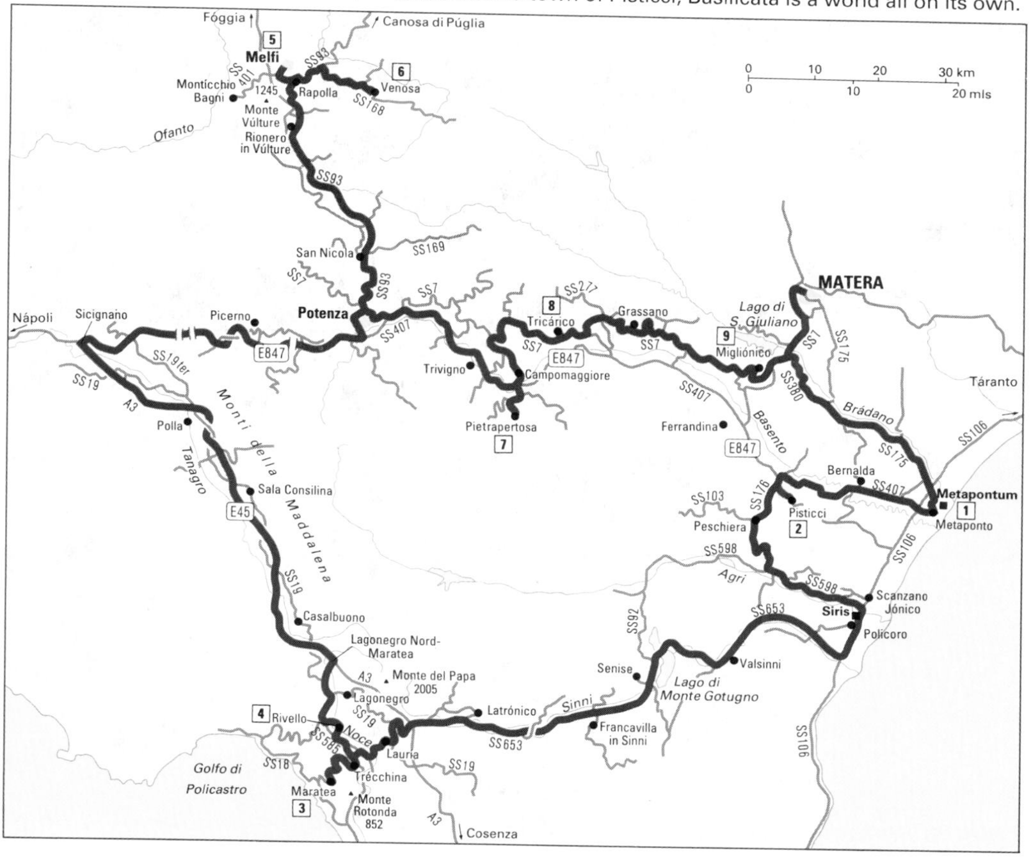

The glory that was Greece: the Temple of Hera at Metapontum

FOR HISTORY BUFFS

1 At **Policoro**, about 19km (12 miles) south of Metaponto on the **SS106**, are the remains of the ancient colony of ***Siris-Heradeia***. It has the remains of living quarters and a Temple of Demeter. An outstanding museum of antiquities from the area – **Museo Nazionale della Siritide** – contains sculpture, metalware and some fine Greek painted pottery.

SPECIAL TO . . .

Matera holds its **Festa della Bruna** on 2 July, an event linked to the fertility of the earth and an abundant harvest. It involves a procession in which a large wagon containing the Madonna is dragged around the town by eight mules. Although the wagon, constructed by the same family each year, takes a laborious four months to complete, it is destroyed during the procession each year (as a part of the rite and not the work of vandals), everybody hoping to grab a piece of it as a relic. This is a strange festival in which the whole town takes part.

BACK TO NATURE

Basilicata is predominantly a mountainous region. The most peculiar rock formations found in the area are the *calanchi* around Pisticci, strange dry hillocks of rock.

4 Other than that there is the **Sirino Range**, the highest peak of which is Monte Papa (Mount Papa) 2,005m (6,578 feet), visible as you leave Rivello and join the **A3**. It is densely wooded with hazelnut, oak, chestnut, alder and beech and it harbours forest birds, foxes and wolves.

Look out for the ancient fertility statues.

*From Metaponto, take the **SS407** west, turning left on to the **SS176** after about 22km (14 miles). A further 2km (1 mile) along this road, a minor road leads off to Pisticci.*

Pisticci, Basilicata

2 The country town of Pisticci, built on an incline, has a colourful daily market. Go in the morning, because that is when you will see the women of the town shopping in their traditional costumes, with huge wide skirts and strange headgear. The streets are lined with houses, linked together with whitewashed walls and dusty brown terracotta roofs. The **Chiesa Madre**, the parish church (1542), was built on the ruins of a 13th-century building and there is also a ruined medieval **castle**.

*From Pisticci, return to and take the **SS176** going south. Turn left at the junction with the **SS103** and continue for about 19km (12 miles) until you hit the **SS598**. Go east along this for about 16km (10 miles) until you reach the coastal **SS106**. Follow this for about 9km (6 miles), going south, until you reach the **SS653**. This latter goes inland again – follow it for about 85km (53 miles) until you reach the autostrada **A3**. Go under this and turn left on to the **SS19**. After 5km (3 miles), turn right and follow the country road through Lauria to the **SS585**. Turn right on to this and very shortly left on to the minor road which leads, via Trécchina, to Maratea.*

Maratea, Basilicata

3 This is perhaps the best known part of Basilicata. The coastline is unspoilt and is studded with little rocky coves where you can swim in complete privacy. The Marina di Maratea and the old port have a number of restaurants and little hotels. The old town, climbing up a hill, is still mostly intact. You can visit the picturesque **medieval quarter** with its loggias and small doorways. Maratea is the kind of place to explore on your own, discovering the odd café for a quick drink or cappuccino. you can also visit the 17th-century former **Convento di San Francesco** with its two-storeyed cloister of pointed arches. On a peak just above Maratea you cannot fail to notice the enormous **statue of the Redeemer** – 22m (72 feet) high.

[i] Piazza del Gesù 40

*From Maratea, retrace the route of the **SS585**. Turn left and after a short distance you come to the minor road off to Rivello.*

Rivello, Basilicata

4 This must be one of the prettiest towns in southern Italy. It straddles the spine of two hills and, because of its shape, is thought to look like a dragon. Rivello coils itself around the top of the hill, each little street thick with outside staircases and small galleries and overhung with wrought-iron balconies. At each end of the town is a – mainly Byzantine – church. **Santa Barbara** has a very pretty apse decorated with tiny hanging arches, while **San Nicola dei Greci** seems more like a fortress than anything else. The lovely, frescoed 15th-century **Convento dei Minori** has a wooden choir carved by local monks, and depicting various trades.

*Take the **SS585** to its junction with the autostrada **A3**, then follow the latter for about 70km (44 miles) until you hit the autostrada going east to Potenza from the Sicignano junction. At Potenza, go north on the **SS93** for about 50km (31 miles) towards Melfi before branching off on the **SS303** for the final 6km (4 miles) of the journey.*

Melfi, Basilicata

5 Melfi is crammed with the remains of its illustrious past, in particular those from the Norman and Hohenstaufen periods. You can see part of the old perimeter wall, the Norman **castle** with its eight towers, each one different (the castle contains a museum of antiquities), and the **cathedral** of 1155, with its Norman Sicilian **belltower**. The old city gate, the **Porta Venosina**, is Norman though Frederick II (Hohenstaufen) tampered with it. A walk around the town would include a handful of little churches including the very much restored 17th-century San Lorenzo.

*Return via the **SS303** to the **SS93** at Rapolla. Turn left and proceed for about 8km (5 miles) before turning right on to the **SS168** for Venosa.*

Venosa, Basilicata

6 Venosa belongs, visually, more to the nearby region of Puglia than to Basilicata. As in Melfi, you can trace the town's history in the streets, but here the various periods are more easily distinguishable. It was particularly favoured by the Romans, whose *Via Appia* passed through it, and it was the birthplace of the poet Horace. Others who came here include Byzantines, Saracens, Normans, Hohenstaufens, Angevins and the Spanish. The **castle** dates from 1470 while the **cathedral**, which shows Catalan influence, is early 16th-century. Wander around the medieval centre with its huge old paving slabs and carved doorways. Behind the Church of **San Rocco** you can see the even older remains of **Roman houses and baths**, while further on appear some fragments of an **early Christian baptistery** and a **Roman amphitheatre**. Perhaps the most interesting of all is the Abbey of **La Trinità**. Begun around 1050, it is in three parts, having an old church, an abbey and a later (1135), but unfinished, 'new' church. It became the final resting place of the five De Hauteville brothers who were responsible for conquering southern Italy for the Normans (while William the Conqueror was doing the same to England).

*Return to the **SS93** and thence to Potenza. Then take the **SS407** going east for about 30km (19 miles), branching inland for about 11km (7 miles) to Pietrapertosa.*

Pietrapertosa, Basilicata

7 This rock town, poised way above deep surrounding valleys, is, at 1,088m (3,570 feet), the highest town in Basilicata. The road climbs up to it in a series of hair-raising bends. It is surrounded by strange irregular rock formations with names like Áquila Reale (Golden Eagle), Rocca Saracena (Saracen's Rock) and Grande Madre (Big Mother). Like many of the other towns of the region, Pietrapertosa is full of little wrought-iron balconies and tiny houses with carved doorways of great antiquity. If you do not want to visit the town's several little churches, you can just sit on a wall and gaze out over the surrounding hills and the woods. However, the Church of the **Minori Osservanti** is well worth a visit with its 15th- and 16th-century art, and also **San Cataldo**, which has a fine 16th-century altarpiece and carved wooden choir.

*Return towards the **SS407**. This time pass under it and take the minor road through Campomaggiore to the **SS7**. Turn right and drive to Tricárico.*

Tricárico, Basilicata

8 Tricárico has a strange Arab quarter, the **Rabatana**, which even today is more reminiscent of Morocco than the Italian mainland. You enter it via the **Porta Saracena** (Saracen Gate). The Rabatana is full of chickens running about and old women in black sitting in doorways. On the whole, however, Tricárico is a town of medieval houses with ancient sculpted doorways and old balconies. Many of these houses have the evil eye symbol embedded into their stonework. The **cathedral** is 11th-century, though much restored, and there is a variety of other churches, notably **Sant'Antonio** with its frescoed cloister. Although much of the old centre is dilapidated, Tricárico has an air of faded grandeur, much of it owed to the wealthy Carafa family.

*From Tricárico, take the **SS7** for about 42km (26 miles) to Miglionico.*

Miglionico, Basilicata

9 Miglionico is still a fortified town, its Norman defences and 11th-century castle partially intact. The **castle** dominates the town and was the scene of a notorious plot late in the 15th century, in which the local barons conspired to overthrow the king, Ferdinand of Aragon. It failed and the castle acquired the nickname 'Malconsiglio' – 'bad counsel'. If you are short of time, go straight to the Church of **San Francesco** and see the **altarpiece** painted by Cima di Conegliano, an important early 16th-century Venetian painter much influenced by Bellini. It has 18 sections and is Basilicata's most important painting.

*From Miglionico it is only about 22km (14 miles) back to Matera via the **SS7**.*

Matera – Metaponto 50 (31)
Metaponto – Pisticci 31 (19)
Pisticci – Maratea 169 (105)
Maratea – Rivello 24 (15)
Rivello – Melfi 192 (120)
Melfi – Venosa 25 (16)
Venosa – Pietrapertosa 110 (68)
Pietrapertosa – Tricárico 45 (28)
Tricárico – Miglionico 42 (26)
Miglionico – Matera 22 (14)

Rivello dominates the Noce valley

RECOMMENDED WALKS

5 Just south of Melfi, around the base of the extinct volcano, Monte Vúlture, are some good walks that follow the paths used by brigands in the past. However, there is nothing to fear today: the paths are quite safe, and the only thing that will cross your path will be wild game and maybe shepherds and their flocks. Walks in this area take you around the beautiful **Laghi** (Lakes) **di Monticchio**. You can also use horses on the longer routes and local people sometimes act as guides.

SCENIC ROUTES

Monte Biagio, way above Maratea, affords magnificent views of the Gulf of Policastro. The drive to the top of the mountain is worth every crippling hairpin bend. Bagni, on the western slopes of Monte Vúlture, gives you some stunning views of the extinct volcano.

FOR CHILDREN

In a variety of places you can stay on a farm in self-contained accommodation. Most have farmyard animals, some have swimming pools. Ask the tourist office for the *Guide to Rural Hospitality* (*Guida dell'Ospitalità Rurale*) for details of locations.

3/4 days – 314km (196 miles)

ANCIENT PUGLIA

Bari • Bitonto • Molfetta • Trani • Barletta
Canosa di Puglia • Minervino Murge
Castel del Monte • Ruvo di Puglia • Alberobello
Locorotondo • Monopoli • Polignano a Mare • Bari

From towns with hefty, solid Norman cathedrals and castles, to villages with curious, prehistoric-looking, conical-roofed houses and farmsteads, central Puglia is packed with the evidence of a rich and diverse past. The gently rolling fertile countryside is criss-crossed with high stone walls enclosing ancient groves of gnarled olive trees. From one end of Puglia to the other, these are the region's most common sight. Bari is one of the biggest cities in Puglia, and the most cosmopolitan spot on this tour with a large variety of shops and restaurants as well as a medieval centre and a busy port.

i Piazza Aldo Moro 33a, Bari

*Bitonto is about 16km (10 miles) from Bari. Take the **SS96** from the city centre, then branch along the **SS98**.*

Bitonto, Puglia

1 Right in the centre of Bitonto is the fine Puglian Romanesque 13th-century **cathedral**. Its best features are the women's gallery, the carvings of animals on the entrance portals, and the pulpit with its primitive bas-relief portraits of Emperor Frederick II and Isabella of England. Go down into the crypt and see the lovely column supports there. Other interesting churches are **San Francesco** with its late 13th-century façade, and the Church of the **Purgatorio** which has a sculptured relief of human skeletons just above the main entrance portal. Most of the centre of town is either Renaissance or baroque. See in particular the **Palazzo Sylos-Labini** and its Renaissance courtyard.

*From Bitonto, travel north to the **A14**. Take the autostrada northwest 11km (7 miles) until the Molfetta exit.*

BACK TO NATURE

4 The **Saline di Margherita** is a large area of saltpans and wetlands just along the coast from the town of Margherita (a few kilometres west of Barletta). Birds such as black-winged stilts, Kentish plovers, pratincoles and short-toed larks breed in the area, and migrant waders, including curlew sandpipers, spotted redshanks, and wood sandpipers, pass through on passage.

Molfetta's domed 'old cathedral' gazes benignly over the harbour

Molfetta, Puglia

2 Molfetta is an active fishing port – its fleet is one of the larger ones on the Adriatic. Predominantly medieval, it has a lovely 12th- to 13th-century cathedral, the **Duomo Vecchio**, dominated by three domes – a Byzantine feature. There is also the **Duomo Nuovo** (new cathedral), though in this case 'new' means late 18th-century. This building has a baroque façade. The town has two museums. The **Archaeological Museum** contains the finds, including some Hellenistic ceramics, from local excavations. The **Museo Diocesano** (Diocesan Museum) is housed in the bishop's palace.

*Take the coastal road **SS16** going northwest via Bisceglie to Trani, about 17km (11 miles).*

Trani, Puglia

3 Trani has always been an important port. Trade with the Orient in the 11th century drew into its orbit merchants from Genoa, Pisa and Amalfi and also created a large Jewish community. Still a large and prosperous port, it is full of little restaurants serving seafood. The **cathedral**, which sits in an open-ended piazza facing the sea, is a fine building. Puglian Romanesque in style, it contains the remains of two other, earlier, structures on the same site. The oldest of these was an early Christian **catacomb** which you can still see with its marble columns and frescos: above that, though below the existing nave, are the remains of **Santa Maria**, the earlier Byzantine cathedral. The most noteworthy element of the present building is the pair of 12th-century bronze doors by a local master. Two other buildings that should not be missed are the Church of the **Ognissanti**, built by the Knights Templar as a hospice and, near the harbour, the **Palazzo Caccetta**, a 15th-century palace in the Gothic style – unusual in Puglia.

i Corso Cavour 140

*Continue up the coast on the **SS16** to Barletta, 13km (8 miles).*

Barletta, Puglia

4 In Barletta is the largest known bronze statue in existence. Called the **Colosso**, it is 5m (15 feet) high and represents a Roman emperor, possibly Valentinian, who died in AD375. You can see it on its pedestal at the end of the Corso Vittorio Emanuele. In the Middle Ages Barletta was an important and prosperous port. Like Trani it still retains much of its prosperity and has a pretty, if somewhat dilapidated medieval centre. As usual, the cathedral is the town's most interesting building. Built in the 12th century, the **Duomo** has a lovely rose window and there is an inscription above the left entrance portal which records how the English king Richard Coeur de Lion was involved in its construction (he came here on his way to the Crusades). You must visit the 13th-century Church of **San Sepolcro**, the design of which recalls the Church of the

Conical-roofed trulli, *the traditional houses of Puglia*

Holy Sepulchre in Jerusalem, and the former convent building of **San Domenico** which now houses the **Museo Civico** (Civic Museum) and picture gallery. The **Castello** (castle) is a massive structure, originally built by Emperor Frederick II and enlarged by Charles of Anjou.

i Via Gabbiani 4

*The **SS93** branches inland from Barletta and goes to Canosa di Puglia, about 22km (14 miles).*

Canosa di Puglia, Puglia

5 Standing in the Tavoliere Plain, this town was an important Roman centre, called *Canusium*. Remains of Roman baths, amphitheatres and basilicas can be seen, and there is a Roman bridge over the Ofanto river which only survives because its arches were rebuilt in the Middle Ages. There are two later items of interest in the town's Romanesque **cathedral**: the marble 11th-century bishop's throne, which rests on the backs of two elephants, and the Tomb of Bohemund, Prince of Antioch, who was the son of Robert Guiscard and who died in 1111. The tomb's doors were made from a single slab of bronze. Other relics of the town's past are kept in the **Museo Civico** (Civic Museum).

*From Canosa di Puglia, take the **SS98** towards Ándria, turning off right after 7km (4 miles) on the **SS97** to Minervino Murge, a further 12km (7 miles).*

SPECIAL TO . . .

The district around Bari has a particularly fine brand of **olive oil**. If the label says it comes from Bitonto in particular, then buy it.

Bari holds its **Festa di San Nicola** (Feast of St Nicholas) on 7 May. Recalling the arrival in Bari of the bones of the saint, brought from the Far East by sailors in 1087, an antique icon of the saint is carried in procession to the Basilica of St Nicholas. The following day the saint's statue is mounted on a boat which leads a water-borne procession.

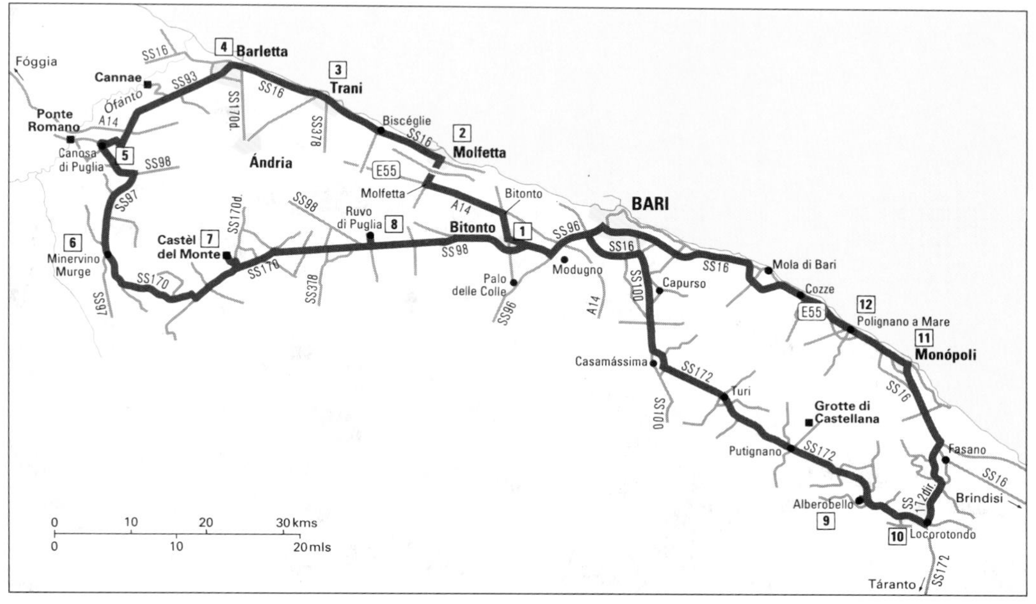

FOR HISTORY BUFFS

4 The site of *Cannae*, where Hannibal gained his last great victory over the Romans, lies between Canosa di Puglia and Barletta on the Ofanto river. The remains of a huge necropolis can be seen here and traces of the former city of *Cannae*. An Antiquarium houses finds from the site. On a hill above is the Cittadella (citadel) which has yielded mainly medieval remains.

SCENIC ROUTES

The most scenic parts of this tour are the following:

6 – the views from Minervino Murge to the surrounding countryside; here the landscape is most typically Apulian – a gently rolling, almost flat landscape;

10 – the views from Locorotondo across the *Trulli* Zone of the Itria Valley. Here it is easy to imagine yourself in a prehistoric landscape: the *trulli* (beehive-like buildings) which dot the countryside are the kind of houses that the long-ago ancestors of present-day Puglians might have lived in;

12 – the coastline from Polignano a Mare to Mola di Bari, going along the **SS16**. This is lovely unspoilt coastal scenery (though not suitable for swimming except from the rocks).

Minervino Murge, Puglia

6 Minervino Murge is known as the 'Balcony of Apulia' because of its wonderful position at the edge of the Murgia Alta, the rolling hills on Apulia's southern border. 'Minervo' derives from an ancient temple dedicated to the worship of Minerva on whose remains rises the present-day Church of the **Madonna del Crocifisso**. Apart from the church and the panoramas of the countryside, this little town has a 12th-century **castle**, a **Palazzo Comunale** built in local style and a Norman **cathedral**, re-embellished in the Renaissance.

*Take the **SS170** eastwards for 22km (13½ miles) until the **SS170dir** branches off to the left. Follow the latter for 1km (½ mile) to the turning for Castel del Monte on the left.*

Castel del Monte, Puglia

7 This huge isolated castle is one of the most impressive monuments surviving from the reign of Emperor Frederick II and is well worth a special excursion to visit it. With its eight Gothic corner towers, you can see it from miles away, crowning an isolated peak way above the surrounding countryside. It was built around 1240 and in plan is a perfect octagon – the number eight being the symbol of the crown. You can wander through huge rooms, eight on each floor, that were once decorated with reliefs in Greek marble, porphyry and precious stones, now mostly disappeared. The castle may have been used originally as a centre for astronomy as its proportions are supposed to relate to the movements of the planets. But it was also the very grim prison of Frederick II's grandsons, who were incarcerated here for 30 years. Notice the beautiful carved entrance portal and, among what is left of its decoration, the signs of classical, Gothic, Persian and Arabic influences.

*Return to the **SS170** and follow it eastwards. It joins the **SS98** 2km (1 mile) before Ruvo di Puglia.*

Ruvo di Puglia, Puglia

8 Ruvo di Puglia was a town celebrated in ancient times for its pottery. As long ago as the 5th century BC, its terracotta vases were highly sought after and some of these can be seen in the **Palazzo Jatta**. Here, too, is the magnificent red-figured Greek vase known as the 'Crater of Talos'. It is an important collection which you should not miss. Ruvo's **cathedral** is an important Puglian Romanesque building – one of the best in Puglia. Built in the 13th century, it has a richly decorated façade and a superb 16th-century rose window. In particular, notice the griffins surmounting the columns on either side of the main entrance. Around the sides of the building are little sculpted figures of ancient, pagan gods, which it is thought may have been copied from classical pottery.

*Return to Bari via the **SS98**. Skirt round the southern edge of the city on the **SS16** and turn right on to the **SS100**. Take the latter as far as Casamassima, about 15km (9 miles), then branch left along the **SS172** to Alberobello, about 35km (22 miles).*

Alberobello, Puglia

9 Alberobello is a very curious town. Clustered together in its centre is a collection of the prehistoric-looking local buildings called *trulli*. These small, circular, stone buildings with

Castel del Monte is one of the great medieval buildings of Europe

cone-shaped tiled roofs look a bit like upside-down ice-cream cornets. There is nothing quite like them in any other part of Italy. Once such houses were quite common in Mediterranean countries – the beehive-shaped prehistoric Sardinian *nuraghi* are not dissimilar – but in Puglia, for some reason, they are a living tradition. Wander through the narrow streets of the **Rione Monti** and **Aia Piccola** quarters of Alberobello, where most of the *trulli* (there are over 1,000) are whitewashed and still inhabited. Even the style of the Church of **Sant'Antonio** seems to have derived its looks from the *trulli*. Most of Alberobello is a national monument, so that what has survived of its strange appearance is in very good condition. One or two of the *trulli* are open to the public or have been turned into shops and restaurants.

*The **SS172** leads straight to Locorotondo.*

Locorotondo, Puglia

10 Locorotondo was laid out in concentric circles around the pinnacle of a low hill, and takes its name ('round place') from this plan. From the town there are wonderful views out over the Itria Valley in which you can see clumps of *trulli* scattered about – generally farmhouses and barns. In Locorotondo everything is covered with whitewash and gleams in the scorching Puglian summer sun. Small Greek-looking houses cluster around secret courtyards. There are geraniums in pots on the balconies, and the cobbled alleys and passages make this one of the more picturesque towns of Puglia. If you want to get out of the sun for a while, visit the churches of **San Giorgio** and **San Marco della Greca**, the former neo-classical, the latter a much earlier, possibly late Gothic, building.

*The **SS172dir** leads via Fasano to the **SS16**. From Fasano, take the **SS16** to Monopoli, about 12km (7½ miles).*

Monopoli, Puglia

11 Monopoli is the most beautiful port on this strip of the Adriatic coastline. In the older quarter, tall medieval houses are built right up to the quay, overlooking the port and the little brightly painted fishing boats. The old centre is full of churches and other buildings which bear the traces of Byzantine and Venetian invaders. There is a **castle**, a Romanesque **cathedral** of 1107, with an impressive baroque façade and belltower, and the Church of **San Domenico**, perhaps the most magnificent building in the town. The Renaissance façade of San Domenico is split into three parts by columns and decorated with statues, and there is a fine rose window. At various points beneath Monopoli, there are underground chambers and places of worship. One such is the **Chiesa-Grotta**, a natural cave, decorated in Byzantine times.

From Monopoli, take the coast road northwest to Polignano a Mare, about 8km (5 miles).

Portal of Ruvo di Puglia's fine Puglian Romanesque cathedral

Polignano a Mare, Puglia

12 Polignano a Mare is a delightful old city with little alleyways and flights of stepss. In the old quarter is the **parish church** dedicated to Our Lady of the Assumption. Although Romanesque in style, it was added to during the Renaissance period. Ask to see the painting by the 15th-century Venetian artists Vivarini, in the sacristy. Just outside town are the **Grotte Palazzese** (Palazzese Caves), set into the cliffsides. These are two huge sea caves, reached by climbing down precarious steps set into the rock just below the town.

*The **SS16** leads back to Bari.*

Bari – Bitonto 16 (10)
Bitonto –Molfetta 19 (12)
Molfetta – Trani 17 (11)
Trani – Barletta 13 (8)
Barletta – Canosa di Puglia 22 (14)
Canosa di Puglia – Minervino Murge 19 (11)
Minervino Murge – Castel del Monte 24 (15)
Castel del Monte – Ruvo di Puglia 21 (13)
Ruvo di Puglia – Alberobello 87 (54)
Alberobello – Locorotondo 9 (6)
Locorotondo – Monopoli 25 (16)
Monopoli – Polignano a Mare 8 (5)
Polignano a Mare – Bari 34 (21)

RECOMMENDED WALKS

7 On a visit to the **Castel del Monte**, walk some way from the castle to appreciate the full impact of this extraordinary building. All around is a pretty, agricultural and virtually empty landscape, called the Tavoliere, splendid for walks and also for picnics.

FOR CHILDREN

Puglia is really not an area to bring children. However, they might enjoy looking into the *trulli* – built, it seems, more for hobbtis than for humans. Everything in these igloo-like structures is in miniature. In both Alberobello and Locorotondo, one or two of them are open to the public.

At Fasano, a developing holiday centre about 10km (6 miles) from both Alberobello and Locorotondo, there is a zoo/safari park, where animals of the African plains, such as giraffes, can be seen in the rough, dry terrain not far removed from their natural habitat.

3 days – 352km (219 miles)

THE HEEL OF ITALY

Brindisi • Ostuni • Mesagne • Grottaglie • Oria Lecce • Otranto • Gallipoli • Manduria • Brindisi

Scattered all over southern Puglia are monuments that seem more Greek than Italian, while others look as though they should be in northern Europe rather than in the hot sunny Puglian countryside. Greeks, Arabs, Normans – these were just some of the inhabitants of Puglia in the past. And from baroque Lecce, Puglia's architectural gem, to Grottaglie with its ceramic workshops, and to the busy coastal port of Brindisi, stepping-stone to Greece and North Africa, southern Puglia's attractions are eccentric and varied.

FOR HISTORY BUFFS

6 Right down on the very tip of the Salentine Peninsula, at Patu, near Leuca (reach it from Otranto or Gallipoli), is the so-called **Centopietre** (Hundred Stones). This is a mysterious small building made of flat stone slabs with a pitched roof. It has two aisles divided by columns, and may be a Messapian (local pre-Greek civilisation) temple ... or some think its is medieval.

[i] Via C Colombo 88, Brindisi

*From Brindisi, the **SS16** leads via San Vito dei Normanni to Ostuni, 35km (22 miles).*

Ostuni, Puglia

1 Ostuni is built on three hills about 200m (600 feet) above sea-level. The oldest part of the town, also the highest, is the most interesting, dominated by the huge Gothic **cathedral**. This building, which seems more Spanish than anything else, has three lovely rose windows in its façade. Near by is the **Palazzo Vescovile** (Bishop's Palace), the two parts of which, on two sides of the square in

Details of carving to be seen in Ostuni's Piazza Libertà

which it stands, are connected by a little honey-coloured stone bridge. Further down the hill is the baroque Church of **Santa Maria Maddalena**, topped by a patterned majolica cupola. All around these three buildings, and leading down to the huge dusty Piazza Libertà in the 19th-century part of the town, are little alleys burrowing through the gleaming whitewashed buildings of the old quarter.

[i] Via Continelli 47

*Take the **SS16** back to San Vito, where you should turn on to the **SS605** to Mesagne, about 28km (17 miles) in total.*

Mesagne, Puglia

2 Mesagne sits in the middle of the Tavoliere di Lecce, a large, flat plain heavily cultivated with figs, olives and vineyards. Nowadays, Mesagne prospers from the fertility of the surrounding landscape and its **market** should be one of the stopping points on this itinerary. The **castle** is worth taking an hour or two to look at. Built originally in 1062 by the Norman adventurer Robert Guiscard, various attackers destroyed it over the years and the last time it was rebuilt was in the 17th century. It is a spectacular construction with a rather lovely Renaissance loggia which runs along its north and east sides. The parish church, the **Chiesa Madre**, is baroque and the Church of **Sant'Anna** is rococo; both are worth a visit – in fact the latter is the best example of its style in the area.

*Join the **SS7** on the north edge of town which leads west to Grottaglie, about 38km (24 miles).*

Grottaglie, Puglia

3 This town is one of the most renowned centres for **ceramics** in southern Italy. Many of the items for

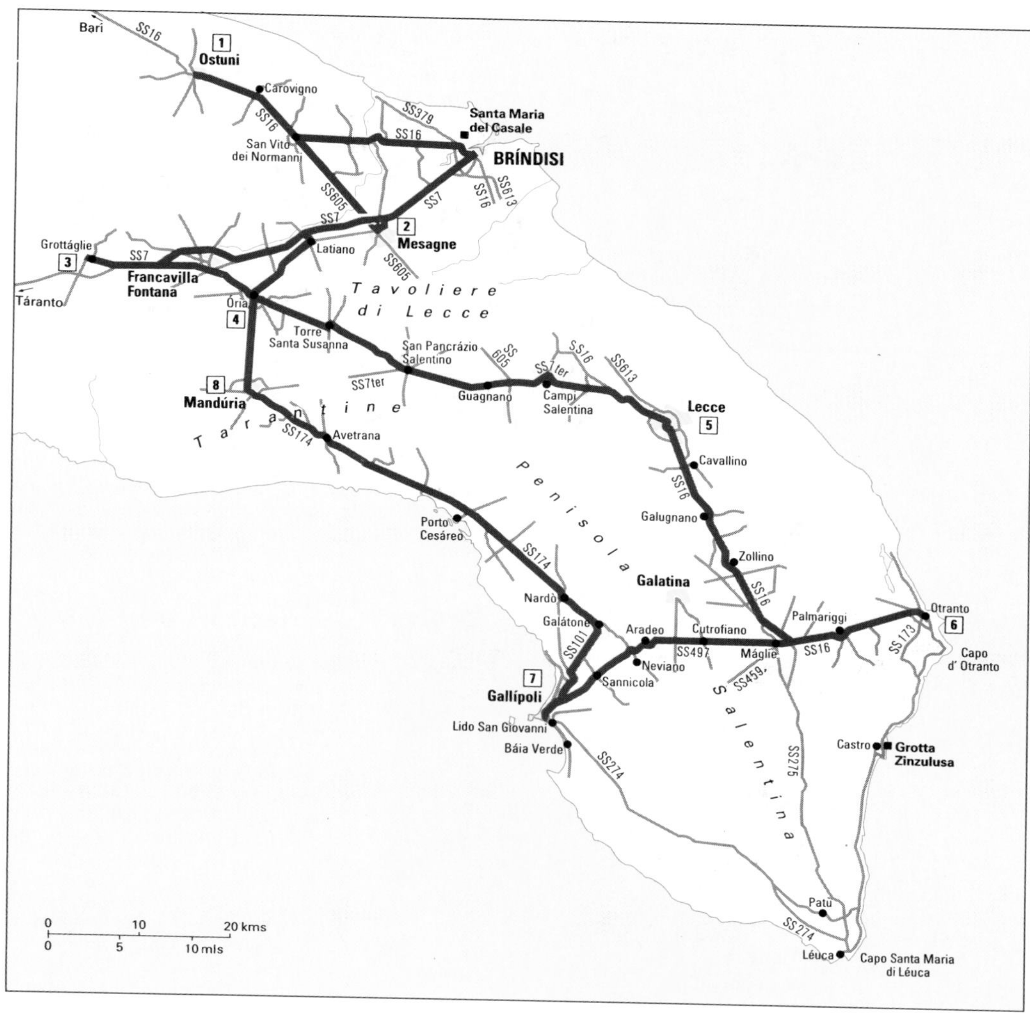

sale are traditional and well-tried designs, long abandoned by more up-to-date craftsmen elsewhere. The ceramicists' quarters lie behind the massive castle. Here you can still see people making things in the traditional-always and their wares line practically every flat surface in sight – including roofs. This is an excellent – and inexpensive – place to buy ceramics. You can visit the Church of the **Carmine** which has a traditional **Presepio** (Christmas crib) of 1530. The early 12th-century **Chiesa Matrice** is a very decorative building. Its Chapel of the Rosary is topped by a cupola decorated with local coloured tiles, and the church also has an exotic Puglian Romanesque entrance portal.

*Return along the **SS7** branching off to Francavilla Fontana, about 14km (8½ miles), at which head towards Oria, only about 6km (3½ miles) – follow the signs in the south of the town.*

Oria, Puglia

4 Oria is yet another Puglian town dominated by a castle built by Emperor Frederick II. Although over the years it has been altered and enlarged, it still retains its basic triangular shape. In its vaulted hall is a small museum. Not far away is the **Cripta dei Santi Crisante e Daria**, a small subterranean basilica dating from the 9th century topped by a series of shallow domes and decorated with frescos. Oria's **cathedral** was rebuilt in the 18th century following an earthquake; its most noteworthy element is its ceramic covered dome. In the old town, with its winding streets and whitewashed houses, search out the Jewish quarter – the **Giudecca** – which is still very much as it was in the Middle Ages when a large community of Jews lived here.

The Roman amphitheatre in Lecce, known to the Romans as Lupiae

*From Oria, continue along the country road for about 20km (12 miles), via Torre Santa Susanna, to the **SS7ter** which runs to Lecce, about 50km (31 miles), joining and becoming the **SS16** shortly before the town.*

Lecce, Puglia

5 Lecce is to southern Italy what Florence is to central Italy. The city is an architectural gem and is filled with magnificently decorated, ebullient, baroque (mostly late 16th- and early 17th-century) buildings built from a soft, golden sandstone called 'Pietra di Lecce'. The most notable architects were Antonio and Giuseppe Zimbalo who, between them, were responsible for most of the **Basilica di Santa Croce**, begun in 1549. In particular, notice the more florid parts of the façade and the rose

SPECIAL TO . . .

The western coast of the Salentine Peninsula, that is, between Gallipoli and Capo Santa Maria di Leuca, has some of Italy's best beaches. Gallipoli itself has good places for bathing, and there are other places at nearby Lido San Giovanni and Baia Verde, both within 10km (6 miles) of Gallipoli.

BACK TO NATURE

Wooded and shrub-covered hillsides in southern Italy are favoured by several species of birds of prey. They nest in the trees and use thermals generated off the land to gain lift. Species such as short-toed eagle, buzzard, sparrowhawk and goshawk are widespread and there is always a chance of seeing a golden eagle or Bonelli's eagle. Regrettably, birds of prey are much persecuted by Italian 'sportsmen'.

RECOMMENDED WALKS

6 The Salentine Peninsula – the southernmost part of the Italian mainland – is good for walks, in particular just to the south of Otranto (Capo d'Otranto). The coastline leading to Otranto is fairly rugged but beautiful, with caves and places to swim.

SCENIC ROUTES

The approach road (either the **SS605**, the **SS16** or the narrow country road that leads from the coast) to Ostuni is scenically outstanding, principally for the stunning views to the town itself. Rising on to a little hill and bleached white in the sun, it looks more Greek than Italian.

window. Next door, the **Palazzo del Governo** was also designed by Giuseppe Zimbalo ('Zingarello'), as was the **Duomo** (cathedral) in Piazza del Duomo. Not everything is baroque in Lecce. In Piazza Sant'Oronzio are the remains of a Roman **amphitheatre** which at one time could probably seat about 25,000 people, and a Roman column topped by a statue of St Oronsius. There is also a lovely example of Puglian Romanesque architecture in the Church of **Santi Nicolò e Cataldo**. Lecce is a busy, thriving town with good ceramic shops selling the more expensive end of Grottaglie's range of wares. There are antique shops, restaurants and an indoor market selling local produce.

i Via Monte San Michele 20

Take the ***SS16*** *south as far as Maglie, about 29km (18 miles). From the road bypassing Maglie, branch to the left along the* ***SS16*** *to Otranto, about 19km (12 miles).*

You can enjoy fresh seafood in the little port of Gallipoli

Otranto, Puglia

6 In the 11th century this little town was one of the leading Crusader ports. Nowadays it is better known as a port for ferries going to Greece. However, Otranto does have a good **cathedral** with one of the most stunning rose windows in Puglia. Founded by the Normans in 1080, it was added to and embellished over the years. This is the only medieval building in southern Italy to have preserved its entire original **mosaic floor**. There are scenes from the scriptures, depictions of animals and mythological subjects. In the oldest part of Otranto is the small Church of **San Pietro**, a delightful Byzantine building which may have been the town's old cathedral. There is also a **castle** here, built by Ferdinand of Aragon at the end of the 15th century. Inside you can see the remains of Roman brickwork and some very early medieval masonry.

i Lungomare Kennedy

Retrace the route to Maglie, then continue on the ***SS497*** *as far as Neviano, about 17km (11 miles), then follow the signs for Gallipoli.*

Gallipoli, Puglia

7 Gallipoli is a remote place, on an island just off the west coast of the Salentine Peninsula. The oldest part of the town, with its narrow little streets, is joined to the mainland by a causeway. On the edge of it, and dominating it, is the **Castello**, the oldest part of which is Byzantine. There is also an elaborate baroque **cathedral** of 1630. The interior is sprinkled with works by local artists – see in particular the *Madonna with Sant'Orontius* by Giovanni Coppola. If it is open, go into the Church of the **Purità** and see the richly decorated ceramic paving tiles of 18th-century majolica.

From Gallipoli, take the ***SS101*** *to Galatone, turning left on to the* ***SS174*** *proceeding northwards via Nardo to Manduria, a further 47km (29 miles).*

Manduria, Puglia

8 Manduria was an important centre of the local Messapian civilisation which long predated the coming of the Greek colonists to the area. The Messapians here fiercely opposed the Greeks, and the ruins of their ancient settlement can be seen to the north of the 'new' town. There is a **necropolis** and a stretch of ancient **city walls**. The oldest of the latter (there are three sets of walls concentrically sited around what was the old city) date from the 5th century BC and the latest from about the 3rd century BC. Carefully cut blocks of stone, a strange **triple gate** and 2,000 rock-cut tombs survive. In the middle of the excavations is the famous **Pozzo di Plinio** (Well of Pliny – so called because Pliny himself mentions it), in which the water remains at a constant level however much you draw out of it. The most interesting part of the town itself is the **Jewish quarter**, the confines of which are marked by three large tufa arches. The houses here have no windows. See also the impressive 1719 **Palazzo Imperiale**, in Piazza Garibaldi.

From Manduria, go across country to Oria, about 11km (7 miles), then from there to the ***SS7*** *via Latiano, also about 11km (7 miles), then follow the* ***SS7*** *to Brindisi, about 21km (13 miles).*

Brindisi – Ostuni 35 (22)
Ostuni – Mesagne 28 (17)
Mesagne – Grottaglie 38 (24)
Grottaglie – Oria 20 (12)
Oria – Lecce 50 (31)
Lecce – Otranto 48 (30)
Otranto – Gallipoli 30 (19)
Gallipoli – Manduria 60 (37)
Manduria – Brindisi 43 (27)

FOR CHILDREN

If you can make it to Ostuni for **La Cavalcata di Sant'Oronzo** (St Oronzo's Cavalcade) – check with the local tourist office for dates – the children will be good for the rest of the trip. Horses and riders trundle through the streets colourfully dressed in Saracen attire – both animals and riders decked out in embroidered cloth and plumes.

3 days – 366km (228 miles)

THE GARGANO PENINSULA

Its ruined 15th-century castle dominates Monte Sant'Angelo

Foggia • Manfredonia • San Giovanni Rotondo Monte Sant'Angelo • Vieste • San Severo Lucera • Tróia • Bovino • Foggia

While most of Puglia is relatively flat, the Gargano Peninsula, a rocky, partially wooded outcrop, constitutes what is possibly the only really scenic stretch of Adriatic coastline since Venice. It is the spur of Italy's boot which rises unexpectedly from the sea, an area of saints and mystic legends. It has a handful of sanctuaries to which devoted pilgrims flock, very much as they have always done. All the towns on this tour, except Foggia, are small historic centres, dominated as usual by an ancient cathedral or castle. Foggia was bombed in World War II and, while it is still a lively and important city, its old monuments have been replaced by modern buildings.

[i] Via Senatore E Perrone 17, Foggia

From Foggia, take the ***SS89*** *to Manfredonia, about 39km (24 miles).*

Manfredonia, Puglia

1 This lively port takes its name from Manfred, the son of Emperor Frederick II and King of Sicily and Naples. Not much is left from that period in the 13th century, apart from the hefty remains of Manfred's **castle**, which now houses the **Museo Archeologico del Gargano** (National Archaeological Museum of Gargano), displaying artefacts from the remains of nearby ancient *Sipontum*. There is an undistinguished **cathedral**, built in 1680. More interesting is the Church of **San Domenico** with its Gothic doorway flanked by two stone lions and, inside, 14th-century frescos. Manfredonia is a base for ferries to the **Tremiti Islands** on the other side of the Gargano Peninsula. These tiny resorts are wonderful places to swim and sunbathe and consequently are extremely popular.

[i] Corso Manfredi 26

From Manfredonia, follow the signs inland to San Giovanni Rotondo, about 23km (14 miles).

San Giovanni Rotondo, Puglia

2 The little town of San Giovanni Rotondo drifts down the side of **Monte Calvo** (Mount Calvo) and is one of the principal pilgrimage centres of Italy. Here lived Padre Pio da Pietralcina, a 20th-century miracle-worker who, like St Francis, received the *stigmata* – the wounds of Christ on his hands and feet and in his side. This modern saint (1887–1969) is buried in the newish church near the 16th-century **Convent of Santa**

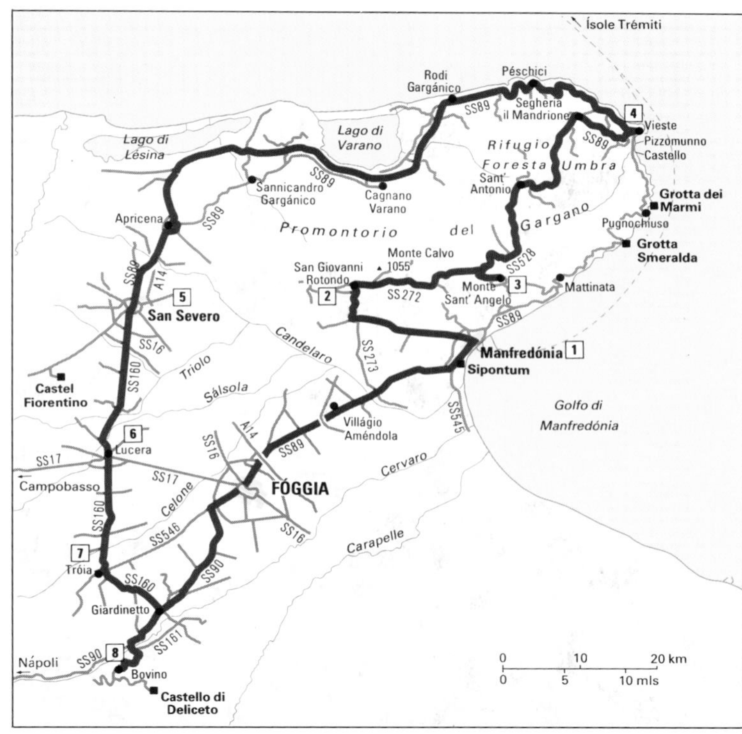

FOR HISTORY BUFFS

1 Outside **Manfredonia** (about 2km/1 mile to the south) are the remains of ancient *Sipontum*, abandoned in the Middle Ages because of malaria. Hannibal conquered it in the 3rd century BC, only to lose it to the Romans. There is a **museum** here as well as the lovely **Santa Maria Siponto**, an 11th-century church that survives from the very last period of the town. Near the museum is a recently discovered Christian catacomb (for details of access, ask at the museum).

Maria delle Grazie and his tomb is the object of much veneration today. The town takes its name from a round temple, possibly dedicated to Jupiter, which became the Rotonda di San Giovanni, a baptistery of uncertain date. There are plenty of hotels and restaurants, and souvenir shops by the dozen.

[i] Piazza Europa 104

*From San Giovanni Rotondo, the **SS272** winds eastwards to Monte Sant'Angelo, about 24km (15 miles).*

Monte Sant'Angelo, Puglia

3 This is another of Italy's important pilgrimage sites. St Michael is supposed to have appeared, in the 5th century, in a cave set deep within the ground – the same **Santuario di San Michele** (Sanctuary of St Michael) that you can visit today. A church was built in front of the grotto in 1273 and its contemporary **belltower** copies the plan, though in miniature, of the Castel del Monte (see page 110). On your way down to the dark, damp cave, you will pass a set of beautiful bronze doors dating from 1076. Reputedly made in Constantinople, they depict scenes from the Old Testament. In the grotto itself is a statue of St Michael by Andrea Sansovino, a Renaissance Florentine sculptor much under the influence of Raphael. The oldest quarter of Monte Sant'Angelo is the medieval **Junno** district, which would have been known by illustrious visitors of the past, such as St Thomas Aquinas and St Francis. In another part of town is the '**Tomb of Rothari**', in fact a very early, and rather unusual, baptistery building. It stands next to the late medieval Church of **San Pietro**.

*Retrace the route for 6km (4 miles) before turning right on the **SS528** through the centre of the Gargano for 24km (15 miles) to Sant'Antonio. Here branch right, following the signs to Segheria il Mandrione, about 17km (11 miles), at which take the **SS89** to Vieste.*

Vieste, Puglia

4 Vieste, beautifully situated on a tip of the Gargano Peninsula, surrounded by coves, cliffs and beaches, is a popular resort. The town is dominated by a **castle** and a **cathedral**. There are no saints here, and fewer monuments, but who cares? There is plenty to do. Apart from shops and restaurants, there are all sorts of caves within reach of the town, accessible either on foot or by boat (tours) – just to the south are the **Grotta Smeralda** (Emerald Cave) and the **Grotta dei Marmi** (Cave of the Marbles). South of the town are the beaches of **Pizzomunno** and **Castello** – both long. From Vieste ferries run to the **Tremiti Islands**.

[i] Corso Lorenzo Fazzini 8

*Take the coastal road going north to join the **SS89** at Peschici. Continue along the coast on the **SS89** to Rodi Gargánico before striking inland. Follow the main road to the turning for Apricena and San Severo.*

San Severo, Puglia

5 Much of San Severo has a baroque overlay. For example, the town's main landmark, the medieval **cathedral**, looks anything but ancient, having been revamped in a baroque style. The important Romanesque Church of **San Severo** did not escape. It retains its rose window, but manages to combine it rather cleverly with some baroque details. Other churches include **San Giovanni Battista**, also Romanesque but with a baroque belltower and **Santa Maria degli Angeli**. About 13km (8 miles) from San Severo, you can visit the ruins of **Castel Fiorentino**, where the Emperor Frederick II died in 1250.

The old fishing port of Vieste sits on a rocky promontory

BACK TO NATURE

The **Rifugio Foresta Umbra** (Umbra Forest Nature Reserve) on the Gargano promontory, is an area of woodland comprising mainly beech interspersed with field maple, yew and hornbeam. *Macchia* (scrub) vegetation flourishes in the forest clearings and includes species such as mastic, tree heather, cistuses and laurel. These are visited by numerous insects – look out for chafer beetles and hairstreak butterflies. Birds of prey and many woodland species such as woodpeckers and flycatchers inhabit the woods.

SCENIC ROUTES

The eastern extremity of the Gargano Peninsula, as it thrusts into the Adriatic, is the region's most scenic area, with fine coastal views. Although the tour takes you from Monte Sant'Angelo to Vieste along an inland road, a very much longer alternative would be the coastal route. Apart from its great natural beauty, it is studded with beaches and tourist villages and is the kind of stretch you might like to complete very slowly, staying overnight where you can.

*Take the **SS160** to Lucera, about 22km (14 miles).*

Lucera, Puglia

6 Lucera was once the town in which the Emperor Frederick II preferred to live. It contains the remains of the biggest **castle** he ever built (1233), one of the most magnificent in Puglia. The turreted walls survive, extending for about 900m (½ mile) and dominating the town and the great Tavoliere plain beyond. Charles I of Anjou transformed the castle (1269–83), and today there are only ruins of Frederick II's palace inside the walls. Lucera has a strange history. Cosmopolitan Frederick lured here from Sicily about 20,000 Saracen subjects who transformed Lucera into an Arab city. In 1300 most of these were massacred by Charles II, but there are traces of their existence around the town. The 14th-century **cathedral** is an impressive building and thought to be one of the least altered of its date anywhere. More French Gothic than anything else (people from Provence replaced the Saracens after 1300), its high altar is made from a slab of marble that was once Frederick II's dining table in his Castel Fiorentino (see page 116). In Lucera's **Museo Civico** (Civic Museum), you can see ceramics from the doomed Saracen period as well as some fine remains from the old Roman settlement of *Luceria Augusta*, in particular, a marble statue of Venus.

*Take the **SS160** south for 18km (11 miles) to the turnoff for Tróia, a further kilometre (½ mile).*

Tróia, Puglia

7 Tróia is one of the loveliest towns on this tour. It owes its fame to a splendid Romanesque **cathedral**, of which the rose window – its most noteworthy adornment – is slightly Arabic-looking and dates from Frederick II's time. There are two bronze doors, that at the front of the building dates from 1119 and the one on the south side from 1127. They show classical and oriental influences. Inside, you should look at the 12th-century carved pulpit as well as the illuminated manuscripts in the cathedral treasury. A **museum** in the Convent of **San Benedetto** contains part of the treasure from the cathedral, church paintings and some baroque furnishings.

*Take the **SS160** for to the junction with the **SS90**. Branch slowly for 7km (4 miles) then turn left on to the **SS161** for 1km (½ mile) before taking the winding country road on the right for 9km (5½ miles) to Bovino.*

Bovino, Puglia

8 Bovino was once a Roman settlement called *Vibinum*. Its claim to fame, until about 80 years ago, was that it was an infamous centre of brigandage. Up on its hill, its remoteness protected its reputation. Bovino is a good centre for excursions into the surrounding countryside. At **Giardinetto**, about 17km (10½ miles) on the return to Foggia, is a wonderful 11th-century cathedral. Take care to examine its bronze doors. Then, closer to Bovino, is the **Castello di Deliceto** (about 8km/5 miles).

*Retrace your route to the **SS90** which leads to Foggia.*

Foggia – Manfredonia 39 (24)
Manfredonia – San Giovanni Rotondo 23 (14)
San Giovanni Rotondo – Monte Sant'Angelo 24 (15)
Monte Sant'Angelo – Vieste 59 (37)
Vieste – San Severo 109 (68)
San Severo – Lucera 22 (14)
Lucera – Tróia 19 (12)
Tróia – Bovino 28 (17)
Bovino – Foggia 43 (27)

Peaceful in the sunlight, Bovino belies its disreputable past

RECOMMENDED WALKS

4 Surrounding Vieste are extensive beaches, good for long, hard walks after a drowsy lunch. In particular head south from town towards the Grotta Smeralda.

SPECIAL TO . . .

1 Manfredonia is noted for its delicious red wine called Orta Nova. If you can stand up after a lunch including this, then good luck to you.

2 In San Giovanni Rotondo, is the **Festa dell'Ospite** (the Guest's Festival). For a week there are lively folklore celebrations, exhibitions and displays, local gastronomic treats and a great deal of local – and very potent – wine is consumed (usually 11–20 August, but check for any changes to these dates).

FOR CHILDREN

If the children deserve a treat for sitting still and not complaining, then give them *cassata di ricotta*, a richer version of ice-cream made from fresh, light *ricotta* cheese.

INDEX

References to captions are in *italic*.

ACKNOWLEDGEMENTS

The Automobile Association would like to thank the following photographers and libraries for their help in the preparation of this book, and the Italian State Tourist Office (London), Agip Motels, Magic of Italy and Italiatour who assisted the photographer, Anthony Souter.

ANTHONY SOUTER took all the photographs in this book (AA PHOTO LIBRARY), except those listed below.

SPECTRUM COLOUR LIBRARY 8/9 Milan Duomo, 19, 20 Emilia Romagna, 22 Rimini, 84 Caserta Palace.

WORLD PICTURES 9 Verona.

ZEFA PICTURE LIBRARY UK LTD Cover Florence, 9 Turin, 16 Lago di Garda, 17 Cremona, 35 San Remo, 54/5 Perugia, 68/9 Napoli.

Edited by Audrey Horne.